Learned Lady

Letters from

Robert Browning to Mrs. Thomas FitzGerald

1876–1889

THE CARL H. PFORZHEIMER LIBRARY

The publication of this volume has been aided by a grant from
The Carl and Lily Pforzheimer Foundation, Inc.

Distributed in Great Britain by
Oxford University Press

Library of Congress Catalog Card Number 66–11358

Printed in the United States of America

TO

Mabel Purefoy FitzGerald

Preface

THIS BOOK CONSISTS OF sixty-six letters in The Carl H. Pforzheimer Library, for the most part heretofore unpublished, supplemented by eight letters or portions of letters previously published. They constitute one of the best of the primary sources we have for the last fourteen years of Browning's life. Written to a dear friend who was also a "learned lady," they shed light on his poetry, his social life, and his friendships; and they give as well some of his views on the nature of poetry, of art, and of religion.

Letter 1 of this collection is at Stowe School, Buckinghamshire. Letter 69 was purchased by the late Carl H. Pforzheimer from Meyers & Co., London, in 1946 and is now in the Pforzheimer Library. Letter 71 is owned by Mr. Richard L. Purdy of Yale University. Six letters (4, 6, 44, 46, 49, and 74) were used by Mrs. Sutherland Orr in her *Life and Letters of Robert Browning* (1891) and subsequently lost, although number 4 appeared in the J. H. Benton sale catalogue of the American Art Association, March 12, 1920, and a half sheet of number 44 is in the possession of Miss Mabel Purefoy FitzGerald.

The remaining sixty-five letters are in The Carl H. Pforzheimer Library. "The Property of the Rev. H. Purefoy FitzGerald Grandson of the original recipient," they were sold at Sotheby's on July 28, 1913, to Joseph Hornstein, for £155. (By coincidence, Browning's letters to Mrs. Skirrow were sold on the same day for £140.) At the Hornstein sale of February 25, 1918, again at Sotheby's, they were purchased by Sotheran's for £100. They were next sold at the Anderson Galleries in New York City on February 17, 1919, and finally purchased by Mr. Pforzheimer from Gabriel Wells on May 5, 1920.

When Browning and Mrs. FitzGerald were both in London, he called on her every Sunday. When either of them was not in London, he wrote or intended to write to her every Saturday. There must be, therefore, letters not accounted for in this volume. Mrs. FitzGerald sometimes kept a letter in an appropriate book, and her granddaughter has a few of these. She left to a kinsman her fine autograph collection from various correspondents, and surely Browning must be represented in it. She also gave letters away; pinned to letter 69 is her note, "Would you like this letter as an Autograph written 3 years before his death in Decr 1889—he wrote to me, till the last week of his life." Four of the letters in the Pforzheimer collection (38, 45, 47, and 61) are incomplete; perhaps Mrs. FitzGerald gave away the last page of each as an autograph. It is known that she destroyed parts of some letters because of allusions therein to contemporaries. There is one Browning letter to her postmarked April 12, 1875, at Harvard University; there is another at Baylor University. I have found some Browning letters addressed to "Dear Friend" and written on a Saturday, but there is not enough internal evidence to prove that they were addressed to Mrs. FitzGerald. (One such brief note, dated July 27, 1878, is in the Mary S. Harkness collection of the New York Public Library.)

W. R. Nicoll and T. J. Wise in their *Literary Anecdotes of the Nineteenth Century* (London, 1895, I, 470–471) print four sentences from a Browning letter about his *Ferishtah's Fancies* (1884), concluding, "The Hebrew quotations are put in for a purpose, as a direct acknowledgement that certain doctrines may be found in the Old Book which the Concocters of Novel Schemes of Morality put forth as discoveries of their own." In the copy of *Ferishtah's Fancies* that Browning presented to Mrs. FitzGerald on November 20, 1884, she wrote the four sentences later quoted by Nicoll and Wise, and, *in addition,* the date, "Octr 19, 1884," and a further sentence: "I have put them in English characters with the proper pronunciation that they may go properly into English verse but that is done only for private information." Surely one may suspect that the letter quoted was written to Mrs. FitzGerald.

Even though Browning tried to write to Mrs. FitzGerald every Saturday when either of them was away from London and he could not pay his Sunday call, we cannot tell how many letters he did write. We do not always know when she was away from London, and Browning did not always live up to his resolution. Of the seventy-two dated letters in this volume, only forty-two were dated on a Saturday. While he was on the Continent in 1888, Browning deliberately did not write for over four months: ". . . she found such fault with what she called my 'scolding her,'" he wrote to Mrs. Skirrow, "that I thought a little stopping in our intercourse would have a soothing effect" (D&K, p. 363).

The text of sixty-seven letters in this volume are taken from the holographs in the Pforzheimer Library and at Stowe School. The remaining seven letters are from the previously published sources. The introduction aims to acquaint the reader with Mrs. FitzGerald and her family, with the social background of the letters, and with Browning, his sister, and his son. The notes are intended to identify persons, events, and obscure quotations. This is the first edition of Browning correspondence to contain bibliographical descriptions of the physical characteristics of his letters (see appendix). These descriptions should make it possible for future editors to date, at least approximately, some of the letters Browning left undated.

For permission to edit these letters, I am grateful to Mr. Carl H. Pforzheimer, Jr., on behalf of The Carl and Lily Pforzheimer Foundation, Inc.; to Mr. John Temple and Mr. John C. Saunders of Stowe School; to Mr. Richard L. Purdy; to Dean W. C. DeVane, Professor K. L. Knickerbocker, and the Yale University Press; and to Sir John Murray.

New York, January 1965 Edward C. McAleer

Acknowledgments

THE LIBRARIES I USED MOST are the New York Society Library, the New York Public Library, the Bodleian, and the British Museum, and I thank the staffs of these libraries for their kind help. I am especially indebted to Miss M. C. Stanley-Smith of the Oxfordshire County Library, Miss Gwenda Jones and Mr. Ray Fowkes of the Buckinghamshire County Library, Mr. Jack W. Herring of the Armstrong Browning Library, Mr. J. Gewritz of the library of the *Jewish Chronicle,* Mr. Herbert C. Schultz of the Huntington Library, Mr. William H. McCarthy, Jr., of the Rosenbach Foundation, Mr. Jefferson T. Warren of Vizcaya in Miami, Mr. G. F. Willmot of the Yorkshire Museum, and Dr. Kenneth N. Cameron and Dr. Marcelle Thiébaux of The Carl H. Pforzheimer Library.

I take this opportunity to thank friends and colleagues who have helped me to track down facts and to identify quotations: Mrs. Giuliana Artom Treves, Mr. Howard Comrie, Professor Leon Edel, Mr. Lawrence Evans, Mr. Lachlan Phil Kelley, Professor Cecil Lang, Professor James McNally, Mr. Geoffrey Purefoy (great-grandson of Mrs. FitzGerald and the present owner of Shalstone Manor, Mrs. Mary Lillias Geraldine Purefoy having in recent years made over the property to her eldest son), Mr. Malcolm Quantrill, Mr. Vincent Quinn, Mr. James Toole of Lamlash, Mr. Howard Twelvetrees, Mrs. John Hall Wheelock, Professor John Wildman, and Professor Carl Woodring. Colleagues at Hunter College who have been particularly helpful are Dr. Mirella L. D'Ancona, Dr. Mariella Cavalchini, Miss Elsie M. Fugett, Professor Elio Gianturco, Professor E. Adelaide Hahn, Professor Leslie Marchand, Professor Helaine

Newstead, and Professor Constantine Trypanis. The City University of New York allowed me a research assistant, and I gratefully acknowledge the invaluable help of Miss Beverly Goldberg.

Especially do I wish to thank Miss Mabel Purefoy FitzGerald of Oxford, the last surviving grandchild of Mrs. FitzGerald. Miss FitzGerald was born in 1872; she knew Browning and, of course, her grandmother. She also knew Mrs. Sutherland Orr and recalls with great interest the visit Mrs. Orr paid to Shalstone in June of 1890 when she went through the letters she later used in writing her life of Browning. Miss FitzGerald has access to books, diaries, and papers that belonged to her grandmother, all of which she examined for any information that would shed light on these letters. I spent the summer of 1962 in Oxford working in the Bodleian and daily I called on Miss FitzGerald, who would have ready for me answers to problems I had left with her the day before. In addition to the pleasure of using the Bodleian, I had the pleasure of meeting daily with a gentlewoman who knew the writer of these letters, the recipient, and many of the people mentioned in them, and whose face would light up as she brought them to life for me.

E. C. M.

Contents

Illustrations

following page 110

(all from the collection of Miss Mabel Purefoy FitzGerald)

Introduction

ABBREVIATIONS USED IN THE NOTES

BM	British Museum
BSP	*Browning Society Papers,* London, 1881–1891
DAB	*Dictionary of American Biography*
DNB	*Dictionary of National Biography*
D&K	*New Letters of Robert Browning,* ed. W. C. DeVane and K. L. Knickerbocker (New Haven, 1950)
Dearest Isa	*Dearest Isa: Robert Browning's Letters to Isabella Blagden,* ed. Edward C. McAleer (Austin, Texas, 1951)
Hood	*Letters of Robert Browning Collected by Thomas J. Wise,* ed. T. L. Hood (London, 1933)
MPFG	Mabel Purefoy FitzGerald
Orr	Mrs. Sutherland Orr, *Life and Letters of Robert Browning* (Boston, 1891)
Sotheby	Sotheby, Wilkinson, and Hodge, *The Browning Collections: Catalogue of . . . the Property of R. W. Barrett Browning, Esq.* (London, May 1, 2, 5, and 8, 1913)
***	Triple asterisks indicate the beginning or end of a letter that exists only in part.

Introduction

After the death of Mrs. Browning in Florence, on June 29, 1861, Robert Browning took from her finger the ring Isa Blagden had given her and put it on his watch chain, where he wore it until his own death twenty-eight years later. He returned to England, ministered to on the way by Isa Blagden, his dearest woman friend, who went back to Italy and corresponded with him every month thereafter until she died in 1873. Grief-stricken by the death of his wife, he lived in London quietly with his son, first on Chichester Road then at 19 Warwick Crescent, a house that he began by despising but which he later learned to love, especially after the furniture, paintings, books, and tapestries from Florence had been installed there. Gradually he began to go into society again and to make new friends. "I have been much favoured in friendships — especially from women," he wrote,[1] and among the women who valued his friendship during the last decades of his life were Miss Julia Wedgwood, Miss Annie Egerton Smith, Mrs. Ernest Benzon, Mrs. Sutherland Orr, Mrs. Bloomfield Moore, Mrs. Charles Skirrow, Mrs. Arthur Bronson, and Mrs. Thomas FitzGerald of Shalstone Manor, Buckinghamshire, and 22 Portland Place, London — the recipient of these letters.

Mrs. FitzGerald — Sarah Anna Elizabeth Purefoy Jervoise — was born on April 25, 1809, at Herriard Park, Basingstoke, Hampshire, the only child of Major Richard Purefoy Jervoise (formerly Purefoy) of the First Royal Dragoons and Anna Victoria Story, daughter

[1] D&K, p. 241.

of the Rev. Joseph Story of Bingfield, County Cavan.[2] (The Purefoy family had added the name of Jervoise upon inheriting the estate at Herriard in 1795.) When Elizabeth, or Eliza as she was known, was two and a half, her father resigned his commission; he was on his way home from the Peninsular Wars, accompanied only by his faithful soldier servant, when he contracted a fever resulting from a wound received in battle and died at Abrantes, in September 1811.

As an infant Eliza lived with her mother at Herriard and Shalstone, another of the family estates. From her fifth to her eleventh year (1814–1820) they lived simply, first in Winchester, then in Bath, and subsequently in London. During her early years she spent the winter months in the family home, The Moat, Britford, Wiltshire, or with her grandmother in the close at Salisbury. Seemingly her childhood was spent more in the company of the elderly than the young, and she was influenced particularly by the Rev. William Coxe (1747–1828), historian, Rector of Bemerton, and a canon of Salisbury. Her accomplishments — proficiency in foreign languages and able performance on the piano — and her sensitivity to literature indicate the quality of her early education, which was assured by her mother's wisdom and the substantial sum of money allowed annually for this purpose by her uncle and guardian, George Purefoy Jervoise. While serving in the House of Commons, Eliza's uncle had lodgings at 42 Bridge Street, Westminster, and it was there, as a child of twelve, that she first met Thomas FitzGerald.

Like Eliza, Thomas FitzGerald had been left fatherless at an early age. He was in Jamaica when his soldier father, Edward, who owned property on the island, died there. Subsequently he came to England — where his Irish aunts, the widowed sisters of his father, were then living — and to the care of his relative Keane FitzGerald, a Bencher of the Inner Temple. Thomas became a barrister at law, Lincoln's Inn, and joined the Northern Circuit. He was the principal

[2] Burke's *Landed Gentry, sub* Purefoy of Shalstone.

heir of Keane, who died on October 14, 1831, aged eighty-three, leaving Thomas property in the City of London and in the counties of Middlesex, Surrey, and Hertford, and making him lord of the manor of Mortlake.[8] This branch of the FitzGeralds was related in some degree to Mary Frances FitzGerald, the mother of the translator Edward, but there had been at one time a family quarrel and generally speaking the two branches were not on friendly terms.

Thomas FitzGerald was many years Elizabeth's senior, and she looked to him for advice. There is a family story that she went to him with the problem of which husband to accept from among the many young men who had proposed to her, for she was a beautiful and cultivated woman as well as an heiress. Thomas is said to have thought for only a moment and then to have replied, "Marry me!" On September 25, 1832, she did, in Herriard Church.

The FitzGeralds' London house was at 48 Dover Street. Their country houses they rented: at first, Woolhampton House, Berkshire, a handsome brick mansion set in a wooded park not far from Newbury. Then, in the mid-1830's, they lived in Purley House near Reading and also near Three Mile Cross where it was easy for Miss Mitford and her "dearest Mrs. FitzGerald" to exchange visits. From 1836 to 1846 they lived at Muntham Court, Findon, near Worthing in Sussex, a house they loved, where three of their children were born. Upon the death of her uncle George in December 1847, Mrs. FitzGerald inherited landed property in Hampshire, Wiltshire, and Warwickshire, as well as Shalstone, which was after 1849 her country seat and where her youngest son was born. The FitzGeralds had eight children: Thomas Keane (1833–1887), Robert Allan (1834–1881), Richard Purefoy (1836–1895), Maurice George Beaufoy (1837–1901), Geraldine (1840–1850), Henry Jervoise (1842–1852), Mary (1845–1860) and Alfred William (1849–1871).

[8] Will of Keane FitzGerald in Somerset House. See also *The Victoria History of the County of Hertford* (London, 1908), II, 336.

Shalstone is situated about four and a half miles northwest of the town of Buckingham and near the grounds of the former seat of the Dukes of Buckingham, which is now Stowe School. The Purefoys, among the oldest of the county families, acquired the estate by marriage in the year 1418 and held it until the death of Henry Purefoy in 1762.[4] He was a bachelor who "conversed more with Books than with Men," as we are told by his memorial in Shalstone church, and being childless he left the estate to his cousin, the Rev. George Huddleston Jervoise, who took the name of Purefoy and later became the rector of Shalstone. His eldest son, George Purefoy Jervoise, uncle of Mrs. FitzGerald, inherited the property in 1803 and left it to her with remainder to her third son, Richard Purefoy FitzGerald, with the provision that after her death future heirs should "use the surname of Purefoy only and bear the arms of Purefoy only."[5] When Mrs. FitzGerald inherited it, the manor house was described as a "very unostentatious residence" and the village as "one of the most retired and least interesting" of Buckinghamshire villages, with irregular and "meanly built" houses.[6] But the owner had been living elsewhere, at Herriard Park, and had divided his attention between more than one country house and estate.

There were 186 parishioners living on Mrs. FitzGerald's estate, which occupied 1320 acres—including arable land, land given to permanent grass, and about seventy-one acres of woodland. A brook spanned by a bridge runs at the bottom of the village street, and there is but one street. Although the village was described as unattractive in 1847, Mrs. FitzGerald entered upon her inheritance with a deep sense of responsibility, shared by her husband, and from the

[4] G. Eland, F.S.A., ed., *The Purefoy Letters, 1735–1753* (London, 1931), Introduction.

[5] Will of George Purefoy Jervoise in Somerset House.

[6] George Lipscomb, *The History and Antiquities of the County of Buckingham* (London, 1847), III, 70–75.

beginning of 1848 they were improving landlords and devoted much of their energy to the village — he for the last twelve years of his life, and she, as lady of the manor, for the thirty-nine years she survived her husband. Four years after their occupancy they built a school to accommodate forty pupils — a white brick building with Bath stone dressing, dark blue tiled roof, and ornamental chimneys copied from some at Wells. They then built several new houses for the villagers — comfortable houses of stone with tiled roofs — extending the village to the north. In the 1850's Thomas FitzGerald purchased Evershaw, a copse, from the trustees of the Duke of Buckingham, and also some more land in and near Shalstone,[7] making provision in his will for their addition to the Purefoy property held by his wife. With encouragement from the manor house, the villagers took pride in their cottages and gardens, so that later commentators refer to the village as "remarkably neat" and as "this model village," and there were many tenants from other villages who wanted to move to Shalstone.

In August 1860, Thomas FitzGerald died in his eighty-third year, having been deputy lieutenant of the County of Buckingham, justice of the peace, and lord of the manor of Mortlake in Surrey. The sermon preached in his honor quoted him as often saying, "The rich must pay for the poor."[8] Among his bequests to his wife he left the London house in Portland Place, with its contents; the house in Bath at 15 Edward Street; his possessions on the premises and in the Shalstone house including all his "plate, books, maps, charts, globes, philosophical and other instruments, pictures, prints, statues," etc. To his eldest son he left FitzGerald property in Ireland, and in addition left to his sons property in Surrey, Hertfordshire, and Middlesex, including with the land in London on which they were built a

[7] Will of Thomas FitzGerald in Somerset House.

[8] *A Sermon Preached in the Parish Church of Shalstone, August 19, 1860, being the Sunday after the Funeral of Thomas FitzGerald, Esq.* (Oxford, 1861).

riding school, coach houses, twenty-two stables in Queen's Mews and Kensington Garden Square, Bayswater, and fourteen houses, numbered one to fourteen, in Kensington Garden Square.[9]

As a widow, Mrs. FitzGerald was responsible for the management of her property, and she demonstrated that among her other virtues was that of being a good businesswoman. As evidence of her success, it may be noted that the rateable value of Shalstone, which was £1260 in 1862,[10] had become £1696 by 1883,[11] in spite of the fact that in the 1880's rents were falling and landed property was in serious decline, especially after the dreadful rains of 1879, in which year the rector of Shalstone returned to the glebe tenants fifteen per cent of the last half-year's rent on arable land.[12]

In 1862, Mrs. FitzGerald restored the parish church of St. Edward the Confessor, in the Gothic style under the superintendence of Sir Gilbert Scott, R.A. Her five surviving sons presented five bells in memory of their father. Each bell was inscribed with the name of the donor; ringing a peal of great charm, they were called the Brother Bells. Mrs. FitzGerald put up a stained-glass window in the chancel in memory of her father, depicting him as Cornelius the Centurion, who also had "a devout soldier . . . that waited on him continually" (Acts, x, 1–7).[13] In 1889, she added a vestry and organ in memory of her eldest son, who died in 1887.

✣

As testimony of his associations with Shalstone Browning included hidden references to the estate in his *Pacchiarotto* volume of 1876.

9 Will of Thomas FitzGerald.

10 James Joseph Sheahan, *History and Topography of Bucks* (London, 1862), p. 301.

11 Kelly's *Directory of Berkshire, Bucks and Oxon* (London, 1883), p. 380.

12 Buckingham *Express,* June 28, 1879.

13 The original church was of the fifteenth century, remodeled in 1828, with only a few fifteenth-century details remaining. On his visits to Shalstone, Browning would have noted among the memorial tablets one to Stephen Skirrow, a FitzGerald friend who died in 1864, for Mrs. Charles Skirrow was Browning's indulgent hostess in the 1870's and 1880's (D&K, *passim*).

If he took a morning walk south from the brook on one of his many visits he would have passed the forge, the seventeenth-century thatched stone cottages of the villagers, the one shop, the spring-fed drinking fountain presented to the village by Mrs. FitzGerald in 1861, and the wall box which the postman from Buckingham cleared every weekday at 4:25 P.M. Continuing his walk, he would have passed on his right the school built by the FitzGeralds in 1852, the new houses built for the tenants, the rectory, and the parish church. On his left, opposite the church, he would have found the manor house and its accompanying pleasure grounds. The walk, though uphill, might have taken him ten or fifteen minutes.

The manor house that Browning visited was a seventeenth-century plastered-stone building of two stories with attics. A lime tree grew on each side of the entrance, denoting that the owner was a Tory (a Whig would have planted elms). Despite remodeling and enlarging in the eighteenth and nineteenth centuries, the original seventeenth-century oak staircase, with its square balusters and its walls later lined with family portraits, led from the entrance hall to the first floor, on which there were twenty-eight rooms, counting those of the original house and those of the extensive wings later added. Looking south from the house, one saw an avenue of stately elm trees planted in the seventeenth century; looking to the west, a lawn with a fine old cedar tree; and looking east, an extensive formal garden, the design of the flower beds being a copy of that on the molded ceiling of the drawing room. In one garden there were daffodils grown from bulbs sent from Tennyson's Farringford on the Isle of Wight.

From Shalstone Browning was sent figs from the fig trees growing against the east wall of the walled garden, cuttings from the Virginia creeper growing on the south wall of the oldest part of the manor house, varieties of ferns from the glass-roofed fernery, rhododendron, pomegranate flowers, and other plants for his garden at Warwick Crescent. Through Mrs. FitzGerald's kindness his "sluggard's garden" was in 1881 transformed into a garden worthy of a poet. While he and his sister were absent on the Continent, Mrs. FitzGerald arranged to have choice flowering shrubs grown at Shalstone by her skilled gardeners transplanted into the poet's neglected garden.[14]

Browning must have been especially interested in the garden into which Mrs. FitzGerald had introduced many of the plants named in the Scriptures (daffodils and Martagon lilies representing "lilies of the field"), interested also in the two oak trees grown from acorns that came from Mount Tabor and Mount Carmel. In the outer part of the Bible garden were two rhododendron bushes, one bearing the name of Robert Browning, the other of Lord Tennyson. Browning, who loved animals, surely would not have left unnoticed Hecla, the white garden pony that Keane FitzGerald had brought from Iceland in 1860, nor the flock of horned black and white sheep (perhaps Portuguese) that Thomas FitzGerald had begun in 1850 from a flock belonging to his friend Sir Henry Dryden, and he would have paused at the part of the garden that contained the tombs of Mrs. FitzGerald's pets.[15] In 1875 Browning sent his pet geese to Shalstone, where they lived on the farm "The Grounds" rented by Mr. Treadwell and there they died and were buried in 1876.

In his letters to Mrs. FitzGerald, Browning sometimes mentions fêtes at Shalstone. The Buckingham *Express* supplies us with information about these festivals, typical of Victorian village life. There were the annual school treats, when the children enjoyed rowing on the lake and bowling on the green. There were cricket matches with such neighboring villages as Whitfield, Westbury, and Water Strat-

14 Letters 36, 39, and 42.

15 When Hecla died in 1886, Mrs. FitzGerald wrote these lines for his tombstone:

> Born amidst distant ice and snow,
> Thy fate, an English lawn to mow;
> Long years the daisies felt thy tread,
> Now bold they rise above thy head:
> Oft hast thou smoothed my path for me,
> Let this my grateful tribute be.

ford. There was the annual church choir concert and the annual rent supper, and almost annually there was the Harvest Home festival. But especially there was the annual flower and vegetable show.

Late in August, the coach house was transformed into a floral hall, the walls decorated with fern or laurel, with flags, Union Jacks, and family mottoes abundantly displayed. There were prizes for the best-kept gardens and tidiest premises, for the best potatoes, carrots, parsnips, turnips, scarlet runners, peas, cabbages, onions, vegetable marrows, cucumbers, pots of honey, sweet herbs, lettuces, rhubarb, apples, apricots, and plums. There were prizes for the best model garden, garland of flowers, basket of flowers, window plants, and collection of wild flowers. The competition was limited to the villagers, from little children to octogenarians, but the children of the manor house and the rectory and some of the neighbors showed floral displays of their own. By three o'clock the judges, often head gardeners from neighboring estates, had made their decisions. Mrs. FitzGerald, members of her family, grandchildren, and invited guests (about twenty friends from neighboring country houses) came to the coach house to inspect the work of the villagers. Then the public was admitted to the coach house and the pleasure grounds of the manor. At six o'clock Mrs. FitzGerald presented the prizes of money to the winners, almost always adding on impulse some extra prizes for especially good exhibits. There were cheers for "the kindest lady in the land." [16]

[16] Buckingham *Express,* September 13, 1879; August 18, 1883; September 6, 1884; August 22, 1885; August 21, 1886; August 18, 1888. In 1889, when Mrs. FitzGerald was eighty, some of her tenants from Grendon Underwood, where she also owned some property, came to the Shalstone flower show with a tribute that moved her deeply. The tribute was framed and glazed and surrounded by an illuminated border; it read as follows: "We, the inhabitants of Grendon Underwood, beg your acceptance of this small contribution towards the fund for the erection of an organ in Shalstone Church, in memory of your late beloved son, Capt. Keane FitzGerald. And we take this occasion to thank you most warmly and gratefully for your exceeding kindness in providing this parish with a supply of beautiful spring water, which has been, at your expense, brought down into the heart of the village. We feel that we can never

In late September or early October, the village celebrated Harvest Home, a festival rather like the American Thanksgiving. At noon, divine service was held in the parish church, and the offertory collection, amounting to five or six pounds, was presented to a charity such as the Buckingham Nursing Home. At two o'clock the men and boys of the village gathered for dinner in the coach house, where they were joined after dinner by Mrs. FitzGerald and the women. There were toasts to the Queen, to the bishop and clergy, to the army and navy. As evening fell, Chinese lanterns were lighted, the band played, and the villagers danced until midnight.[17]

In the manor house at Shalstone there were well over ten thousand volumes — "books everywhere," in the front drawing room, the study, the dining room, on the landing of the staircase, in bedrooms and dressing rooms, the upper book room, recess room, and passageways — collected in the eighteenth century by Henry Purefoy and later by Mrs. FitzGerald and her husband. A friend could hardly mention a book that she had not read, and she had the ability to summarize a book in a few sentences. Whenever she learned that a literary friend was writing, she would ransack her library for material that might be of assistance to him. Browning himself profited.

As she read, Mrs. FitzGerald often penciled notes in the margins, and they tell us something about her. For example, on the fly-leaf of her copy of *Dramatis Personae* she wrote, "How I have read & reread this Volume." Beside "James Lee's Wife" she wrote, "EFG put into Italian for Signor Adelmaan to sing — he composed the music"; beside "Abt Volger," "Knox Little's favourite quotation." In the margin by "A Death in the Desert" she noted: "re-read Feby 1, 1872 . . .

sufficiently thank you for your kindness, but sincerely pray that every blessing may attend you, and that you may finally drink of that water of life, which shall prevent you from ever thirsting again" (*ibid.*, September 21, 1889).

[17] *Ibid.*, September 25, 1880; October 14, 1882; September 29, 1883; October 4, 1884; October 16, 1886; September 24, 1887; October 5, 1889.

May 12, 1884 . . . July 30, 1893: A little more understood—but how long." From her comment on "Caliban upon Setebos" we know that it was "greatly praised by Lord Tennyson." Where Rabbi Ben Ezra said "Be our joys three parts pain," Mrs. FitzGerald added *"assuredly* they ARE." In another volume, beside Mrs. Barbauld's lines, "Say not good-night, but in some brighter clime Bid me 'Good morning,'" she noted, "quoted by R. B.—his favourite poem."

Mrs. FitzGerald's interests and good will extended far beyond Shalstone, her library, and her friends. During the American Civil War, raw cotton could not be delivered to the English mills, and the unemployed cotton workers suffered the utmost distress. In spite of their starvation, and to their credit, they wrote to President Lincoln endorsing his aims. There were some private subscriptions to help them, and callous things were said in the House of Lords. Two ladies, and only two ladies, entered the Lancashire mills, coming face to face with the anguished unemployed. One was Mrs. Gladstone; the other was Mrs. FitzGerald. In the autumn of 1862, Mrs. FitzGerald, sixteen little girls, and forty villagers worked for nineteen days in the Shalstone school, making clothing for the Lancashire workers. The bill for the materials and the inventory of the finished clothing still exist. Such items are 2 dozen women's flannel petticoats, 12 little girls' petticoats, 8 sets of baby clothing, 12 men's shirts (the gift of Mr. Skirrow), 4 beautiful shirts (the gift of Mrs. Pitman, the housekeeper at Portland Place), skirts, gloves, pillows, blankets, etc., indicate the work accomplished. At the end of the nineteen days, Mrs. FitzGerald took the clothing and £100 to distribute among the Lancashire workers. The bill for the materials, bought of Robert Bartlett of Brackley, amounted to £20.14.5½. The bill is dated November 1862, and on it Mrs. FitzGerald has written, "When I think that all this would be but the price of one velvet dress!"

At the end of the war, cotton again arrived in Lancashire, and the workers knelt to kiss the first bales. When prosperity returned, they remembered Mrs. FitzGerald with a medal and a huge counterpane knitted by fifteen hundred mill girls, each girl doing a portion of the work.[18]

In 1871, nine years after the Lancashire visit, Mrs. FitzGerald made another pilgrimage. The early months of the year she had spent nursing her youngest son Alfred. When he was sent to Madeira, accompanied by his brother Purefoy, Mrs. FitzGerald was freed to work for the sick and wounded lying in Berlin hospitals as a result of the Franco-Prussian war. Again the women of Shalstone sewed, and in March Mrs. FitzGerald went to Berlin with gifts for the hospitalized soldiers and with cigars for French prisoners. She returned to England on March 23 after a fortnight's absence.

These two journeys differ from her other generosities only in being more dramatic. To the poor of the parish she was a "veritable Dorcas," according to the *Workmen's Messenger*. The aged were given tidy houses rent free; the villagers were provided with public pleasure grounds called the People's Park; in 1895 she gave land for a reading and recreation room; she was one of the largest subscribers to the Buckingham Nursing Home and the District Nursing Association. In 1887, she gave each child of the village a little mug commemorating the Queen's golden jubilee, and Caroline Tew, later Mrs. Caroline Greaves, housekeeper of the manor house, still treasures her mug—in fact her second mug, a finer one, for Mrs. FitzGerald gave her one of her own possessions when Caroline was unhappy because she had broken the first.

✣

Mrs. FitzGerald spent almost every forenoon in the morning room, writing to her friends. If they were traveling abroad they had only to call at *poste restante* to find letters and papers from her awaiting them. She followed them on the map, and if they visited a place she did not know, she read up on it in order to be "quite in

18 Obituary in *Workmen's Messenger*, September 1899, pp. 136–137.

sympathy with her friends' experiences."[19] As Browning and his sister traveled on the Continent every autumn, they received the current papers and journals from her. The letters of this volume contain repeated thanks for her "traditional kindness" in sending the *Academy,* the *World,* the *Times* and whatever other journals Mrs. FitzGerald thought would interest them. Among her friends and correspondents were Tennyson (who said, "Mrs. FitzGerald, I like your forehead"),[20] Lady Tennyson, and Hallam; Browning, his sister, his son, and his son's wife; Richard Whately, Archbishop of Dublin; Tommaso Salvini (whose *Hamlet* Mrs. FitzGerald saw three times, once, on May 31, 1884, with Browning and Miss Spedding); Gustave Doré; Lord Selborne, lord chancellor and neighbor; Samuel Wilberforce (who at a memorable dinner party at Portland Place in May 1873, discussed with Browning Lord Houghton's *Monographs*); Lord Leighton; the Rev. William Rogers; Sir Richard Owen, the anatomist; Mary Russell Mitford; Richard Chenevix Trench, W. H. Thompson, J. W. Blakesley, G. S. Venables, and James Spedding among the Cambridge Apostles; Aubrey deVere; Dr. Whewell of Trinity College, Cambridge; Thomas MacQuoid, R.I.; Dr. John Ella; Barry Cornwall; and Charles Tennyson Turner.

As a girl Mrs. FitzGerald had learned to speak French and Italian, becoming fluent during the two years (1830–1832) she spent on the Continent with her mother. While in Paris she daily walked with a cultivated French woman, and she was given dancing lessons by Mlle. Mélanie of the Paris Opera. Her Italian was good enough to enable her to put "James Lee's Wife" into Italian verse. Her mastery of German came later. In 1876 she tried her hand at reading the Greek Testament, and three years later, when she was seventy, she secured Joseph B. Mayor's *Greek for Beginners* and began working at the grammar with a will. She sent her exercises to Browning, who

19 Obituary in *Athenaeum,* August 29, 1899.

20 Obituary in Buckingham *Express,* July 22, 1899.

gave her some instruction,[21] although his own Greek was what Jowett called "homespun." At the end of six diligent years, she had mastered the grammar and thereafter read some Greek every day. Later she enjoyed sharing her Greek studies with her grandson Henry, who was an invalid.

"Do you know Spanish?" Browning asked her.[22] She did not at the time, but she studied the language until she was able to read Calderón with ease and pleasure.

Emily Harris, who wrote the obituary for the *Jewish Chronicle,* gave an interesting account of Mrs. FitzGerald's interest in things Jewish and in the Hebrew language. Miss Harris was a young Jewish author and social worker associated with Lady de Rothschild and her daughter, Lady Battersea, in visiting the London poor. She had written a little book of Bible stories for the children of Leopold de Rothschild, and, knowing the book, Mrs. FitzGerald called on her, asking to be taught the Hebrew words for "The Lord is my shepherd." The girl found the elderly lady an apt pupil and then a dear friend. "Of so delicate an understanding and profound reverence for forms in faith," Miss Harris wrote, "that I declare in dining with her, her table was so guarded in her anxiety not to offend orthodox habits, her dishes appeared to consist of roses and peaches." [23] In gratitude, Miss Harris dedicated *Estelle* (1878) to her.

In 1883, when Mrs. FitzGerald was seventy-four, she found a new impetus for the study of Hebrew in Browning's *Jocoseria* and in letters 51 and 52 Browning explained a bit of Hebrew to her, although his own knowledge of the language was shaky, and, we are told, his use of Hebrew did not convey the meanings he intended.[24]

[21] Letters 31 and 56.

[22] Letter 10.

[23] Obituary in *Jewish Chronicle,* August 4, 1899.

[24] Judith Berlin-Lieberman, *Robert Browning and Hebraism* (Jerusalem, 1934), p. 76.

In 1891, when she was eighty-two, a stroke of luck sent the Rev. Mr. Stanley, a converted Viennese Jew, to take the duty at Shalstone while the rector was away. He gave her Hebrew lessons, was surprised at her fluency in reading German, and reveled in her German books.

❖

When Mrs. FitzGerald wrote that the joys of this life assuredly are three-parts pain, she had reason for the sentiment. She was left fatherless at two; she was a widow for thirty-nine years; only one of her eight children survived her. Yet she had lived a most useful life as wife, mother, and grandmother; she had given sons and grandsons to the army, the navy, and the church (three of her sons fought in the Crimean War and two in the Indian mutiny); and she had delighted in the education of her granddaughters, children of her third son, Richard Purefoy — Geraldine, Mary, Laura, Catharine, and Mabel — whom she adored and who adored her. She spent her ninetieth birthday with her granddaughters, who resided in Oxford. During the afternoon reception, two of her oldest Oxford friends and contemporaries came to pay her tribute: Dr. James Edward Sewell, Warden of New College, aged eighty-nine, and Sir Henry Acland, Regius Professor of Medicine, aged eighty-five. During her last year she read the Brownings' love-letters, published by their son, who sent a copy to her. Three weeks before her death she was still writing long, old-fashioned letters to her friends. On July 19, 1899, she died in her manor house at Shalstone, in her ninety-first year. There were obituaries in the Buckingham *Express,* the *Times,* the *Athenaeum,* the *Annual Register,* the *Workmen's Messenger,* and the *Jewish Chronicle.* All mentioned her literary endowments, her skill in languages, and her friendship with Victorians eminent in literature and science.[25]

[25] *Times,* July 27, 1899, p. 6c; *Annual Register* for 1899, p. 159; see also notes 18, 19, 20, and 23.

Mrs. FitzGerald possessed to a rare degree the qualities that made her worthy of Browning's friendship: dignity, beauty, charm, learning, conversational vivacity, and religious faith. Although she disliked publicity, her influence for good was widely felt, and more than once biographers requested permission to write her life. She refused, and her wishes were regarded when a similar request was made after her death.

Mrs. FitzGerald first became acquainted with Browning's poetry in 1864 when she was visiting on the Isle of Mull and learned to love "Saul." She later met the poet at a dinner in the London house of James Spedding, her closest friend among the Cambridge Apostles. The date of the first meeting is not certain, for in later years she gave different dates, but it was in January or February of 1872. She refers to the "birthday of the friendship" as having taken place a year later. On February 23, 1873, when Browning paid his Sunday call he gave her a photograph of the Field Talfourd portrait of Mrs. Browning; he had already given her a copy of Mrs. Browning's *Greek Christian Poets*. Isa Blagden, to whom he had written on the nineteenth of every month, had died in Florence in January 1873; now he had a new friend to whom he could write on Saturday whenever he could not make his Sunday visit.

On her birthday in 1875 Browning presented Mrs. FitzGerald with a copy of his recently published *Aristophanes' Apology,* and thereafter he sent her all his volumes as they came out. Sometimes he remembered her birthday with a book not his, such as The *Book-Lover's Enchiridion* (1883), which he gave her on April 25, 1885. It is a small volume bound in white vellum with gold lettering and gilded edges, and, facing the half-title, Mrs. FitzGerald has inserted the ending of a letter from Browning with his autograph. She remembered his birthdays with a book, such as the first edition (1611) bound in old calf of T. Coryat's *Crudities Hastily Gobled up in five Months Travells in France, Savoy, Italy, etc.* On the fly-leaf

Browning has written "given to me as a Birthday present, by my friend, old and dear, Eliza FitzGerald, May 7, '87."[26]

When the Browning Society was formed in 1881, Mrs. FitzGerald was a charter member; at one time she doubled her subscription and at another she donated £3.16 toward the expenses of the society.[27] On the last Friday of every month when she was in London she went to the meetings of the society, walking from Portland Place to University College, accompanied by the tall footman without whom she never walked abroad in London. On one occasion, Browning had to be severe with her for catching cold as she went to a meeting on foot in bad weather.[28] One year after the poet's death she resigned from the society and received as a parting gift a copy of William Sharp's *Life of Browning* (1890).

✣

The virtues of Mrs. FitzGerald, whom Browning called "learned lady," account for the quality of these letters, among the best that he wrote during the last fourteen years of his life. He could discuss with her better than with other friends (except Mrs. Orr, and his letters to her have not been found) such things as the Schopenhauer doctrine that the "soul is above and behind the intellect," a doctrine that he was sure permeated the whole of his own poetry;[29] the superiority of imaginativeness over technicality in art;[30] or the somewhat more recent view that attention should be given to a poem itself and to extraneous matter not at all.[31]

The letters also show how priceless to her Browning's friendship was. Nothing could be more satisfying or comforting than his letters to Mrs. FitzGerald during the mental illness and ultimate death of her second son, Bob FitzGerald, the most popular cricket

26 Sotheby, no. 594, p. 90.
27 *BSP,* I, xii.
28 Letter 45.
29 Letter 2.
30 Letter 25.
31 Letters 51 and 52.

player of his day. On the other hand, Browning would spare no effort to scold her into the "truth," with no suspicion that his scolding might give offense.[32] When a friend of his was present, he could raise his voice; when absent, he was obliged to bully by mail. Browning's quickness to anger at what he considered error or anything less than the whole truth on the part of his friends received considered approval from no less a sage than Rabbi Ben Ezra: "This rage was right i' the main," said the rabbi after examining his conscience, "That acquiescence vain."

William Grove, the poet's servant for seven years, has given an account of Browning's most regular habits.[33] He rose daily at seven and remained in his room reading until eight, during which time he ate some fruit that had been left for him over night. At eight he bathed and at nine came down to breakfast. After breakfast he read the *Times* and the *Daily News,* and then from ten to one he was in his study writing. Luncheon was light, generally only a pudding, and after luncheon he went out to pay calls on friends or to visit the private showings at the art galleries. Tuesdays and Fridays at two o'clock he called on Mrs. Orr; Saturdays he went to the Athenaeum Club; Sundays he called on friends. At half past five or six he returned home to dress for dinner. On Mondays, he tells us in these letters,[34] he generally dined with Dean Stanley and then assisted the dean in showing tradesmen around Westminster Abbey, but he blessed his lot whenever he found himself at home of an evening with book, lamp, and fire.[35]

"I have dined out — and been to a 'Ball' — on each of the two days since I saw you," Browning wrote in the first letter of this volume. It was the height of the London "season," and during the season Browning dined out every day for weeks on end. During the

32 Letter 47.
33 *Pall Mall Budget,* December 19, 1889, p. 1625.
34 Letter 17.
35 Letter 41.

1870's and 1880's the season began after the Easter recess of Parliament and lasted until August. Although the Queen came to London early in February for the opening of Parliament she returned almost at once to Windsor, and society remained in the country. Society was a landed hierarchy to which literary men were admitted and from which actors and physicians were debarred.[36] During Holy Week society descended upon London from the country houses, unshuttered its town houses, made preparation for the season — and immediately left London for the ten-day Parliamentary recess, most people going to Paris. Parliament reassembled, the Queen removed to Buckingham Palace, and then began the round of dinners and balls and concerts and art exhibitions and plays, most of which Browning seemed to enjoy. Parliament generally adjourned for Derby Day, and there was a respite during the Whitsuntide recess and consequent holiday, after which the whirl began again.

London hostesses found their duties much simpler when they could get Browning as a dinner guest, for he was infinitely talkative and could easily dominate a small dinner party of ten or a large one of forty. The guests assembled; the gentlemen took the ladies down to the dining room in order of rank; the hostess provided Browning with a decanter of port; and the poet began to talk. C. E. Hallé tells of a dinner at the Benzons when Browning talked throughout the meal without eating a bite. When he did pause, the Rev. W. Brookfield had something to say; whereupon Browning leaned across Hallé, seized Brookfield's arm, and began talking all over again.[37] The meal finished, the ladies retired, the gentlemen fell to their claret (if they were conservatives) or port (if they were liberals), Browning talked, and the ladies waited anxiously in the drawing room until the men rejoined them. Browning was at home by twelve-thirty at the latest.

Sometimes he read his poetry, as he did on July 26, 1880, at a small

[36] Lady Mary J. St. Helier, *Memories of Fifty Years* (London, 1909), p. 180.
[37] Charles Hallé, *Life and Letters* (London, 1896), p. 9.

tea Lady Knightley gave for about thirty-five of her friends. "I do not think that he reads well," Lady Knightley said, "but everyone seemed to like it." [38] Grateful as the hostess was, an occasional guest was less tolerant. Disraeli thought Browning "noisy" and "conceited"; [39] but Disraeli was impatient of literary men when he thought they were socially ambitious or pushing.[40] Browning realized his propensity: "I know I am too noisy," he told Leveson-Gower, "but I cannot help it." [41] He himself did not do any entertaining, although he sometimes had a guest or two in for the simplest of luncheons, but he was much sought: "if the family had been allowed to commandeer the presence of whom they would, as guest," Archbishop Benson's son wrote, "the vote would probably have been cast for Browning." [42]

The Victorians had not discovered the week end and devoted Sundays to visiting. The ladies stayed at home, and from three to seven an endless stream of gentlemen called upon them. Most ladies did not know what gentlemen would call on any particular Sunday, but Browning was regular in calling on Mrs. FitzGerald before calling on Mrs. Procter and on Carlyle.

Sometimes Browning mentions that he has attended a ball. Victorian balls opened with a stately quadrille, followed by a waltz, a polka, a mazurka, or lancers; and at some houses and at Court balls there were vigorous Scottish reels. Browning, who would much prefer to talk, found all this a bore and bided his time on a sofa philosophizing over the scene.[43]

[38] Julia Cartwright, ed., *The Journals of Lady Knightley of Fawsley* (New York, 1916), p. 340.

[39] W. F. Moneypenny and G. E. Buckle, *Life of Benjamin Disraeli* (London, 1929), II, 1155.

[40] George W. E. Russell, ed., *Letters of Matthew Arnold* (New York, 1895), II, 219.

[41] Edward F. Leveson-Gower, *Bygone Years* (New York, 1905), p. 280.

[42] E. F. Benson, *As We Were* (New York, 1930), p. 125.

[43] Letters 1 and 62.

From Easter until August, then, this was the life that Browning led. About August first, women and children began to leave London for their country houses in England or Scotland, and on August 12 Parliament rose, M.P.'s appeared at once on the grouse moors, the ministers had their annual Whitebait Dinner at the Ship in Greenwich, and Browning departed for the Continent, exhausted.

Browning's autumn holiday of secluded quiet was the complete opposite of his frenzied spring and summer in London. With his sister Sarianna ("poor thing, she is often alone in the London season")[44] he would go to the remotest of villages — such as Blairbeg, Lans, or St. Pierre de Chartreuse — where they lived in the most inexpensive quarters[45] and where they could walk for hours without encountering a single person. The air and quiet replenished the energy Browning had spent during the season, and sometimes he wrote poetry. In 1878, the Brownings began to include Italy in their holiday. After five or six weeks in the remote village they would spend several weeks in Venice. There they took gondolas, walked on the Lido, and Browning became the darling of such Americans as Mr. and Mrs. Daniel Sargent Curtis (of Boston) and Mrs. Arthur Bronson (of Newport), who outdid themselves in beneficent effort to make the poet comfortable.

Nobody thought that Browning looked like a poet. Physically he was a sturdy little man, "compact," and in dress "almost a dandy," one journalist said.[46] He might have been a banker, and his talk on financial matters would bear out the impression.[47] He watched his money, the man who had to borrow to pay for his honeymoon, and there is on record the remark that a cab driver made when he re-

44 Henriette Corkran, *Celebrities and I* (London, 1902), p. 165.

45 Browning's Account Book, in the British Museum (Ashley MS 5716), shows that he planned generally on "Board wages for 3 at 12^{s} a week each" on August 12, 1878, and in other years.

46 Letter 40.

47 Mrs. Andrew Crosse, *Red Letter Days of My Life* (London, 1892), I, 270.

ceived the poet's tip: "You may be a damned good poet, but you're a bad paymaster." [48]

He was constantly receiving gifts, ranging from writing paper (from Mrs. Skirrow), to a proffered piano (from Mrs. Bronson), to £1,860 of railroad stock (from Mrs. Benzon); [49] and his gifts in return (and Mrs. Browning's, earlier) were treasured, but they were not costly—a volume of his verse, a letter George Sand had sent his wife (to Mrs. Moore), or a flower from the grave of Keats (to Mrs. Eckley). Thus one is puzzled in examining his account book,[50] in which he meticulously recorded pounds, shillings, and pence, by comparatively expensive gifts for an unidentified "A":

	L.	s.	d.	
Ring for A	3	10		Dec. 15, 1877
Brooch for A		10		July 19, 1880
Solitaires for A	1	5		Dec. 19, 1881
Bracelet		15	6	" "
Clasp for A's br		6	6	Jan. 13, 1881
A's Bracelet	3	5		Dec. 21, 1881
R. Acad		2		Jan. 4, 1883
A's coachman		5		" "

Perhaps "A" was Mrs. Sutherland Orr, whose Christian name was Alexandra and who, Browning told Furnivall, was "simply the dearest woman friend I can boast of in the world." [51]

Browning was surprised, he says in these letters, to hear that Julia Constance Fletcher thought him to be her "very best friend." [52] A Virginia Marsh, who has but one reference in his letters, "ejaculated repeatedly" as she parted from him, *"Good friend!"* [53] But Browning

48 *Ibid.*, p. 274.

49 Letter 10, n. 7.

50 In BM, see note 45.

51 Unpublished letter of November 28, 1885, in Huntington Library.

52 Letter 45, n. 3.

53 Letter 6, n. 4.

had a charm, a "caressing kindness," which made some people think that he cared more for them than his genuine interest should warrant. W. H. Mallock tells how Browning, in a "dazzling white waistcoat," at their very first meeting held out both his hands to the young man "with an almost boisterous cordiality."[54] Emily Harris, whom he met through Mrs. FitzGerald, never forgot how the poet, with tears in his eyes, spoke "with infinite reverence in the lowest tone, his feeling for the mysterious RUACH, that animates the very core, and the essence of Judaism."[55] His desire and ability to be all things to all people, while it elicited friendship also elicited the charge of insincerity from Mrs. Carlyle, who wrote in her journal that Browning dropped on one knee and kissed Mrs. Montagu's hand "with fervour," although she had heard him speak slightingly of Mrs. Montagu.[56] It was, however, possible for Browning to be sincere and to remain within the bounds of verbal truth on each occasion, to be sincere when he befriended Miss Fletcher at one time and equally sincere when he gossiped about her mother at another.[57]

✣

Mrs. FitzGerald's friendship for Browning included his sister Sarianna and his son Robert, known as Pen. Browning's sister, Sarianna, who was two years younger than he, made her home with the poet after the death of their father in Paris in 1866 and appears in these letters as the dear friend and correspondent of Mrs. FitzGerald. As a member of Browning's household, she was unobtrusive, loyal, and proud of mentioning the grandees with whom her brother dined. Besides being the perfect traveling companion for Browning's autumn holiday, she also acted as his censor: "He so feared the turbulence of his own nature, that all his correspondence

[54] W. H. Mallock, *Memoirs of Life and Literature* (New York, 1920), p. 71.

[55] Quoted by Berlin-Lieberman, *Robert Browning,* p. 18.

[56] T. and A. Carlyle, eds., *New Letters of Jane Welsh Carlyle* (London, 1903), II, 108–109.

[57] Letter 45, n. 5.

passed through her hands, as a safeguard against such expression as might stir up newspaper warfare."[58] Unselfish as she was with members of her own family, there was in her relation with outsiders an "unloveableness" detected by Michael Field, who affirmed that it was "useless to think that Brownings will act gracefully."[59] After her brother's death she lived in Italy with her nephew Pen.[60]

The Pen Browning whom Mrs. FitzGerald first knew was a slender young man in his twenties, an artist, who sometimes came back from the Continent where he was studying to visit his father and aunt in London. Their first recorded meeting (although they must have met earlier) was on April 12, 1875, at a party at Madame Schwabe's, on which occasion Jenny Lind was also present. When Pen went abroad to study art, in 1874, he became in his father's eyes a "dear good and absolutely satisfactory fellow,"[61] but before that time, Browning had thought himself only the "manger" at which Pen fed and that the greatest good he could do his son would be to die and leave him "just enough to keep him from starving."[62]

Pen's industry changed all that. From Dinant in Belgium and later from Paris he shipped enormous canvases, which Browning hung in an empty house in Queen's Gate Gardens, whither he invited his friends — Tennyson and Carlyle among them — to view and approve the work. The paintings were quite ordinary, really, but to please Browning Victorian artists said kind-hearted things about them, and

58 T. Moore and D. C. Sturge Moore, eds., *Works and Days: From the Journal of Michael Field* (London, 1933), p. 28.

59 *Ibid.*, p. 217.

60 Ungraceful, certainly, is an admonition in her letter to Pen dated April 24, 1888: "Luckily, I recollected in time that to-morrow is Mrs. F.G's birthday, and I have sent her a small remembrance — a little Venetian glass cup. I do not know if you are in the habit of 'remembering' it, — if not, pray don't begin." (Extract from an unpublished letter sent to the editor by Lachlan Phil Kelley.)

61 Paul Landis, ed., *Letters of the Brownings to George Barrett* (Urbana, 1958), p. 304.

62 *Ibid.*, p. 295.

Mrs. FitzGerald, Pen's "original patroness,"[63] purchased one, a self-portrait, and hung it over the mantel in the morning room at Shalstone. "Do you know," Browning said to Mrs. Bronson, "if the thing were possible, I would renounce all personal ambition and would destroy every line I ever wrote, if by so doing I could see fame and honor heaped on my Robert's head."[64]

As the son of illustrious parents, Pen was the object of more attention and more attentive gossip than he would have otherwise attracted. The story went the rounds that he had taken a Belgian wife, the daughter of his landlord at Dinant. Dr. Furnivall, who was addicted to printing things about the poet and his kin, wrote to Browning for the facts, which Furnivall volunteered to publish. Yes, Browning wrote, there had been an attachment a few years back, but he had persuaded the twenty-six-year-old Pen to break off the engagement because of the hindrance it would be to his career. "Friends of my own," Browning wrote, "with vigilant eyes enough, visit him occasionally, and have long ago set my mind at rest."[65] Here Mrs. FitzGerald's diary for 1875 appears to dovetail with the reported events in Dinant. She left Shalstone on June 22, crossed to Belgium, met Pen, took him away from Dinant for a few days, returned to London on July 12, had luncheon with Browning and Sarianna, and returned to Shalstone on July 14 "for good." Can this be other than a further example of kind graciousness to her friend the aging poet, who was also a worried father?

In 1887, to Browning's thinking, all Pen's problems were solved, despite what his father called his "many peculiarities."[66] In a time

[63] Letter 10, n. 5. Browning elsewhere said that Frederick Lehmann was Pen's "very earliest patron" (Rudolph C. Lehmann, *Memories of Half a Century* [London, 1908], p. 125); but it is possible for a man to be the earliest patron and a woman to be the original patroness.

[64] *Cornhill,* 1902, p. 152.

[65] Unpublished letter of January 5, 1882, in Huntington Library.

[66] D&K, p. 349.

when American heiresses were marrying European titles, Pen, at thirty-eight, wooed and won his heiress, Fannie Coddington of New York City. Fannie tells how, shortly after her parents' death, Pen called on her and greeted her warmly with both his arms extended—rather like the cordial way his father had.[67] Then followed marriage, honeymoon, trip to New York, miscarriage, return, settlement in Venice, and lavish expenditure. Fannie was the ideal daughter: in the two years before Browning died, she wrote to him or to Sarianna every day, giving news of Pen. When Fannie bought Pen the Palazzo Rezzonico in Venice, he discovered his true gift, a flair for interior decoration. "What Pen Browning has done here . . ." Henry James wrote to his sister, "transcends description for the beauty, and, as Ruskin would say, 'wisdom and rightness' of it. It is altogether royal and imperial." [68] Into the royal household Pen introduced Ferdinando Romagnoli, the manservant of Florentine days, whom Browning had rediscovered, after nineteen years, serving as cook for an American family in Venice. The Rezzonico also offered shelter to Ferdinando's wife, Lily Wilson, now old and crazy, but forty years earlier Mrs. Browning's faithful maid and then Pen's nurse.

Soon there were money quarrels, even in the presence of visitors.[69] Pen was vexed when Fannie wanted to know the price of everything in dollars. "They're dollars to begin with," Fannie said. Still more vexing, even maddening, was her passion for building Christian chapels in Japan. American colonists in Venice said that Pen had not wanted to marry anybody, but that his father, who was worldly, had made him. Pen was more inclined to conspicuous waste than to the thrift of his father. Surely he had to pay too much

[67] Fannie B. Browning, *Some Memories of Robert Browning* (Boston, 1928), p. 8.

[68] Percy Lubbock, ed., *The Letters of Henry James* (New York, 1920), pp. 168–169.

[69] Unless otherwise noted, information in these paragraphs is taken from conversations the editor had with people who knew Pen well, including the Cavaliere Ingegnere Cantoni, Pen's best friend at Asolo.

(2,000 lire) to induce an Italian circus to part with its python, or an organ grinder with his monkey, or *contadini* with their furniture. After the inevitable separation, Fannie wanted her furniture back, and Pen had to give up the Rezzonico. As far as she was concerned, his aunt Sarianna, who lived in the Rezzonico with him, would not part with a thing; but in 1895 Marie Coddington, Fannie's elder sister, threatened to call in "outside help" unless Pen delivered the goods with deliberate speed. Sarianna "pecked and raved and repeated herself, but Pen was patient with her." [70] To add to his difficulties, a friend identified only as N, to whom Pen had let a house at nominal rent, disappointed the friendship and brought a lawsuit: the "dastard" used "mean threats." [71]

Pen continued with his hobby of purchasing, restoring, furnishing, and then abandoning old houses. At one of his houses in Asolo he had seven horses and five dogs; at another near Florence he had scores of dachshunds, which he allowed to interbreed, to grow longer and longer, and finally to become monstrous. He no longer exhibited, but he continued to paint, requiring two models, Camilla, who had beautiful features, and Fasana, *la brutta,* whose beautiful body nature should have assigned to Camilla's face. He was kindhearted, *"buono di cuore, buonissimo,"* loved his inferiors, and everybody loved him in spite of the fact that he owed everybody, that physically he became too fat—a "curly ball," a grotesque—and that aesthetically he dressed like a Paris jockey with impossible waistcoats and yellow chamois gloves. Italians explained it all by saying that Pen was a changeling. Knowing his mother's love for Italy, her desire for a son, and her history of miscarriages, her attendants had substituted a peasant boy for the baby she had lost. Charming as is this indication of the Italian desire to please, the story is not true: Pen was the image of his mother.

On his deathbed, Browning had told Pen to seek the advice of

[70] Moore and Moore, *Works and Days,* pp. 206–209.
[71] *Ibid.,* p. 210.

George Smith, his publisher, whenever in need of good counsel. Smith looked after Pen. He used to go to Italy, make inquiries of friends (as Browning had done), and give Pen checks. In 1898, Pen made another mistake: he gave Smith permission to publish the love-letters of the Brownings,[72] only to bring down upon himself the wrath of the Barretts. His uncle, C. J. Moulton-Barrett, wrote to the London *Standard* making public his view that not many a son "either for gain or love of notoriety, would make public the confidential letters of his mother." [73] In spite of all, Pen was, it is gratifying to learn, *felicissimo* — in a state of grace that even his father had not achieved.

When he was sixty-three, in 1912, Pen suffered a heart attack and died after three weeks' illness. The next year his effects were auctioned at Sotheby's. The £27,934 realized went to pay off his debts.

✣

Mrs. FitzGerald's records for 1876 indicate that Browning and Pen were visiting at Shalstone in July. They returned to London on July 10, and the letters of this volume begin on July 13.

[72] *The Letters of Robert Browning and Elizabeth Barrett Barrett (1845–1846)*, in two volumes (London: Smith, Elder & Co., 1899; New York: Harper, 1899).

[73] Reprinted in *The Critic*, June 1899, p. 499.

Letters from

Robert Browning to Mrs. Thomas FitzGerald

1876–1889

Letter 1

[*19, Warwick Crescent, London, W. July 13, 1876*]
Thursday M[*ornin*]*g.*[1]

So, dear Friend, I am to have "salt & mustard" besides all the other good things, and charming photographs of Balliol,[2] and a pleasant letter from Miss Bairnfather [3] with the last news of you! Thanks—whatever warm feeling can be put into the little word! It does not express the earnest wish I have that your Son's [4] health may be amending, and the anxieties which grow out of it may abate. Probably they find you more inclined to entertain them than if you were in London: those quiet beautiful lawns and trees and flowers shut you in upon yourself, while—so to speak,—there are outlets of escape in London. I can do so little, and would fain do so much!

Pen [5] is just gone: he saw his friends to his satisfaction,—especially Millais,[6] who painted goodnaturedly while he sate and looked on for two hours. He was unable to see Leighton.[7] He will proceed to Dinant to-morrow, stay a fortnight, then return to Antwerp: (he has left "all his things" at Dinant, it appears:) the day is propitious for a voyage. He sent the kindest of loves to you,—what need to say?

I have dined out—and been to a "Ball"—on each of the two days since I saw you: the two "Balls" I supposed to be mere evening receptions, or I should have kept away from them. At L^{y} Howard's [8] last night I sate on a sofa with Mr. Lowe [9] and philosophized over the scene. To-day is very hot and I am tired. I duly gave your message to Mrs Bayne [10]—who was greatly pleased to receive it.

She had the Bishops of Winchester [11] and Ely [12] for guests,—good, but *not* the best!

Won't you write and tell me how you are—which will imply—how your Son is? but not about that subject exclusively,—write of Shalstone, and books at Shalstone, and whatever suits Shalstone: and, though you need not think to be *repaid*—you shall have an acknowledgement, if only a poor sheet like the present.

I saw yesterday, in the course of my walks, Mr. Gladstone [13]—who said that the sitting of Parliament would be prolonged,—A. Trollope,[14] who confided to me his profound dislike of "Deronda",[15] L[d] Coleridge,[16] fresh from the Trial,—who expressed a hearty admiration for the abilities of Grant,—and L[d] Acton,[17]—who had just been correcting a strange blunder of the said Trollope's, who, it seems, has just told the story of the Spartan boy with the—not "fox" but—wolf concealed in his bosom! [18] Such flowers one plucks in dusty London!

Be happy, dear Friend, & satisfy the true heartfelt wishes of

Yours affectionately

RBrowning.

Manuscript: Stowe School, Buckingham

1. The holograph of this letter was found at Stowe School, in a volume of *The Gentleman's Magazine,* a set of which had been bought in a sale at Shalstone Manor in 1944. The letter was published in the school magazine, *The Stoic,* in March 1955, and edited by John C. Saunders, who assigned the date on internal evidence, specifically that of the trial.

2. Balliol College, Oxford, of which Browning was made honorary fellow in 1867.

3. Georgina Bairnsfather, friend of Mrs. FitzGerald, pianist, and daughter of George Bairnsfather of the Honorable East India Company Society (MPFG).

4. Robert Allan FitzGerald (1834–1881), second son, barrister at law, married (1867) Harriet Agnes Rigby and had three sons. He was for many years the honorary secretary of the Marylebone Cricket Club and went with the first English cricket team to America. He was the author of *Jerks in from Short Leg* (London, 1866) and *Wickets in the West: Tour of the All-England Eleven in America* (London, 1873). During the last few years of his life he suffered from a mental illness that caused his

mother much sorrow. (See *A Supplement to Allibone's Critical Dictionary of English Literature* [Philadelphia, 1891], I, 598; Burke's *Landed Gentry* sub Purefoy; and *The Victoria History of the County of Hertford* [Westminster, 1902], I, 374.)

5. Robert Wiedemann Barrett Browning (1849–1912), the Brownings' only child.

6. In the autumn of 1873, Millais was with Pen at Birnam in Scotland (T. L. Hood, ed., *Letters of Robert Browning Collected by Thomas J. Wise* [London, 1933], p. 162), and, while Millais painted his *Scotch Firs,* Pen tried his hand at the same subject, impressing Millais enough to have him recommend that Pen devote himself to art (Felix Moschelles, *Fragments of an Autobiography* [New York, 1899], p. 320). See Letter 62, n. 8.

7. Sir Frederick Leighton (1830–1896), artist, president of the Royal Academy (1878), and first Baron Leighton of Stretton (1896).

8. Perhaps Lucy Joan Cavendish (1808–1899), fourth daughter of the Duke of Portland and wife (1828) of Charles Augustus, sixth Lord Howard de Walden.

9. Robert Lowe (1811–1892), leader writer for the *Times* (1850), M.P. from 1852 to 1880, first Viscount Sherbrooke (1880).

10. Alicia (Pryme) Bayne (1814–1883), a cousin of W. M. Thackeray. (See Genealogical Table II in *The Letters and Private Papers of William Makepeace Thackeray,* ed. G. N. Ray [Cambridge, Mass., 1946], IV, 462.)

11. The Rt. Rev. Edward Harold Browne (1811–1891), Lord Bishop of Winchester from 1873 to 1890.

12. The Rt. Rev. James Russell Woodford (1820–1885), Lord Bishop of Ely (1873), and chaplain to Queen Victoria (1872).

13. William Ewart Gladstone (1809–1898), prime minister. Browning's friendship for Gladstone was warm at the time of this letter but later cooled.

14. Anthony Trollope (1815–1882), whose political novel *The Prime Minister* appeared in 1876.

15. George Eliot's novel *Daniel Deronda* appeared serially between February and June of 1876 in *Blackwood's Magazine.*

16. John Duke Coleridge (1820–1894), eminent lawyer, fellow of Exeter College from 1843 to 1846, Attorney General from 1871 to 1873, first Baron Coleridge (1874), and Lord Chief Justice of the Common Pleas (1880). On July 7 and 11, 1876, he presided in Guildhall during "The Lisbon Steam Tramways Company Case" (Twycross vs. Grant and Others), when Grant appeared in person without counsel, addressed the court, and earned the public praise of Lord Coleridge (*Times,* July 14, 1876, p. 10e).

17. John Emerich Edward Dolberg (1834–1902), eighth baronet, first Baron Acton of Aldenham (1869), historian, and moralist.

18. "The Spartan boy did not even trouble to make a grimace when the wolf bit him beneath his frock, and these were all Spartan boys," (Trollope, *The Prime Minister,* chap. xx — III, 241 in 1893 edition).

Letter 2

Blairbeg, Lamlash, Arran. N. B.[1]
Aug. 28. '76

Dear Friend, I got your letter on Saturday — too late however for a proper reply — and there was no post yesterday. I should think it a privilege beyond my other poor powers of writing if I could indeed be of any comfort to you: yet I seem to see that there are very many comforting circumstances: the complete absence of pain or fear at the enforced seclusion — which perhaps amounts to positive *happiness,* — surely *that* is a blessing. I confess I wonder, dear friend, that you could entertain for a moment that doubt which you express — & which Mr Hussey[2] so strangely declares he cannot solve — as to the liabi[li]ties of any soul deprived by the visitation of God of that reason which is given as a guide to its actions. WHO has said *"I* will be eyes to the blind"?[3] — and may not the soul want sight much more than the body? What struck me so much in that Life of Schopenhauer[4] which you gave me, was that doctrine which he considered his grand discovery — and which *I* had been persuaded of from my boyhood — and have based my whole life upon: — that the soul is above and *behind* the intellect which is merely its servant. I first met with this doctrine's enunciation in a memoir of Robert Hall the Baptist Minister,[5] who was subject to fits of mental alienation, and expected to be eventually deprived altogether of his reasoning faculty. The memoir went on to say that he had a correspondence with some eminent friend on this subject — I believe, Macintosh[6] — who pressed on his consideration that the instrument was not the craftsman, the intelligence — not the soul. The consequences of this doctrine were so momentous to me — so destructive of vanity, on the one hand, — or undue depression at failure, on the other — that I am sure there must be references to and deductions from it throughout the whole of my works: and I wrote a letter to this effect to a friend & relation of Miss Zimmern,[7]—at the request of that friend. Now, in the case of any one deprived, by no fault of his own, of those *eyes* of the soul—the reasoning powers—could we wrong the justice as well as the goodness of God more offensively than by supposing that He will ignore the consequences of his own act and punish the blind for blindness? In your son's case,[8]—the letters which I read contained positive proof that his religious feeling was very earnest—*that* is the *soul:* and if, like poor L[d] Lyttelton[9] who was similarly afflicted, in the absence of his *soul's eyes* he should commit the worst of excesses against himself or others—I should never dare attribute to God what would be injustice in a human being—nay, in a *less* degree,—and think Him capable of punishing what Himself was the agent in producing. That is my opinion, and it is inexplicable to me how people with a belief in the Mercy and Rectitude of God can have any other. Trust in these, dear Friend,—and dismiss all such fancies as derogatory to the All-good and All-wise.

Now, let us turn our own servants,—our own intelligence and thoughts,—from the morbid employment about such matters, and make them do legitimate duty by bearing us above what sorrow may be so surmounted. You fortunately have much to employ you—many to care for and make happy—and, even in your own present affliction, there are others claiming your love. Moreover, there is still abundance of hope—most rational hope.

Our days go by swiftly here. We are half-way in the *fourth* week of our residence—which yet seems as if it had just begun. The beauties of the little isle are abundant: we had, till yesterday, continued fine weather, and employed the time to advantage: yesterday was rainy, and to-day broke in torrents: but already the sun is shining again. I walk for two hours before breakfast,—and afterward walk or drive (even then, descending and walking) till dinner time—at 8½: the middle of the day is for reading—and no writing at all. Nothing can exceed the purity of the air, and general sense of pleasantness: it ought to do me a world of good, and may really help me through the winter without the usual penalty I pay in the shape of a "cold". Sarianna [10] does not fare so well, unfortunately. She is much troubled with pains in the face—cheek & gums: and, two days ago, had a swollen face which would have frightened you. She is better, I hope, today. Miss Smith [11] is getting abundantly strong—walks well—and enjoys the place—as who would not? She begs to be most kindly remembered to you. Thank you much for the "Academy": [12] I put it aside always—and you will receive it in due time not much the worse for its journeying. I hope you don't lay to heart—indeed, don't mind one straw the howlings which my stone flung among the critics has caused—as I was prepared for.[13] I always intended, for the benefit of my successors, to leave on record some memorial of my feeling for the authorities which have sate in judgment on me this long while—especially the "poets" who, dropping out of the ranks, condescended to hide behind a wall, throw a handful of mud at their so-called "rival": and then slink out and stand by his side as a "fellow-poet" just as if nothing had happened: and one man, who has been playing these tricks with me for I can't tell how long, seemed the most perfect specimen of the "little man" I ever met with or imagined: [14] I gave him one fillip in return for fifty or more flea-bites. It seems, he *is* little—physically as well as morally & intellectually: but you may be sure that had he equalled Golia[t]h in stature such a creature would figure in my eyes as a pygmy. Enough of him! I leave myself no room but for the most earnest and affectionate of farewells. God bless you, dear friend. I am ever yours RB

Manuscript: Carl H. Pforzheimer Library, RB 31

1. In 1876, Browning, his sister, and Miss Annie Egerton Smith spent their holiday near the village of Lamlash on the coast of the Isle of Arran, North Britain (Scotland). They stayed, it appears from this heading, at Blairbeg House (now the

Bay Hotel) on Blairbeg Farm. They left London on August 3 (W. C. DeVane and K. L. Knickerbocker, *New Letters of Robert Browning* [New Haven, 1950], p. 235) and had returned there by October 25 (Hood, p. 176).

2. The Rev. Henry Walford Hussey, Rector of Shalstone (1873–1878), left Shalstone for a poor London parish (*Buckingham Express,* Sept. 21, 1878) and was succeeded by the Rev. William Cotton Risley (*ibid.,* Oct. 12). He returned to assist Mr. Risley at Mrs. FitzGerald's funeral (*ibid.,* July 29, 1899).

3. "I was eyes to the blind, and feet was I to the lame" (Job, 29:15).

4. Helen Zimmern, *Arthur Schopenhauer, His Life and His Philosophy* (London: Longmans, Green), 1876.

5. Robert Hall (1764–1831), Baptist minister and pulpit orator, whose mind twice lost its balance between 1804 and 1806. *The Works of the Rev. Robert Hall, A.M., with a Brief Memoir of His Life* by Dr. [Olinthus] Gregory was published in 1832 in six volumes. The doctrine Browning presents in this letter is very much like Hall's discussion of "The Spirituality of the Divine Nature" (American edition of *The Works* [New York, 1842], III, 295–310).

6. Sir James Mackintosh (1765–1832), Scottish publicist and physician, and Robert Hall's closest friend when they were undergraduates at Aberdeen. He was the grandfather of Julia Wedgwood, with whom Browning corresponded in the 1860's (Richard Curle, ed., *Robert Browning and Julia Wedgwood: A Broken Friendship* [New York, 1937]).

7. Helen Zimmern (1846–1934), author and translator from the German. Her books include *Homes and Haunts of Famous Authors* (1906), which contains a chapter on the Brownings. She corresponded with Browning and thanked him for encouragement and sympathy in the preface to her *Firdusi: Epic of Kings* (1882), a book which he used in writing *Ferishtah's Fancies* (1884).

8. Robert Allan FitzGerald (see Letter 1, n. 4). In her copy of *Bread from Heaven: Scripture Texts for Every Day in the Year in Greek and English* (London, n.d.) Mrs. FitzGerald wrote beside August 16, "On this day 1876 our poor Robert came home to P[ortland] P[lace]," and beside August 17, "only to leave us/Most sad day." Beside the text "And yet I am not alone for the Father is with me" she wrote that Robert had quoted these words when she was once obliged to leave him for a little while.

9. George William, Lord Lyttleton (1817–1876), died on April 18, 1876, having flung himself downstairs "while of unsound mind" (Cokayne, *Complete Peerage*). His town house, 24 Portland Place, was near Mrs. FitzGerald's, which was at 22.

10. Sarianna Browning (1814–1903), the poet's sister.

11. Browning first met Miss Annie Egerton Smith, part owner of the Liverpool *Mercury,* in the 1850's in Florence (Mrs. Sutherland Orr, *Life and Letters of Robert Browning* [Boston, 1891], II, 441), where her sister Mrs. William Bracken lived. She made her home not in Liverpool but at 1 Holland Park Terrace, Notting Hill (according to her will at Somerset House). Browning, his sister, and Miss Smith

spent four summer holidays together (1874–1877), and her sudden death on the last of these occasioned his *La Saisiaz* (1878), which he dedicated to her.

12. Mrs. FitzGerald regularly sent Browning her copy of *The Academy: A Weekly Review of Literature, Science and Art.*

13. Browning's *Pacchiarotto* (published on July 18, 1876) was a fierce reply to the critics who had been hostile to him for many years. Some of the reviews were fierce in return, notably that in the *Saturday Review* of August 12.

14. Alfred Austin (1835–1913), critic and poet, had earned the implacable enmity of Browning when he published an article on the poet in *Temple Bar,* 26:316–333 (June 1869), criticizing the poetry as not being poetry at all and criticizing Browning for his inordinate cultivation of high society. Browning had hoped to be offered the laureateship for the pleasure of refusing it (Mary Sturgeon, *Michael Field* [London, 1922], p. 43); his death in 1889 spared him the knowledge that Austin became laureate in 1896.

Letter 3

W[arwick] C[rescent] Dec. 30. '76.

Dear Friend, I have had many memorials of you this last week of one or another kind,—how shall this one paper-utterance return thanks for them all? You know how I wish you to "prosper as the soul prospereth": [1] it is a coincidence that when I wrote to Tennyson last week I used the same words with reference to his dear and invalided wife.[2] They were greatly impressed on me once—many years ago—when, being with my wife on a short visit in the country, we went together to a little dissenting chapel, on Sunday, when the preacher took that text for a very admirable discourse on the possible advantages of sickness. I remember, Kingsley came over and spent the previous day with our hosts, and walked with us all the afternoon. When next I saw him, at the Deanery, just before his death, I failed to recognize the strong fresh man who jumped up a hillock to pluck barberries for my wife, and, when we inspected the ruins of an abbey in the neighborhood, lay down in the stone coffin embedded still in its earth there.[3] He knew me, however.

To-day is the private-view of the exhibition of Old Masters:[4] I reserved a ticket for you,—on the chance that you *might* come to town,—till two hours ago. The day is dismal, and unpropitious enough for picture-seeing: Altogether a disspiriting Christmas time: no Pen, no jollity of any kind.

I rejoice to hear that you come up for Thursday: on that day I will take you to see the portrait[5]—on condition that you dine with us afterwards: shall it not be so? And pray forgive a stupid inadvertency of mine with respect to the last letter of S.[arianna] which she entrusted to me not only for posting but *stamping:* and which I wisely dropped into the box *stampless!* As the oversight would have been the same had the cost to you been far greater—I feel humbled about it, and apologize sincerely. And now, all good go to you, dear Friend. We are rightly meant to foresee *nothing* (nor good, nor evil[)]. I trust you will see good in your & my heart's content. Ever aff^y yours RB.

Manuscript: Carl H. Pforzheimer Library, RB 32

1. "Beloved, I wish above all things that thou mayest prosper and be in health, even as thy soul prospereth" (3 John, 1:2).

2. Lady Tennyson was an invalid after 1874 (Charles Tennyson, *Alfred Tennyson* [New York, 1949], p. 414).

3. Charles Kingsley (1819–1875), novelist, socialist, muscular Christian, and rector. Mrs. Browning tells of meeting Kingsley in 1852 at the home of her friends the Paines in Farnham, Surrey (F. G. Kenyon, ed., *The Letters of Elizabeth Barrett Browning* [New York, 1897], II, 83). Near Farnham, on the bank of the Wey, are the thirteenth-century ruins of Waverley Abbey, the earliest Cistercian foundation in England. "In the middle of the nave is a stone coffin, with black and yellow tesserae . . ." (Thomas Allen, *A New and Complete History of the Counties of Surrey and Sussex* [London, 1830], II, 235–240).

4. The exhibition of old masters at Burlington House was opened to the public

on January 1, 1877, and included paintings by Van Dyck, Reynolds, and Gainsborough (*The Academy*, 10:636 [December 30, 1876]).

5. Perhaps one of the many portraits that Pen painted of his father. (See appendix for description of cross-writing from the word "portrait" to the end of the letter.)

Letter 4

[*19, Warwick Crescent, W.*]
January 20, 1877

Dear Friend,—I have our letter of yesterday, and thank you all I can for its goodness and graciousness to me unworthy. . . . I returned on Thursday—the hospitality of our Master [1] being not easy to set aside. But to begin with the beginning: the passage from London to Oxford was exceptionally prosperous—the train was full of men my friends. I was welcomed on arriving by a Fellow who installed me in my rooms—then came the pleasant meeting with Jowett, who at once took me to tea with his other guests, the Archbishop of Canterbury,[2] Bishop of London,[3] Dean of Westminster,[4] the Airlies,[5] Cardwells,[6] male and female. Then came the banquet (I enclose you the plan, having no doubt that you will recognize the name of many an acquaintance: please return it)—and, the dinner done, speechifying set in vigorously. The Archbishop proposed the standing *Floreat domus de Balliolo* [7]—to which the Master made due and amusing answer, himself giving the health of the Primate. Lord Coleridge,[8] in a silvery speech, drank to the University, responded to by the Vice-Chancellor.[9] I forget who proposed the visitors—the Bishop of London, perhaps Lord Cardwell. Professor Smith [10] gave the two Houses of Parliament,—Jowett, the Clergy, coupling with it the name of your friend Mr. Rogers [11]—on whom he showered every kind of praise, and Mr. Rogers returned thanks very characteristically and pleasantly. Lord Lansdowne[12] drank to the Bar (Mr. Bowen),[13] Lord Camperdown[14] to—I really forget what: Mr. Green[15] to Literature and Science, delivering a most undeserved eulogium on myself, with a more rightly directed one on Arnold, Swinburne, and the old pride of Balliol, Clough:[16] this was cleverly and almost touchingly answered by dear Mat Arnold. Then the Dean of Westminster gave the Fellows and Scholars—and then—twelve o'clock struck. We were, counting from the time of preliminary assemblage, six hours and a half engaged: *fully* five and a half nailed to our chairs at the table: but the whole thing was brilliant, genial, and suggestive of many and various thoughts to me—and there was a warmth, earnestness, and yet refinement about it which I never experienced in any previous public dinner. Next morning I breakfasted with Jowett and his guests, found that return would be difficult: while as the young men were to return on Friday there would be no opposition to my departure on Thursday. The morning was dismal with rain, but after luncheon there was a chance of getting a little air, and I walked for more than two hours, then heard service in New Coll.—then dinner again: my room had been prepared in the Master's house. So, on Thursday, after yet another breakfast, I left by the noonday train, after all sorts of kindly offices from the Master . . . [Note the care I][17] observe in detailing all these sayings and doings, because you lay the injunction on me so to do. There were no reporters suffered to be present—consequently (as I was assured) no account could appear in the Oxford papers: I take it, that in yesterday's "Times"[18] was furnished by one or more of the guests: it is quite correct as far as it goes. There were, I find, certain little paragraphs which must have been furnished by "guessers": Swinburne, set down as present, was away, through his Father's illness: the Cardinal[19] also excused himself, as did the B^{p} of Salisbury[20] and others. There, have I tired you? I will remember, and do what is possible about Miss Zimmern, whom I hope to see next week. I am crammed into a corner indeed: but it will hold the assurance that I am ever affy

Yours R Browning

Text: Orr, II, 449–452. The elliptical dots are in the source.

1. Benjamin Jowett (1817–1893), Regius Professor of Greek and Master of Balliol College from 1870 to 1893. Browning spent two days (January 16–18) at Oxford on the occasion of the opening of New Hall at Balliol College, commemorated by a grand banquet on the sixteenth at which some 250 senior members of Balliol were present (*Times,* January 17, 1877, p. 10e).

2. Archibald Campbell Tait (1811–1882), fellow of Balliol, and Archbishop of Canterbury (1869).

3. The Rt. Rev. John Jackson (1811–1885), Lord Bishop of London from 1868 to 1885.

4. Arthur Penrhyn Stanley (1815–1881), Dean of Westminster Abbey (1864).

5. David Graham Drummond Ogilvy (1826–1881), seventh Earl of Airlie, and his wife, Henrietta Blanch, daughter of the second Lord Stanley of Alderley.

6. Edward Cardwell (1813–1886), one time fellow of Balliol, statesman, and first Viscount Cardwell (1874).

7. "May the house of Balliol flourish," a traditional toast.

8. John Duke Coleridge (1820–1894). See Letter 1, n. 16.

9. James Edwards Sewell (1810–1903), warden of New College from 1860 to 1903 and vice-chancellor of Oxford from 1874 to 1878.

10. Henry John Stephen Smith, brilliant mathematician and classicist, fellow of Balliol. In 1878 Browning endorsed his unsuccessful candidacy for Parliament (D&K, p. 245).

11. William Rogers (1819–1896), M.A., Oxford (1844), chaplain in ordinary to Queen Victoria (1857), rector of St. Botolph's, Bishopsgate (1863).

12. Henry Charles Keith Petty-FitzMaurice (1845–1927), fifth Marquis of Lansdowne.

13. Charles Synge Christopher Bowen (1835–1894), fellow of Balliol (1857), lawyer and judge, knighted (1879), Baron Bowen (1893).

14. Robert Adam Philips Haldane (1841–1918), third Earl of Camperdown.

15. Thomas Hill Green (1836–1882), fellow of Balliol (1860), Jowett's right-hand man, Whyte professor of moral philosophy from 1878 to 1882 and the "Mr. Gray" of Mrs. Humphrey Ward's *Robert Elsmere* (1888) (*DNB*).

16. Matthew Arnold (1822–1888), Algernon Charles Swinburne (1837–1909), and Arthur Hugh Clough (1819–1861), all Balliol men.

17. The remainder of the text is taken not from Mrs. Orr but from the catalogue

of the J. H. Benton sale of the American Art Association, March 12, 1920, number 109, which includes a facsimile page of the letter.

18. *Times*, January 19, 1877, p. 4a.

19. Henry Edward, Cardinal Manning (1808–1892).

20. The Rt. Rev. George Moberly (1803–1885), Bishop of Salisbury (1869).

Letter 5

Trin[*ity*] *Coll*[*ege*] *Cam*[*bridge*].
March 10. '77.

Dear Friend, I snatch a minute to speak my usual word which reaches your kindness at Shalstone: I shall hardly be able—indeed shall *not* be able to arrive in time at London for the longer letter I would write if I could. This then is only to tell you that I return presently to Town after a very pleasant, if somewhat wearying visit—wearying, inasmuch as I have been engaged during the whole of it—(on the first day, to six *meals!*). but the kindness of everybody has been extreme. Joachim's [1] investiture as Doctor, his Concert, his company—were even & all worth the pains of the journey. Our weather too has been fine, though cold,—at all events, propitious for walking and sight seeing. I come in, after a long morning in the Library, where I have glanced at most of the rarities—Milton's Manuscripts,—and Bentley's,—Newton's,—Porson's books.[2] But I soon get fatigued with even such kind and more than attentive society as I have had here—being, inspite of appearance very owl-like in my predilection for the shady & the still. I am also anxious to hear about Pen, who was suffering from sore throat; I should have heard, I think, in any case of necessity: but no letters were forwarded here, by my desire. It transpired at the dinner-table yesterday that it was Pen's birthday: and his health was kindly drunk by the

Master [3] and guests in proximity. Good bye, dear Friend. All that this scribble aims at is to assure you that I am

Ever yours affectionately
Robt Browning.

Manuscript: Carl H. Pforzheimer Library, RB 33

1. On March 8, 1877, Cambridge University conferred the honorary degree of Doctor of Music on the violinist Joseph Joachim (1831–1907). Browning was one of the distinguished guests at the ceremony, which included a magnificent concert in which Joachim played Beethoven and Bach and conducted the first English hearing of Brahms' *Symphony in C Minor* (*The Academy,* March 17, 1877, pp. 239–240). Sir Charles Villiers Stanford wrote: "There was a most interesting gathering in Coutts Trotter's rooms at Trinity, when Joachim . . . Browning [and others] had a warm controversy on the subject of Beethoven's last quartets. The member of the party who talked most and knew least about the subject, was, curiously enough, Browning" (*Pages from an Unwritten Diary* [New York, 1914], p. 176).

On page one of this letter there is an annotation in Mrs. FitzGerald's hand: "E. FG was there to see him take the H degree." (See appendix for description.) The nature of this letter indicates that Mrs. FitzGerald was *not* there, but she was present when Browning himself received the honorary LL.D. from Cambridge in 1879. (Letter 18, n. 5).

2. John Milton, Richard Bentley, Isaac Newton, and Richard Porson — all distinguished sons of Cambridge, the last three of Trinity College.

3. William Hepworth Thompson (1810–1886), Master of Trinity College, Cambridge (1866–1886).

Letter 6

[*Chalet du Dr. Roussel,*
La Saisiaz]
August 17, 1877.

*** How lovely is this place [1] in its solitude and seclusion, with its trees and shrubs and flowers, and above all its live mountain stream which supplies three fountains, and two delightful baths, a marvel of delicate delight framed in with trees—I bathe there twice a day—and then what wonderful views from the chalet on every side! Geneva lying under us, with the lake and the whole plain bounded by the Jura and our own Salève, which latter seems rather close behind our house, and yet takes a hard hour and a half to ascend—all this you can imagine since you know the environs of the town; the peace and quiet move me the most. And I fancy I shall drowse out the two months or more, doing no more of serious work than reading—and that is virtuous renunciation of the glorious view to my right here—as I sit aerially like Euripides,[2] and see the clouds come and go, and the view change in correspondence with them. It will help me to get rid of the pain which attaches itself to the recollections of Lucerne and Berne "in the old days when the Greeks suffered so much," as Homer says.[3] But a very real and sharp pain touched me here when I heard of the death of poor Virginia Marsh,[4] whom I knew particularly, and parted with hardly a fortnight ago, leaving her affectionate and happy as ever. The tones of her voice as on one memorable occasion she ejaculated repeatedly *Good friend!* are fresh still. Poor Virginia!***[5]

Text: Orr, II, 457–458. The letter is incomplete.

1. In 1877, Browning, his sister, and Miss Smith spent their holiday in Switzerland, staying at La Saisiaz ("the sun"), a chalet a few miles southwest of Geneva. They had intended to remain two months, but Miss Smith's sudden death on September 14 (D&K, p. 240) altered their plans, and they returned almost at once to London.

2. Perhaps Browning had in mind Aristophanes' *The Archanians,* lines 307–310.

3. ". . . for we know everything that the Greeks and Trojans suffered in broad Troy by the will of the gods" (*Odyssey,* XII, 189–190). Browning elsewhere refers to this passage (*Dearest Isa,* Letter 99, May 22, 1867).

4. Mary Anne Virginia Gabriel (1825–1877), composer, wife of George March, of 58 Cadogan Place, died on August 7 as a result of "injuries sustained by a fall from a carriage" (*Times,* August 10, 1877, p. 1b).

5. Three asterisks (***) here and throughout indicate the beginning or the ending of a letter which exists only in part.

Letter 7

Chalet du Dr Roussel, etc.
Aug 30. '77 [*La Saisiaz*]

Dear Friend, Sarianna has just received a letter from you—I suppose, as it was written on Monday, my letter had not then reached you. My notion, you remember, was to manage, by writing on Thursday, to "call on you," as usual, on Sunday: but the arrangement seems unfortunate: you must tell me if *this* succeeds better than its predecessors. Yes, I did get the letter with the bit of Homer: but was I to translate it? My motions, that way, are stiff and slow in this relaxing place. I have brought Homer, however, and read a book occasionally—I ought to have told you how many remembrances of you I brought likewise: this writing-book, the very useful paper-knife memorial of Stonehenge, and, as you wished, Grillparzer:[1] and if they were *not* all here and about me, do you think I should forget you? I think I was disappointed at first with the over cultivated country—and the people,—peasantry,—seem ignoble, and quite prevent that "universal presence of Love" which Byron found apparent.[2] The peasant, absorbed in his money-grubbing, "with a clown's (not even) broad back turned (the reverse of) broadly to the glory of the stars"[3] repels me. But great beauties there are, and I open my heart to them as wide as I can. I have been just hearing the history of this little estate from its owner: it was a borderline between the two communes, Collonges and Bossey—the rivulet, I suppose, making the division. Hence,—perpetual feuds and fighting between the two amiable neighbours, each of whom disputed the right to this and the other inch of the border. Whereupon, the matter being referred to Carlo Alberto of Sardinia,[4] he determined that the little wedge of ground should belong to a third commune, and be constituted neutral ground: this commune sold its rights to a peasant, who transferred them to the present proprietor—and, on the change of masters, the French recognized the ownership: on each side; the forest (poor forest—thicket, say rather) belongs to the respective communes, and cannot be sold—much as our landlord would like to round-off his property. The live little spring-source, from the mountain, is a very real and peculiar advantage: one would value *that* greatly in England: what a vein of life there is in such a streamlet!—and the bath, hemmed in by trees, in which I indulge twice a day, is delightful. So much for this—if not lotos-eating, let us say, lettuce-eating land—there being a sleepiness and satisfaction in θρίδαξ,[5] as in the nobler herb. I shall not be too stupefied by it to get up and go away in due time. We had a pleasant excursion two days ago: took our meal, after a morning's journey, on the top of a mountain in the full view of Mont Blanc and its brethren and found we had made the full circle, or spiral, and were just above our house: if the notch in the mountain-wall behind it were cloven down even half way—we should see that assemblage by turning round our heads simply. As it is, we get the huge cape of shade two hours longer than were the barrier removed. I am glad we are on what I think the preferable side of the Lake.[6] To-morrow we visit Ferney.[7] And is all the sheet to be filled with nothing but—nothings like these? After all, you don't know them till I tell you: and you do know how glad I shall be to hear from you, and gladder still to see you when the six weeks more wear themselves away. Your news continue to be good: may all go well and better! I doubt if I shall catch this post to-day,—but I am trying to do so—and not trying but confident to be yours affectionately ever, RB.

I have not heard from Pen since I left London: does he write to you?[8]

Manuscript: Carl H. Pforzheimer Library, RB 34. There is an annotation in Mrs. FitzGerald's hand: see appendix for description.

1. Franz Grillparzer (1791–1872), Austrian dramatist and poet. E. Frothingham's English translation of his *Sappho* was published in 1876.

2. In his note to canto three, stanza ninety-nine, of *Childe Harold,* Byron speaks of love as "the great principle of the universe."

3. In "Echetlos" (1880) Browning speaks of "a clown's limbs broad and bare," and he called Mrs. Bronson's gondolier "broad-backed Luigi."

4. Charles Albert (1798–1849), King of Sardinia (Piedmont) from 1831 to 1849, and father of Victor Emmanuel.

5. The Greek for "lettuce."

6. Lake Geneva.

7. A village on the Swiss border four miles northwest of Geneva, famous as the residence of Voltaire from 1758 to 1778.

8. Browning's postscript is cross-written: see appendix.

Letter 8

19 Warwick Crescent, W
June 9. '78.

Dear Friend, I am happy that all would seem to be going satisfactorily with you at Shalstone. You know you always have my absolutely best wishes,—so, enough of that assurance. S. will have told you that the exchange has been accomplished,—that the "Roofs" are with us and the "Ruins" with you.[1] We had a pleasant and satisfactory letter from Pen on Saturday: he is at Antwerp and at work: troubled by his old rheumatic affection and other incommodities, but in good spirits apparently. I took luncheon yesterday with an intimate friend of the Mr Fielden who bought the picture—and hear to my great pleasure that that gentleman likes his purchase extremely and was bent on making it.[2] He is described to me as one ignorant of the conventional recommendations of a picture, but very sagacious and self-relying, and "sure of his own mind"—a valuable quality in my eyes. I am invited to meet him at an early day, and shall be very glad to do so. By the way, I have just received an invitation to the Dulwich Banquet given to the President & Council of the R. Academy on the 25th instant.[3] No doubt there will be a general party in the afternoon. You remember the pleasant drive there and back we enjoyed once? Why might it not be again? I have accepted, for my part. You must come and see how pleasantly my sister has brightened up the house. We have hung as many of Pen's early works on the walls of my room as will go there, — and very well they really look, — I shall like to raise my eyes from the paper I stoop over, and, like the patriarch, "taste of the venison of my son that my soul may bless him"[4] — whether he be my true Esau or the supplanter. But the most charming adornment of my room is undoubtedly the creeper which literally embowers the window, just as if it had a purpose — as it may have.[5] I used to admire a little circumstance in a picture by Mantegna in the Gallery of the Uffizi: it represented the "Flight into Egypt": and, as Mary and Joseph were passing by a barren wall of rock, out of a crevice therein came, as if born in full bloom, a lily-flower, — reaching to salute them.[6] And as I look on this bough of wreathy leaves so high above the slender stalk which has somehow managed to introduce itself by a totally invisible chink, it looks like an apparition rather than a mere stray natural offshoot of a Virginian creeper. I will not let curtains be put up there so long as a leaf remains which they may injure. Your ferns were very pretty,[7] and prove how well they are cared for. There was one very fresh green leaf which I did not recognize, — a single great green one: what was that? Send me another, — if it so please you, — when you next incline to pick one. Talking of "sending", Pen received *only* that copy of the "Times" which you had the kindness to send him: the copy I sent never reached him, and he supposed we could not have seen it therefore. Your goodness was not wasted, though you accounted it so, you see. Do you observe that paragraph in the "World"[8] about the price of his picture? Does Lady Violet[9] return to Town soon? Or rather, did she not return for the "Derby" and other delights? I will call on her, according to her desire, when once assured I may find her. What a fresh blowing day we have here,—with sudden droppings-down of blackness, as if the sky would fall! Most people are taking a Whitsuntide[10] holiday, I suppose. Where shall we go, I wonder, this autumn, if we go anywhere—which, for my own part, I should very contentedly decline. I seem to enjoy the rest I am getting even here: but "here" is "here" indeed: for my walks are sadly circumscribed. I never go this way for one reason, nor that way, for another.[11] Well, we who remain to each other, must be thankful for the blessing—and I hope there is no ingratitude in

Yours ever affectionately
Robert Browning

Manuscript: Carl H. Pforzheimer Library, RB 35

1. This may refer to an exchange of books between the two households.

2. Joshua Fielden of Stansfield Hall, Todmorden (1827–?), M.P. from 1868 to 1880, manufacturer and merchant (Henry Fishwick, *Genealogical Memorial of the Family of Fielden* [London, 1884] p. 36). Fielden paid £300 for Pen's *A Worker in Brass,* a life-size portrait of a gray-bearded Antwerpian craftsman engaged in putting the chasing on a dish, shown at the Royal Academy in 1878 (*The Academy,* April 6, 1878, p. 310). Mrs. FitzGerald wrote on page 1 of this letter, "The Poets son sold his picture in the Academy for 300£ which was well for a début & *encouraging.*" See appendix for description.

3. The Dulwich College Picture Gallery, constructed (1812–1814) to the plans of Sir John Sloane, was situated only two miles from Browning's birthplace and, until the opening of the National Gallery (1838), was the principal public gallery in England. The fine collection of 350 paintings was made by Noel Joseph Desenfans for Stanislaus, King of Poland, but was instead bequeathed to Dulwich College, with £12,000 for maintenance of the collection and construction of the gallery. The terms of the bequest required an annual inspection of the gallery by the Council of the Royal Academy, of which Browning was later (1886) secretary for foreign correspondence (*Browning Society Papers* [London, 1881–1891], II, 153*). Mrs. Desenfans subsequently left plate, linen, and £500 to provide an annual dinner for the Council on the occasion of its inspection (*Times,* June 26, 1878, p. 10d).

4. "Bring it near to me, and I will eat of my son's venison, that my soul may bless thee" (Genesis, 27:25).

5. Mrs. FitzGerald sent Browning a cutting of the small-leafed Virginia creeper that grew on the south wall of the Shalstone manorhouse (MPFG). A shoot of this creeper made its way through a crevice in the poet's study window, round the inside of which he had the creeper trained (*Pall Mall Budget,* December 19, 1889, p. 1625). Browning refers to this creeper in the prologue to *Pacchiarotto* (1876) and elsewhere.

6. There is no *Flight into Egypt* by Mantegna in the Uffizi or elsewhere, although there may have been a false attribution in Browning's day. Mantegna's *Adoration of the Magi* (Uffizi, no. 910) has a flowering shoot issuing from a chink in the rock behind the Holy Family.

7. Probably a frond of the Bird's Nest Fern (*Asplenum nidus-avis*) from the fine specimen in the Fernery at Shalstone. Many species of ferns were grown in this grotto-like constructed house, lined with moss and bark. Wide, rough-hewn stone steps led to a lower floor, where there was a fountain and a pool with goldfish (MPFG).

8. "Three hundred pounds or guineas is a good round sum to get from a stranger for a first exhibited work, even if the young artist has had the rare sense not to exhibit until he knew how to paint, and has had the good luck to be the son of a man and woman of genius" (*The World: A Journal for Men and Women,* June 5, 1878, p. 14).

9. Lady Beatrice Violet Greville (1842–1932), daughter of the fourth Duke of Montrose, married (1863) the second Baron Greville. She was a sportswoman, the author of some fourteen volumes, and for two years a contributor to *The World,* which was edited by Edmund Yates. (See her *Vignettes of Memory* [London, 1927] and the supplement to Samuel Allibone's *Critical Dictionary of English Literature* [Philadelphia, 1891].)

10. In 1878, Whitsunday, the seventh Sunday after Easter, fell on June 9.

11. Browning consistently avoided visiting or even passing places and houses associated with dead relatives or friends.

Letter 9

W. C. Aug. 3. '78.

Dear Friend, it is a long time, and even seems longer than it may have been, since I saw or heard from you. My visit to Offington was cut short, or rather, spoiled to a certain degree from the beginning, by the unlucky illness of our poor host, who was in bed from a painful and dangerous inflammatory attack.[1] He was in hopes of so far recovering as to find himself among us in a day or two: but these were disappointed, and we all thought it properly considerate to go — as I did on Tuesday. Had circumstances been favorable I should have greatly enjoyed my visit: the air and pleasant weather did me immediate good (for I was somewhat languid & out of sorts generally) and, the kind and easy ways of the house permitting, I got up early as usual and walked before breakfast — some two hours — and liked the country the more I became acquainted with it, — especially my last morning's stroll on the downs, — I never remember a more *renovating* climb and trudge. But one could not forget that the poor lord of the demesne was laid up and sadly. All the guests were friends of mine, — the hostess an old and charming one, — but there was no enjoying capital materials for enjoyment, and I left the pretty place and the kind people with much regret. The house and garden, and grounds are not too large — but thoroughly cared for and attractive, while the library is large and choice indeed, — such books and such editions of them! I heard much about your house, now Lady Bath's [2] — and as L^y^ Mary Fielding [3] was on a visit to her, I should probably have called there: both ladies called to enquire, a few minutes before I left. Lady B. has cased the house with stone, it appears, at a vast expense. Such cares will never fall to my lot, but I like to take an occasional glance at the bees working, drone as I am. *You* are in a delightful hive indeed, and I hope all is going on there to your satisfaction, both as to swarm and combs, — "Queen-bee", being better than all the "moths" in the world, to my fancy. But here I have to break off — —

And here I remain after luncheon: which was honored by the Miss Probyns,[4] who are just gone; and, I fear, I must go also on my necessary walk after too continued talking: but I have a thing or two yet to say. Here is the letter, — you entrusted me with some time ago, — returned with thanks. I suppose there was no complete

Bunyan[5] found among your books or your goodness would have apprised me. The Dean of Westminster thought he had "Mr Badman"—and took me up to his dressing room to find it,—but the little volume lying on the table did not contain that remarkable work: it is not in our "Athenaeum" Library.[6] We hope to see Pen soon, but I have no decided news about him: he said he was about to write to you. Dear Friend, this poor scribble will suffice to assure you I am

ever affectionately yours R Browning.

Manuscript: Carl H. Pforzheimer Library, RB 36

1. Browning was the house guest of Thomas and Lady Alice Gaisford at Offington, a recently purchased manor house near Worthing on the Sussex downs. Gaisford was the son of Thomas Gaisford, Dean of Christ's Church, Oxford (D&K, p. 204). The magnificent library, which Gaisford inherited from his father, was sold at Sotheby's in 1890. (See Henry Snail, *Notable Houses of Worthing, No. 2: The Story of Offington . . .* [Worthing, 1950].)

2. Harriet Baring (1804–1892), daughter of the first Lord Ashburton, married (1830) Henry Thynne (1797–1837), third Marquess of Bath. In 1850 she purchased Muntham Court, Findon, Sussex (Cokayne, *Complete Peerage,* II, 26), the residence of the FitzGeralds before they inherited Shalstone.

3. Lady Mary Frances Catherine Fielding, daughter of the seventh Earl of Denbigh and sister of the eighth Earl, who married Lady Bath's daughter Louisa.

4. Perhaps Blanche, Evelyn, and Charlotte Eugenia, the unmarried daughters of Edmund Probyn of Huntley Manor, County Gloucester (Burke's *Landed Gentry,* 1879). Browning's address book (BM) lists "John W. Probyn 5 St James Place."

5. Browning wanted to re-read John Bunyan's *The Life and Death of Mr. Badman* (1680) for the story of Old Tod contained therein, which story he adapted and retold in "Ned Bratts," the last poem in his *Dramatic Idyls* (1879). He was unable to find the volume, but, without consulting it, he wrote "Ned Bratts" at the Splügen during his holiday there (Hood, p. 209). Upon his return to London, he acquired Bunyan's complete *Works* bound in old calf (Edinburgh, 1771) and wrote "Robert Browning, Nov. 6, '78" on the flyleaf (Sotheby, no. 530, p. 85).

6. In 1862, Browning was elected to membership in the Athenaeum Club, which possessed the best club library in London (*Dearest Isa,* Letter 45, February 6, 1862).

Letter 10

19. Warwick Crescent, W. Aug. 9. '78.

Dear Friend, I should have greatly enjoyed going to you for a few days—or indeed many a day—had it been possible to foresee the likelihood of your receiving us—but the time seems come for departure in earnest, if depart we really do: we have never been so late in England, I think. For me, I am increasingly lazy, and could well determine to go no farther away than Shalstone exacts in the way of a journey. But S. needs more thorough change,—and perhaps I shall be no worse for it, once forced out of doors. We count on leaving for Paris next Tuesday,—staying a couple of days there at most,—then going northward *somewhere*—to pass the main of the heat-season in some mountain quarter,—and then, we may follow our inclinations as far as they point toward the Italian side,—the only part of the world I seem at present to fancy might stimulate me a little. All this however is hazy enough: you shall know more as I know more, depend on it. The comfort is very great indeed in the knowledge that you are left in circumstances I must consider altogether advantageous for you and, no less, for the poor object of so much tender solicitude.[1] You may be trusted to recover, in your beautiful Shalstone, that quiet and health of which you have so long been deprived. That is all I venture to say. And how shall I put into the fewest words the deep and true gratitude I feel at reviewal of all your kindness to me and mine during your own anxieties of so many kinds? I must give up *that* also. In my own experience, this has been a trying year for me, and I am only now beginning to emerge from the effects of the earlier months.

We—or *I*—had an impression that Pen would come here to reclaim his Picture,[2] and take measures about photographing it, and dispatching it to Mr Fielden,—but he said, rationally enough, that there seemed little use in his leaving off work and making a double journey for a few days only, when the business could be as well settled without him. This is quite true: he would see nobody, — and, if he brought the picture, "St Jerome,"[3] which I am assured, on the authority of at least *one* judge, is "300 times better than the 'Worker in Brass,'" — it would "waste its sweetness in the closet's air," nor do any good till Spring. So, I set to work by myself, and managed to get the picture away from the Gallery on Tuesday (one day in anticipation of the regular Wednesday) — had it photographed the same day — and lo, on that same 7th, it was brought here, packed in its case, and trundled off to Todmorden, — whence, I hope, a letter tomorrow will assure me of its safe arrival. I went on Monday, the closing day, to see it for the last time — for, so far, it has really been productive of nothing but unalloyed pleasure to me. I tell Pen he *must* not expect to have such a pure piece of good fortune another time. He writes a letter, — received a few minutes ago, — directing what is to be done *when the picture arrives* — but I believe nothing material has been omitted. (It is needless to say, one of the photographs is for the Original Patroness.)[4] He adds "I shall do my best to have something for the Academy and the Grosvenor too."[5] Oh, the blessed thing that Work is! I confess to having been quite idle of late: however, as last year I revived my acquaintance with German, so, a few weeks since, I took it into my head to learn Spanish, — which I have so far managed as to read ordinary prose easily enough, and Calderon with no great difficulty. The only stoppages come from the words which are derived from Arabic. Of the pronunciation I know nothing but what the grammar attempts to teach; I have no poor Mrs Benzon[6] to help, as in German: her boast was that she could make *anybody* pronounce properly, and she had certain ingenious devices for effecting it. I shall resort to some Spaniard for a reading-lesson or two, on my return, — if that may be. Do you know Spanish?[7] Of course, like everybody, I had amused myself years ago by stumbling along a few passages, by means of Latin and Italian: but this time I read the grammar (an unpretentious one, to be sure) right through before attempting to construe a sentence.

Dear Friend, I will write no more: a parting word I *will* write—since it will be in answer to some part-word of yours,—*pas vrai?*

I forgot to tell you—Mr Gaisford said that when he asked his new neighbour Trelawney[8] what made him choose Worthing for a residence, he replied gruffly "Figs".—"Why, figs?"—"Why, look there,—that flourishing fig-tree,—and that other in yonder garden, and that other on this side, all leafy and full of fruit! Be sure, where figs flourish, the air is good!"

May figs flourish—as I have good reason to believe they do—at Shalstone,[9] and the best of air sustain you—prays yours affectionately ever

R Browning.

Manuscript: Carl H. Pforzheimer Library, RB 37

1. Her invalid son Robert (see Letter 2, n. 8). At the end of the paragraph, "the earlier months" is an interlinear correction: see appendix.

2. *A Worker in Brass* (see Letter 8, n. 2).

3. Pen seems to have named this picture not *Saint Jerome* but *The Unanswered Question* (see Letter 18, n. 10). The statement about Pen "directing" what was to be done contains a correction: see appendix.

4. Mrs. FitzGerald (see Introduction, p. 25).

5. In 1879 Pen did exhibit at the Royal Academy (Letter 18, n. 2) and at the Grosvenor (Letter 18, n. 10).

6. Elizabeth (Lehmann) Benzon, the sister of Rudolph and Frederick Lehmann, and benefactress of Browning, who received from her about £72 a year (Roma A. King, *Robert Browning's Finances from His Own Account Book* [Waco, 1947], pp. 16–17), the income from £1,860 worth of stock in the London and Northwestern Railway Company (account book in BM, Ashley MS 5716). On December 21, 1877, Browning purchased "Books Mrs. Benzon & Ernst 4s 1d." (*ibid.*); and after July 15, 1878, the income she allowed him is entered after "Schlesinger (Mrs. B)" (*ibid.*). Mrs. FitzGerald noted in a pocket diary that Mrs. Benzon died on February 16 [presumably in 1878]. Her husband, Ernest Leopold Benzon (d. 1873), was a German-American financier; a partner with Frederick Lehmann in Naylor, Vickers & Co., iron-

masters; and an art and book collector. (See *Catalogue de la Bibliothèque de M. Benzon . . .* [Paris, 1875].)

7. Mrs. FitzGerald's diary indicates that she began studying Spanish in the winter of 1891, in her eighty-third year, and that a year later she was reading Calderón easily and a daily chapter of the Spanish Testament (MPFG).

8. Edward John Trelawny (1792–1881), Shelley's friend. He had a cottage and a few acres of land in the village of Sompting, near Worthing, in Sussex. Browning met him occasionally at dinner parties in London, but the Romantic adventurer and the Victorian poet were not really congenial. (See Edward C. McAleer, *The Sensitive Plant: A Life of Lady Mount Cashell* [Chapel Hill, 1958], p. 219.)

9. Well-established fig trees grew against the outer side of the east wall of the walled garden at Shalstone. From these Mrs. FitzGerald sent fruit to Browning (MPFG).

Letter 11

HÔTEL BODENHAUS
SPLÜGEN
Aug. 24. '78.[1]

Dear Friend, you will have heard from S. how happily we have fallen upon this strange place of sojourn,—nothing could suit either of us better. The solitude and yet sense of companionship as the vehicles noiselessly come and go under the windows of the lone house we inhabit is unexampled in my experience. The changes in the face of things are as sudden as extraordinary: this morning, hot sun on the mountain-walk, so that one had to ward it off with an umbrella: a few hours after, intense cold, with storm—rain, thunder and lightning: presently all may be calm again. The effect upon myself has been decided and beneficial,—I am quite relieved from a languor that was coiling about me tightlier every day in London. I most of all rejoice in the evident good done to S: she has never seen such nature, nor breathed such air. We neither of us had any good—rather the reverse—out of the disastrous journey last year:[2]

and even Arran, pleasant as we found it, is incapable of the mountain-power of these altitudes. Did S. tell you how we walked into Italy—a three hours trudge? Or of the two startling appearances made by—first, Hallé [3] and his family, and, yesterday, Mrs. Ford,[4] my old friend, whom I found seated by my side at dinner? Oh, may these "piccolezze" [5] be *all* the adventures in which people I care about are concerned! Our plan is to stay here certainly a fortnight, possibly even longer,—exhausting the renovation of the clouds and crags—and then, descend into Italy—that is, Lombardy, making the most we are able of Venice: if all goes well here and at home there is no need to hurry back. Meanwhile, you—are you at Shalstone, dear friend, and did the Isle of Wight do you good? [6] And is all proceeding favourably elsewhere? Mrs Ford, coming from Chiavenna yesterday, spoke of "the insupportable heat there": as I write, I see snow on the mountain, and could well rub my hands over a wood-fire,—but I shall resist *that* temptation. Only this morning did we get letters &c from Warw^{k} C^{r} though they were sent for six days ago: a letter from you will probably take longer time to reach us, and Pen,—where is he? How much I have seen since the poor *eleven* days ago since I left London! As usual I especially want your aid when I meet with wild flowers,—S. will witness how often I cry out for your help as one exquisite thing follows another on the banks above the streamlets and under the pines. Mrs Ford gave us a piece of information about the culture of *edelweiss* . . but I know S. will have forestalled me here as in all else. So, you were too tired to come, after all, and ascertain whether I "dined out" on that last evening! The *first* letter I have got is from the not-to-be-baffled R. Cholmondeley,[7]—who requires to "know what day I fix in October for going to him." What a "Macédoine," [8] or mash-up of incoherencies I have effected! But you will understand through it all that I want exceedingly to know how you are, and hear your voice: and if my "Macédoine" manages *that* it has done all possible service to yours affectionately ever RB.

Manuscript: Carl H. Pforzheimer Library, RB 38

1. In 1878 Browning and his sister spent their holiday in Switzerland and in Italy. They left London for Paris on August 13, arriving on August 18 in Splügen, a village in east Switzerland, where they planned to stay a fortnight but remained five weeks. They left Splügen on September 23, spent a night at Lake Como, two days at Verona (Orr, II, 469), a few days at Asolo, and a fortnight in Venice. On October 17 they left Venice for Paris, arriving back in London on October 22. In his account book for 1878 (BM) Browning wrote "Aug 12 Board wages for 3, at 12^{s} a week each for eight weeks from Aug. 12 14.8." and later "Returned Oct. 22 Spent about £110."

2. When Miss Smith died (see Letter 6, n. 1).

3. Sir Charles Hallé (1819–1895), pianist and conductor.

4. D&K (p. 165) suggest Mrs. Walter Ford.

5. "pettinesses."

6. Mrs. FitzGerald was probably visiting Miss Laura Bullen Smith, who lived for many years in Ryde on the Isle of Wight. There is reference to another visit to Miss Smith and her sister there in 1885, as well as an undated photograph of Mrs. FitzGerald taken at Ryde (MPFG).

7. Reginald Cholmondeley (1826–1896), third son of the rector of Hodnet, was educated at Trinity College, Cambridge (B.A., 1849; M.A., 1856), was admitted at the Inner Temple in 1850 but received no call, succeeded to the estate of Condover Hall, Shrewsbury, at the death of his brother Thomas in 1864, and married (1867) the Hon. Alice Mary Egerton, daughter of the first Lord Egerton of Tatton. She died in November 1868, and their infant daughter died one month later. (See Burke's *Landed Gentry; Alumni Cantabrigienses;* and Edward Walford, *County Families of the United Kingdom* [London, 1874].)

He loved his friends, Browning and Lady Martin among them (Hudson Long, "Helen Faucit Martin," *Baylor University Browning Interests,* 2nd ser., 34:14–15 [1931]), but he hated the sight of a stranger and indulged his eccentricities and an easily triggered temper. He collected birds of paradise and was a well informed naturalist, many of his specimens being in the Museum of Natural History in South Kensington. His hobby suggested the subject for Millais' *The Ruling Passion,* which portrays an aged invalid lying on a couch, fondling a tiny bird, and surrounded by deferential relatives (John G. Millais, *The Life and Letters of Sir John Everett Millais* [New York, 1899], II, 169–170).

After his death, his brother, the Rev. Richard Hugh Cholmondeley, sold the estate as well as the collections of books, furniture, old masters, and arms (catalogues in the Bodleian dated February 18, March 4, March 6, and April 1, 1897). Although he was a confirmed invalid after 1884, Mrs. Orr errs when she states (II, 530) that he predeceased Browning.

8. A mixture of cut-up vegetables; a hodgepodge.

Letter 12

HÔTEL BODENHAUS
SPLÜGEN
Sept. 7. '78.

Dear Friend, how much I am indebted to you—first for the good news about yourself and your son. I have no sort of doubt that the stay at Shalstone under such perfect superin[ten]dence as only yours could be, did essential good, and that the consequences are evident in the comparatively happy state which you describe: yes, *happy,* —for suppose physical pain,—or, worse,—moral disquietude, intellectual obliquity, were the calamities under treatment? As it is, I see little worse than too ordinary valetudinarianism, such as demands simply greater care and perhaps forbearance than are necessary to perfect health. I would certainly prefer such a state for anyone I loved rather than any degree of mental clearness and even power if dragged down and virtually nullified by the wearing of constant pain. But I venture no farther. You probably have forgetten,—whenever we have talked or written about the case,—that I could not put *you* quite as much out of sight as you seemed to desire: and that it was inevitable I should wish that, if the comfort of the sufferer could be secured without your own being more than jeopardized, *that* course would be the proper one. I am happy to believe that all is now arranged for the best in both instances—and long may the good effects continue! Next, I have to thank you greatly for the letters, the journals, all the proofs that, out of sight is not, with you, out of mind. We are living a strange life here, S and I: it seems almost too delightful to last, but it will not end abruptly through any fault of ours, I think: we shall certainly stay another week—the fourth—and only then go if needs we must: the scenery is so exquisite, and the weather absolutely life-giving.

It occurs to me that neither S. nor myself have *ever* in any former instance "travelled for our health": with *that* particular object in view. It has always been for the conventional "change" — with little contrivance *where* that change should have effect. Our constitutions are much alike, and it is clear that we have needed exactly the reverse of what we generally managed to obtain — sea-air with its effects: this keen pure mountain air was the true tonic — and even in Arran there was, — by comparison, — nothing of the kind obtainable. You would not know either of us with our red faces and elastic limbs, as we come in daily after our morning walk of some five hours. But I have a fear that this sudden and extravagant *rise* may portend a corresponding fall, — and that the return to London may take away all our gains and leave us poorer than ever. Still, what *is* is pure advantage. The union of complete silence and solitude with all that is desirable in the way of material comfort — consequent on our Inn holding communication with the outer world on all sides, — the *seeing* from our windows the silent come-and-go of scores of vehicles and their human lading, — and the passage in a moment on to mountain ways where we walk for hours without meeting a human creature, — all this is what I never experienced before, and could hardly conceive possible. S. will, I dare say, have told you how, for the last four days, we went to Hinterrhein, — at which place, the Rhine proper begins — the higher stream being from another source, while its own descends there from a glacier on the mountain above — which is unluckily difficult — or, at least, long to reach. Our course is up-hill all the way, and the *wine* of the wind really intoxicates one. And to think that none of this was in my mind when I set out — very unwillingly — from London! All that reconciled my laziness to the step was the notion of seeing once again *Venice* — and perhaps Asolo. These seem quite secondary objects now.

I ought to say that no inconsiderable part of the satisfaction we both have in our journey arises from the pleasant tone of the letters we get from Pen: he seems happy, full of his art, and regarding it just as I could desire,—aiming at greater work, not stooping to lower considerations or being satisfied with his present success. He does not seem to have been away, for any considerable time, from Antwerp. He will certainly go to Paris—as he is clearly bound to do—for the extraordinary opportunity given by the Exhibition [1] of studying all the present European notabilities in painting: not that I think him likely to be unduly influenced by any one of them,—he has the "quality of his defects."

So, you have been seeing charming people,—Lady Violet, Miss Probyn, and others my sister tells me about. Your friend Mr Cautley [2] has been emblematizing, and versifying, I see: one specimen, likening his friends,—who go away and after due absence return unexpectedly,—to diving ducks I saw quoted in the "Athenaeum[”]. You have heard of poor Millais' boy—[3] his mother spoke to me with such confidence of his speedy restoration to health four months ago! Millais is a most affectionate heart, and will feel much. And you and William—[4] the good kind young fellow—I am sure he was proud to be noticed by you—as who is not, dear friend? I have scribbled late into the afternoon, and not much to the purpose: but you will help all with your better light. God bless you!

Ever affectionately yours RB.

Manuscript: Carl H. Pforzheimer Library, RB 39

1. *L'Exposition Universelle, 1878* (*Illustrated Catalogue of the Paris International Exhibition, 1878* [London, Virtue & Co.]). Mrs. FitzGerald visited the exhibition (see Letter 16, n. 2).

2. The Rev. George Spencer Cautley (d. 1882), Vicar of Nettleden, published *A Century of Emblems: with Illustrations by Lady Marian Alford, Rear-Admiral Lord W. Compton* . . . (London: Macmillan and Company, 1878). The book contains 38 emblems and 110 poems and was reviewed in *The Athenaeum* for August 31, 1878 (pp. 267–268). The reviewer quoted two stanzas of "Ducks at Play" with hostile comment. Mr. Cautley is listed in Browning's address book (BM).

3. John Everett Millais' son George died in August 1878 at the age of nineteen (Millais, *Life . . . Millais,* II, 92).

4. William H. Grove, a plowboy who used to ring the evenbell for the Rev. Mr. Knox-Little, came up from the country about 1875 to be Browning's manservant (one suspects Mrs. FitzGerald's helping hand; see appendix for her note on this letter). After seven years with Browning, during which time he read *Self Help* and received artistic hints from Pen, he went to work as a photographer with Hollyer's and then in his own studio at 174 Brompton Road. His work includes several fine photographs of Browning and, after a royal warrant in 1899, of the Royal Family. (See T. Moore and D. C. Sturge Moore, *Works and Days: From the Journal of Michael Field* [London, 1933], p. 30; Grace E. Wilson, *Robert Browning's Portraits, Photographs, and Other Likenesses and Their Makers* [Waco, Texas, 1943], *passim;* and L. N. Broughton, C. S. Northup, and R. Pearsall, *Robert Browning: A Bibliography, 1830–1850* [Ithaca, N.Y., 1953].)

Letter 13

Splügen, Sept. 14. '78.

Dear Friend, this is really the first *bad* day—a[l]together so—that we have had; everyday for the last fortnight we have walked resolutely our four or five hours in the morning: but the resolution was only needed because of the sun,—which at this hour yesterday we guarded against with an umbrella: now it is raining heavily, the cold is considerable, and I see snow on the nearer mountain-tops: all this coincides with our plan to outstay the warm weather where we find ourselves: and we shall remain here even another week,—our fifth!—not proceeding on our southward journey till Monday week: then we mean to go as fast as may be to Venice and there pass a week or two. Both of us have gained much by the coolness and quietude of this little village, and the walks I tell you of: we could hardly have done better. You have been, as usual, a great resource to us with your letters and newspapers: I read the account of your fête[1] with great interest and satisfaction—remembering how last year the thunderstorm interfered to spoil what it could. All has been made up to you abundantly this time. There is a sort of grim satisfaction to me in the break up of the weather just to-day — the sad anniversary of the event at La Saisiaz: [2] how fine it was that morning!

Sarianna communicated to me many interesting particulars of your letter. How strange that L[d] Lonsdale [3] should be bound on a voyage already unaccompanied by his wife — as, I judge by what you say, is the case. How does a man say to his wife — and how does she receive the speech — "my health requires that we should part company for a few months — though only the other day we were indissolubly companions?["] It cannot be two months ago since I was at Mrs Lowther's [4] party given on the evening of the marriage, — when everybody was talking about "How it went off" — ominous phrase! She is really charming too — quite above the standard of ordinarily "cultivated" young ladies of her age: I took her down to dinner, last year, at the O'Hagans,[5] and was passably surprised to find how much she knew about — Chaucer! I suppose the lower classes cannot cure their headaches, after a carouse, by absence and yachting — and so they kick their late beloveds to death. I heard from Pen yesterday, — he is exemplary in writing now, — and he mentioned that he had heard from you. Do continue to write to him — I am sure he values your kindness and profits by it. He enclosed to me a letter from poor Mrs Millais, — in answer to a note I sent her husband on becoming aware of his loss: [6] she addressed it — apparently in her confusion to Pen — who had written also, however. She says Millais has suffered much — which I well believe, for he has a heart of his own. From England, all the news (little enough) comes from Mrs Orr,[7] who is in Cornwall: what horrors fill the "Times" [8] however! I don't remember such a generally disastrous year as the present — or the *past,* if I may reckon it from this day twelve months ago. Dear Friend, I am none the less sensible of the comforts that remain — and your sympathy is precious indeed. You will hear what remains to tell next Saturday. Meanwhile and ever be assured of the affectionate gratitude of yours

Robert Browning.

Manuscript: Carl H. Pforzheimer Library, RB 40

1. *The Buckingham Express* for September 7, 1878, reported "The Annual Village Flower Show" that was held at Shalstone on Tuesday, September 3.

2. The sudden death of Miss Smith (see Letter 6, n. 1).

3. St. George Henry Lowther (1855–1882), fourth Earl of Lonsdale, married (July 6, 1878) Lady Constance Gladys Herbert. After his death at twenty-seven, she remarried (1885), becoming the Countess de Grey and then the Marchioness of Ripon. She was a handsome woman, six feet tall, of "matchless grace," and the friend of Edward VII and Queen Alexandra (E. F. Benson, *As We Were: A Victorian Peep-show* [London, 1930], pp. 155–162).

4. Charlotte Alice Parke married (1853) William Lowther, Chargé d'Affaires at Naples. Her father thought that had she been a boy she would have made the name of Parke "illustrious in jurisprudence," and George W. E. Russell applied to her Wordsworth's lines, "A perfect Woman nobly planned . . ." (*Portraits of the Seventies,* [London, 1916], pp. 446–448).

5. Thomas O'Hagan (1812–1885), Lord Chancellor of Ireland, first Baron O'Hagan. "On 11 June 1870 he was raised to the Peerage of the United Kingdom as Baron O'Hagan of Tullahogue, Co. Tyrone, deriving the designation of his title from the ancient seat of his clan" (Burke's *Peerage,* 1884; *DNB*).

6. On the death of his son (see Letter 12, n. 3).

7. Alexandra (Leighton) Orr (1828–1903), the widow (1858) of Colonel Sutherland Orr and subsequently (1891) Browning's biographer. Her photograph in Browning's album, now at Balliol College, shows her as a very beautiful woman.

8. It took two days for London papers to reach Splügen, and, therefore, Browning had just finished reading the *Times* for September 12 when he wrote this letter. That issue reported a collision in the Thames of the *Princess Alice Saloon Steamer* (476 persons drowned); the worst colliery explosion in the history of South Wales (280 men dead); a railway collision at Sittingbourne; and a fatal fire in Birmingham. Abroad, 80 persons died of yellow fever in one day in New Orleans; 115 in Memphis. In Catania, a high wind blew the campanile down upon a dormitory for females. At Verkinondensk, 175 houses were burnt, the charred remains of 35 persons found in the ruins. At Pesth, Mohammedans beheaded the Chevalier Perrod; the Maffia was especially zealous in Sicily; and the Russians were rearming.

Letter 14

Splügen,[1] *Sept. 21. 78.*

Dear Friend, this is like to be the last time I write to you from this pleasant place,—so we have truly found it. Our intention is to leave the day after to-morrow, and get to Lecco by nightfall: proceeding next day to Verona, where we may stop a day or so,—to Vicenza, and, if weather invite us, to Treviso and Asolo,—a place I have a certain longing to see once more, as you know: but if any obstacle is in the way, our course will be through Padua to Venice—where we hope to spend a week or two: thence,—but let us leave the after-journey to be determind as circumstances decide. Here we shall have spent five delectable weeks, making the most of our advantages: but the weather is broken,—after last Saturday, we enjoyed five successively fine days,—warm and bright: yesterday however was altogether rainy and cold,—to-day is no improvement upon it,—though we have managed to walk for above a couple of hours,—and we consider that our summons for departure is plain enough: the genial Lombard temperature will renew the youth of the year. So, think of us as on the road, when you get this—and be sure that, wherever Saturday may find us,—if writing be practicable, you will be written to. Our address will of course be—Venice, *poste restante*. I was about to say again how very unalloyed with any subject of anxiety our stay has been: but I remember I have been pained by the news of three deaths—none that I expected to hear of. Poor Lady Egerton! [2] Nobody was spoken of with more asperity: I never found her otherwise than kind and desirous of giving pleasure; and, last year only, I received three invitations to various places of her abode. I saw her shortly before I left Town,—and certainly observed a great change in her face: but she was gay as usual, and I never thought of the end as so near.

Yesterday, however, I had a sudden shock on seeing in the "Times" that my old friend Lady Cowper [3] was dead. I had noticed the advertised death of the "Dowager Lady Cooper," and convinced myself that it related to somebody else: but a paragraph in the paper of yesterday particularized the birth, parentage, and death of my friend beyond mistake: and I obeyed an impulse in writing a very sincere word of sympathy to her eldest son: the younger, Henry, I met on the steamer between London & Calais, and he reported his mother as perfectly well. She was always most kind to me. So, judge of my surprise and joy when I am informed, by this morning's "Times," that it was all a mistake, and that Lady Cooper [4] was herself and no other! The blunders of this poor Delane-abandoned [5] print are incessant and prodigious. I had just been noticing their repetition of the name "Beufey" instead of "Benfey",[6] the well-known Orientalist scholar, who is President of the Indo-European section at the Florence assemblage. He passed through this place some four weeks ago: and when I found who he was, I almost regretted I did not ask him to write his name in my Homer — almost the only book I boast here. Well, I have nothing more to tell you: for you know, without telling, how much I hope all is going well with you. I heard from Pen yesterday: he proposes to go to Paris, for the end of the Exposition, about the 15 October. I wish he may make some stay there, — for artistic purposes: it could hardly fail of being of some good to him. Your "World" & "Whitehall" and "Light" arrived safely and were received gratefully. I send the "World" to Pen, as you direct. And now what remains but to greet you most affectionately, and express the warmest hope that we may meet at the month's end? — and meet happily, with good news to tell each other! Ever yours R Browning.

X) Oh, no! This place was suggested by nobody: we found it out for ourselves.

Manuscript: Carl H. Pforzhimer Library, RB 41

1. Browning wrote his postscript above this heading (see appendix).

2. Charlotte Elizabeth Loftus (1811–1878) married (1830) William Tatton Egerton, first Baron Egerton of Tatton (1859). She died suddenly on September 11 at Homburg. Irish-born, very rich, and proportionately frank, Lady Egerton was said to have been kind to those who met her standards of propriety. Others feared her tongue (Lady Mary J. St. Helier, *Memories of Fifty Years* [London, 1909], pp. 79–80).

3. Anne Florence (deGrey) Cowper (1806–1880), wife of the sixth Earl Cowper (1806–1856), and the mother of Henry Frederick Cowper (1836–1887) M.P. She is not the Lady Cowper to whom Browning dedicated his *Balaustion's Adventure* (1871), who was Katrine Cecilia, Lady Cowper of Wingham (1945–1913).

4. Elizabeth Harriet (Rickford) Cooper, wife of Sir Astley Paston Cooper (1798–1866), second baronet, died on September 16, 1878 (Burke's *Peerage,* 1880).

5. John Thaddeus Delane (1817–1879) edited the *Times* from 1841 to 1877.

6. Theodor Benfey (1809–1881), German philologist and Sanskrit scholar.

Letter 15

[*The* Stella d'Oro, *Asolo, Italy*]
Sept. 28. '78.

and from *Asolo,* at last, dear friend! So can dreams come *false:* for we got here without hindrance of any kind.[1] I daresay S., who has been writing at the opposite side of the table, has told you about our journey and adventures, such as they were: but she cannot tell you the feelings which which [*sic*] I revisit this—to me—memorable place after above forty years absence,—such things have begun & ended with me in the interval! It was *too* strange when we reached the ruined tower on the hill-top yesterday, and I said "Let me try if the echo[2] still exists which I discovered here (you can produce it from only *one* particular spot on a remainder of brick-work)—and thereupon it answered me plainly as ever, after all the silence: for some children from the adjoining *podere,* happening to be outside, heard my voice and its result: and began trying to perform the feat—calling "Yes, Yes"—all in vain: so, perhaps, the mighty secret will die with me! We shall probably stay here a day or two longer,—the air is so pure, the country so attractive: but we must go soon to Venice, stay our allotted term there, and then go homeward: you will of course address letters to Venice, not this place: it is a pleasure I promise myself that, on arriving, I shall certainly hear you speak in a letter which I count upon finding.

The old inn here,[3] to which I would fain have betaken myself, is gone—levelled with the ground: I remember it was much damaged by a recent earthquake, and the cracks and chasms may have threatened a down-fall. This *Stella d'Oro* is, however, much such an unperverted *locanda*[4] as its predecessor—primitive indeed are the arrangements and unsophisticate the ways: but there is cleanliness, abundance of good will, and the sweet Italian smile at every mistake: we get on excellently. To be sure, never was such another perfect fellow-traveller, for my purposes, than S: so that I have no subject of concern,—if things suit me they suit her—and *vice versa*. I daresay she will have told you how we trudged together, this morning, to Possagno—through a lovely country: how we saw all the wonders,—and a wonder of detestability indeed is the paint-performance of the great man![5]—and how, on our return, we found the little town enjoying high market-day, and its privilege of rowing and screaming over a bargain. It confuses me altogether,—but at Venice I may write more comfortably. Farewell till then, Dear Friend! Remember me ever as yours affectionately

Robert Browning.

Manuscript: Carl H. Pforzheimer Library, RB 42. There is an annotation in Mrs. FitzGerald's hand. See appendix.

1. In June of 1838, during his first Italian tour, Browning spent four days in Asolo, which became his most beloved Italian town. During his forty-year absence, he had a recurrent dream in which he was just in sight of Asolo but was always prevented

from proceeding there (*William Allingham: A Diary,* ed. H. Allingham and D. Radford [London, Macmillan, 1907], p. 248). After the visit mentioned in this letter, the dream did not recur.

2. A good profile photograph of Asolo (facing page 96 of W. H. Griffin and H. C. Minchin, *The Life of Robert Browning* [New York, 1910]) shows the "Turret" or castle at the top of the hill in which Queen Caterina Cornaro of Cyprus lived during her exile. Browning mentions the echo in the opening lines of part III of *Pippa Passes* (1841).

3. Browning told Mrs. Bronson that he had lodged "at the main hotel in the Square,—an old, large inn of the most primitive kind" with a crack in the ceiling of his bedroom caused by earthquake (letter dated June 18, 1889, in possession of the Count Rucellai).

4. "Boarding-house."

5. Antonio Canova (1757–1822) is, of course, best known for his sculpture, but Browning carefully examined the collection of his water colors at Possagno (Katherine Bronson, "Browning in Asolo," *Century Magazine,* 59:923 [April 1900]).

Letter 16

Venice, Hôtel de l'Univers,
Oct. 12. '78.

Dear Friend, Your welcome letter came duly this morning, and my Sister received its predecessor yesterday: I generally count upon her giving you those details of our little daily life which slip away from me: but we have been so pushed up into a corner of the morning by one cause or another that our joint-inkstand allows of only a single pen-dipper at a time—and that, a very short time: you will therefore need to forgive *me f*or claiming the privilege & pleasure of writing an answer for us both. One cause of the hurry is—please acquaint Pen—that his friends, Willy[1] & his wife, called just now: I gave W. the kind love I was desired to take in charge. He leaves on the 15th for Florence. Pen acquainted me with the absolute necessity there was for *not* allowing your desire to be thrust out of your apartment,[2] — through his entry there,— to have its effect: he very superfluously declares that you are "kindness itself" to him, — I expected as much, but am as grateful as if such a fact could still surprise me. Pen is exceedingly happy at seeing so much of you: his meeting the Storys,[3] — after an interval of I don't know how many years, — was fortunate in its way: he has known them all his life, and can hope but seldom to have such a chance. His letters to me continue to be all I could wish: he is clearly an artist born, and, in the doing his nature justice, he will find his comfort and reward in life — or nowhere: I have no longer the least doubt about his success, — so far as it may be said to depend on himself: and I contrast, very much to its advantage, his method of study & work with that of other artistic people who are engaged here in what they consider the same pursuit. He is anxious to be back and at the brush again, — and I shall not detain him very long from that business — indeed, I would return at once: were it not that I cannot think another week spent in the galleries will be a day too much. I should delight in meeting you in Paris: but, since that cannot well be, P. P.[4] must make amends. We propose staying out the fortnight, — starting on Thursday for Paris by Padua, Brescia, Milan, and Turin: managing, by three night-stoppings, to reach it on Monday evening: a day or two will suffice for all we have to do there; and then London will receive us again, it is to be trusted, in the latter part of the week. It seems an age since we left it, one hot yet gloomy morning: hitherto our journey has been most successful and brimful of interest: so that the events, — not vastly important in themselves, — swell out the time actually consumed. You may have heard we have a Hôtel[5] here absolutely to ourselves, and the Lindsays[6] — who make their neighbourship pleasant to the best of their power: we take gondola together, stroll on the Square, and return — all by the brilliant moon fortunately at the full. Dear Friend, my last sand is run out of the hourglass, — but, if I turned it up again, what more could

I say than that I thank you for all your goodness from my heart, & am ever Yours affectionately, RB.

Yes, I remember the Sonnett. Poor Talfourd[7] was always indulgent to me from the first.

Manuscript: Carl H. Pforzheimer Library, RB 43

1. Willy Bracken, nephew of Annie E. Smith, and Pen Browning's boyhood friend. After his marriage (1871), he made his home in Florence (*Dearest Isa,* Letter 5, July 8, 1858).

2. Mrs. FitzGerald was in Paris for the Exhibition (see Letter 12, n. 1) and visited it daily with Pen; there is an annotation in her hand (see appendix).

3. William Wetmore Story (1819–1895), American sculptor, resident in Italy after 1848, when he met Browning and began a life-long friendship. He did not exhibit at the Paris Exposition of 1878, but he was there as one of the United States Commissioners on the Fine Arts (Henry James, *William Wetmore Story and His Friends* [London, 1903], II, 318).

4. Mrs. FitzGerald's town house at 22 Portland Place.

5. Mrs. Orr (II, 473–475) describes the Albergo dell'Universo as a palazzo on the shady side of the Grand Canal, managed by a lady "of good birth and fallen fortunes."

6. Sir Coutts Lindsay (1824–1913), baronet, married (1864) Caroline Blanche FitzRoy (1844–1912). Both were accomplished artists and founders of the Grosvenor Gallery, where Pen exhibited from 1879 to 1889. Lady Lindsay was a water colorist, a musician — a favorite accompanist of Joachim —, and the author of a great many volumes, including novels, essays, poetry, and meditations. George W. E. Russell says that she was a friend of Browning, a great lover of Venice, and that her verses *From a Venetian Balcony* sold almost as a guide book (*Half Lengths* [London, 1913], pp. 99–103).

7. Thomas Noon Talfourd (1795–1854), lawyer, poet, essayist, and dramatist. He was friendly with Browning as early as 1835 (Orr, I, 118), and through him Browning met many influential people, including his benefactor John Kenyon. Talfourd's sonnet to Browning was published anonymously in *Household Words* on Nov. 22, 1851; but Browning discovered who the author was, and thanked him most graciously (Hood, p. 37), having previously (1841) dedicated *Pippa Passes* to him.

Letter 17

19, Warwick Crescent, W
Jan 20. '79.

Dear Friend, you may well have wondered what had become of your correspondent: but Saturday's whole morning was devoted to "Alfred Browning Stanley,"[1] and I returned so late, and found so much to do on returning, that I trusted you would understand a case of necessity was at the bottom of the silence. Not that I have much to tell,—though I rather fancied there might have occurred something fit to be chronicled: the Dean officiated in Henry the Seventh's Chapel, the little fellow behaved capitally, and we had a pleasant luncheon afterwards. The Dean took me to see the window just erected in memory of his wife[2]—really a beautiful thing—I did not think we could produce such a work in England: also, I must not forget, the water employed in the ceremony was veritably a dip from Jordan itself. Were it not that I am engaged this evening I should dine with the Dean, as I usually do, and, afterward help him to do the honors of the Abbey to the tradesmen who assemble for tea in large numbers: somebody else must serve this time.[3] All this while,—not one word about your illness, dear friend! Yet I have not forgotten it for a moment: and on Saturday evening I saw and talked with Pezze[4] (at a quintett-party) and heard that *he* also had been apprised of your illness: how this bitter weather must retard your recovery! Tell me particularly how you are: it *may* happen that I yield to destiny and *at last* go to Condover—[5] my last invitation, consequent of my excusing myself again and again, came two months ago, or more: I could not find a pretext for a refusal. But here is—what Crabbe calls "Truth, terror, and—the Day"[6]—i.e. the 24th when I ought to go—yet—yet—O that people would be more considerate in even their undoubted kindness! I must make up my mind to-morrow. I return poor Salvini's [7] letter. There are some pleasant and unpleasant stories about the poet of the "nimble brethren" and B. Jonson.[8] Pen writes to me,—only mentioning your goodness to him: he is very hard at work [9] and I am anxious about his health. Do write at once however briefly, Dear friend: I shall be impatient to know how you are—and, should I go, you shall be informed of my fate, the last thing: but *hope* still: and am still and ever yours affectionately

R Browning.

Manuscript: Carl H. Pforzheimer Library, RB 44

1. Alfred Browning Stanley Tennyson, son of Lionel Tennyson and grandson of the laureate, was christened on Saturday, January 18, 1879, in Westminster Abbey. Browning was a sponsor (*BSP,* I, 112). Tennyson dedicated his *Ballads and Other Poems* (1880) to this grandson: "Golden haired Ally, whose name is one with mine."

2. Lady Augusta Stanley (1822–1876), daughter of Browning's old friend Lady Elgin, married (1863) Arthur Stanley, Dean of Westminster. The inscription beneath the window in the south apse of the Abbey reads, "To the memory of Augusta Elizabeth Frederica Stanley the beloved wife of Arthur Penrhyn Stanley this window was dedicated by her husband A. D 1877," but the forty-eight panels of stained glass were destroyed during World War II.

3. Dean Stanley had a great love for the Abbey and enthusiasm for its historical associations, acting himself as guide to groups of visitors (*DNB*). Browning was accustomed to assist the dean in these guided tours.

4. Alessandro Pezze (1835–1914), Italian violoncellist, who held the principal cello post at Covent Garden from 1870 to 1873, when he succeeded Piatti as teacher at the Royal Academy of Music. He was acquainted with Mrs. FitzGerald as early as "17 Agosto 1866" when he autographed Beethoven's *Zwei Sonaten* at Shalstone, and he later gave cello lessons to Laura Purefoy FitzGerald. On February 25, 1879, he played Haydn's *Trio in G* with Miss Bairnsfather and Herr Heimendahl in a concert at Mrs. FitzGerald's town house. Madame Pezze sang *"Voi che sapete."* (MPFG has the printed program with a handwritten note, "EFG's last concert in" 22, Portland Place.)

5. The home of Reginald Cholmondeley.

6. From the last line of Letter XXIII, "Prisons," of George Crabbe's *The Borough* (1810).

7. Tommaso Salvini (1829–1916), Italian actor and Browning's friend. Mrs. FitzGerald first met him early in 1875 and saw him in *Hamlet* during his Shakespearean

tour that year. On June 3, he and Browning were the principal guests at a dinner party she gave at 22 Portland Place. They corresponded, and she was given his autographed photograph (MPFG).

8. Not identified.

9. The remainder of the letter is cross-written. See appendix for description.

Letter 18

19. Warwick Crescent, W
May 31. '79.

Dear Friend, I have been tardy in acknowledging & thanking you for your pleasant letter — with the very interesting photograph [1] which, as you say, has a thrilling interest — not *strange,* if one goes to the root of the thoughts it occasions. Byron remarked long ago on the fact that teeth and hair were the first portions of the human frame to decay before — and the last after — death: [2] this hair is, to me, suggestive of a fair face. Do you remember Montgomery's lines —

> O she was fair! — but nought could save
> Her beauty from the tomb! [3]

But I don't remember a more exquisite couplet on the same subject — with a difference —

> Queens drop away while blue legged Mankin thrives, —
> And courtly Mildred dies while country Madge survives.[4]

— two lines which I would rather have written than the whole of what I know of the works of — never mind whom! I am glad you are enjoying yourself — and apparently extending your route: your kind invitation to Shalstone, — as I understand what was recommended for *my* route, — can only be accepted as an agreeable impossibility: I go on the 9th to Cambridge,[5] return to London on the 11th for a trial [6] on the 12th wherein I figure as a witness, —

visit Oxford [7] on the 14th and return on the 16th for another engagement: then engagements must be my excuse for less letter-writing than heretofore — I am more & more wearied out by plying the pen, — and for *such* reasons!

Pen is at Antwerp and, I believe, much the better in every way for what he has done, and been done by — for the more serious critics have been kind to him. I send him, to-day, a nice word or two in the "Athenaeum" [8] — there is a funny caricature of his Fish-picture in the "Piccadilly Peep-Show" [9] — and — I am told — one of the Grosvenor Picture in the "Mask." [10]

Good bye, dear friend: I hope Melrose [11] will delight you as it did me, once on a time. No doubt my Sister will write for herself: (She is far from well, I am sorry to say) [12] I am ever affectionately yours

Robert Browning.

Manuscript: Carl H. Pforzheimer Library, RB 45

1. Mrs. FitzGerald noted: "The Roman coil of hair from York" (see appendix for description). In 1875 a stone coffin was found under the Booking Office of the New Railway Station in York. Inside were the remains of a lady with a beautiful coil of auburn hair and two fine jet pins (Raine's *Handbook to the Antiquities in the Grounds and Museum of the Yorkshire Philosophical Society* [1891], pp. 65 and 68. Mr. G. F. Willmot, Keeper of the Yorkshire Museum, kindly sent me this reference as well as a fine photograph of the hair, which is still in the museum).

2. On November 18, 1820, Byron wrote from Ravenna to John Murray: "I have seen a thousand graves opened, and always perceived, that whatever was gone, the *teeth* and *hair* remained with those who had died with them. Is not this odd? They go the very first things in youth, and yet last the longest in the dust, if people will but *die* to preserve them. It is a queer life, and a queer death, that of mortals." In Mrs. Browning's copy of Byron's *Letters,* edited by Thomas Moore, Browning wrote, "Read for the last time by Robert Browning in June, 1881, June 26 '81, R. B." (Sotheby, no. 536, p. 85).

3. James Montgomery, "The Common Lot" (dated November 4, 1805).

4. Not identified.

5. On May 29, 1879, the Congregation of Cambridge University decided to confer honorary degrees on ten distinguished men, Browning among them (*Times,* May 30, p. 6f). The *Times* noted that the Cambridge Commencement rarely granted honorary

degrees, last having done so in 1874. Browning received the LL.D. on June 10 at a ceremony beginning at noon, the audience being "especially enthusiastic" for Professor Huxley, Mr. Spottiswoode, Sir Frederick Leighton, and Mr. Browning (*ibid.*, June 11, p. 7e). Mrs. FitzGerald was present at the ceremony (see Letter 5, n. 1).

6. In 1887, Richard Herne Shepherd had edited *The Earlier Poems of Elizabeth Barrett Browning,* the poems then being out of copyright. *The Athenaeum* was hostile in its review of this book as it had been in previous reviews of Shepherd's "Literary Revivals." He was finally goaded into bringing suit against *The Athenaeum,* which had used objectionable words ("hack," "insect," "vampire," "bibliographer") and had allegedly injured him professionally. During the trial, Browning testified that he objected altogether to the publication of these poems and that "from what he had now seen of the plaintiff, he thought that the estimate of his abilities formed by the writer in *The Athenaeum* was a very fair one." Browning was crossexamined on the part he had played in the edition of the spurious Shelley letters (1852), and on June 16 the jury awarded Shepherd £150 damages (*Times,* June 17, 1879, p. 6b; leading article, p. 11; and *BSP,* I, 112).

7. Browning's account book (BM) records that he spent £1.2.6 on the trip to Cambridge and £1.4 on the trip to Oxford.

8. In 1879 Pen had two pictures hung at the Royal Academy: *A Stall in the Fish-Market, Antwerp* and *Dinant, on the Meuse, Belgium.* The first (7′2″ x 9′) was later shown at Liverpool in 1879; the International Exhibition, Melbourne, in 1880–1881; and the International Fisheries Exhibition, London, in 1883. Browning mentioned that the picture received gold medals in the last two of these exhibitions (see Letter 58, n. 2), but it remained unsold (Sotheby, No. 75, p. 18). *The Athenaeum* (May 31, 1879, p. 703) called it "One of the most vigorous pieces of brush power" in the Royal Academy show.

The second picture was purchased by Mrs. Bloomfield Moore and presented to the Metropolitan Museum of New York, where it was catalogued as *The Meuse from Bouvigne* (Thieme-Becker).

9. No such caricature was found in the *Peep-Show: Strahan's Magazine for the Young of All Ages* for 1879.

10. Also in 1879, Pen showed his *Unanswered Question* in the Grosvenor Gallery. The picture, which portrays a half-nude saint in a desert contemplating a death's head, was shown in Manchester later in 1879 and in Melbourne in 1880–1881 (Sotheby, no. 20, p. 8). *The Mask* for May 17, 1879 (p. 4) contained a black and white caricature of this picture with the caption, "Shall I boil him for supper or play cricket with him?"

11. In 1879 during a tour of seven English cathedrals, Mrs. FitzGerald crossed the border at Carlisle to view the abbey at Melrose on the Tweed in southeast Scotland. She returned south by the Northumbrian coast and later described the tour in an undated letter to her granddaughter Mary, saying that she could not be sure which she admired most — Durham or Lincoln (MPFG).

12. The comment in parentheses is an interlineated addition. See appendix.

Letter 19

19. Warwick Crescent. W.
June 5. '80.

Dear Friend, I feel, this time, guilty—for you certainly were expecting a letter from me last week: yet if you had seen the incessant calls on my time at the end of it, and the beginning & middle of the present, you would forgive me, I know. I have just sent out seven letters to the post—all & each taking up the minutes of the poor penman who really puts the writing to you as the "pleasure after business" which is always allowable. You would have beeen interested in one of my week's experiences, however,—the representation of the "Agamemnon" at Oxford whereto I was invited on Thursday.[1] I did not expect anything so good: the effect was striking indeed. I am sure that nothing can be better adapted to give an interest in Greek literature—for there was every proof that the actors understood all the verbal niceties of the difficult text. There is an account,—not a bit too laudatory,—in to-day's "Daily News."[2] Dear Jowett gave up his valuable morning to me, and we walked once again through College Gardens & inspected libraries. He is working hard to get done with his translation of Thucydides[3]—or rather the notes to the same, by far the more laborious matter,—he says. I came back yesterday afternoon. Well, to-morrow Pen & my Sister go away, and I shall be left to myself for I don't know how long. You have heard of the portrait:[4] it would seem to be a real success, judging by what people say. I shall transport it to N° 11.[5] with the other works, and there I hope you will see it. My Sister tells me your Son, though better, is still in a darkened room: *that* is very sad to hear,—though I suppose recovery is only a question of time. I thought, while following the play in the little pocket edition I have, wherein the type is none of the clearest,—were it wise to risk even a month's blindness for all the Greek that was ever written? Yet I pored on, and on,—though the Dean of Christ Church,[6] behind me, gave up his big book[7] very early in the evening. (The light was thrown on the stage, and nearly excluded from our part of the Hall.) The Greek was all pronounced purely after Oxford fashion, and all the more intelligible.[8] Dear friend, I shall be happy if you can tell me all is well both where you have been, and where you now are:[9] I shall be free from many hindrances to writing and reading, and in the right mood for a letter,—pray remember—as that I am ever, dear friend, yours affectionately

Robert Browning.

Manuscript: Carl H. Pforzheimer Library, RB 47

1. A performance of the *Agamemnon* of Aeschylus was given in the new hall of Balliol College on June 3 (*Times,* June 5, 1880, p. 11e) and repeated by special request at Eton, Harrow, and Winchester schools (*ibid.,* June 7, p. 11f). Browning had published his own translation of the *Agamemnon* in 1877.

2. *The Daily News* for June 5, 1880, called the production a "complete and almost startling success." "Among the large audience that warmly applauded the play were Mr. Newton and Mr. Robert Browning, perhaps the best possible judges of the success of the revival of the Agamemnon" (p. 3b).

3. Browning received a presentation copy of Jowett's *Thucydides, Translated into English, with Introduction, Marginal Analysis, Notes and Indices,* 2 vols., Oxford, 1881 (Sotheby, no. 1162, p. 136).

4. In 1880 Pen showed his *Delivery to the Secular Arm* at the Hanover Gallery, 47 New Bond Street. The largest composition in the gallery, it portrayed a girl heretic being delivered in 1570 by the Inquisition judges of Antwerp to the secular authorities for execution. Browning supplied five lines of Spanish verse from Calderón and five of English as mottoes for the picture (D&K, p. 256).

At the same time, the portrait here referred to may be "G. F. Watts' masterly portrait of Robert Browning" also exhibited in the Hanover Gallery (*The Academy,* November 20, 1880, p. 373).

5. Shortly before the annual openings in the various galleries, London artists held private showings of their work in their own studios. Since Pen's studio was on the Continent, Browning borrowed for the purpose a vacant house in Queen's Gate Gardens, South Kensington, from his publisher, George Smith (Hood, p. 186; D&K, p. 254). Pen's "other works" there included *Solitude; A Tan Yard, Dinant;* and

Watching the Skittle Players, all three of which were shown at the Royal Academy in 1880.

6. Henry George Liddell (1811–1898), Dean of Christ Church, Oxford, from 1855 to 1891, coeditor of Liddell and Scott's Greek-English lexicon.

7. The word "book" is a correction. See appendix.

8. In Browning's day, Greek was generally pronounced with the English value of the letters, but philologists had already introduced the classical pronunciation, which most scholars now accept.

9. France apparently, since a letter of this time mentions Lisieux (MPFG).

Letter 20

19. W. C. June 19. '80.

Dear Friend,—another break in my really decided purpose to write at once: what shall I say better than that you must be kind and consider the unexpected calls on me which increase strangely. Last Saturday I had to play showman yet once more to Pen's pictures: [1] L[d] Coleridge and his family,—who *did*—and Lowell [2] who did *not*—come by appointment—so went the early afternoon,—the later portion going to A. D. Coleridge's Musical Party,[3]—whence I just got home in time for L[y] Ridley's [4] dinner,—which was supplemented by the D[ss] of Cleveland's [5] Party—"thus runs the world away." Yet people are kind, and I cannot bear to seem ungracious and ungrateful. You were very good to remember and tell me so much of Mr Macdonald's [6] discourse. He was always favorable to me, and once came here as the messenger of Straehan, the publisher, who offered me fabulous terms for the "Ring & the Book." [7] I was pre-engaged however—and, moreover, distrust such "monts et merveilles"—or as the Italians phrase it, "promises of Roma e Toma." [8] Well, I am quite alone—for a few days longer, for my Sister means to return next Tuesday. Her visit has been successful in getting rid of that cough which seemed growing habitual: I could wish she prolonged her stay—but she must decide for herself. Pen is quite well, hard at work already, as he writes this morning from Dinant. The Small-pox is raging at Antwerp, and he has just been re-vaccinated—a wise precaution. He spent his six days at Paris in assiduous study of the pictures—one & all—in the Salon: thinks he has greatly profited thereby, and has a corresponding "fit of work upon him"—its first fury being spent upon—the owls,[9]—in high feather, it appears,—with a young thing: so will he get his hand in for serious work, it is to be hoped. He has had, among many other invitations, an official one to contribute to the Melbourne affair[10]—all expenses paid, even insurance of the pictures: and I incline to send them the Fish-Picture which may—who knows?—allure by its realism! The other pictures will be distributed, as we please, between Liverpool, Manchester, and Leeds—(Leeds, is however done with, I believe.) He is in high spirits—and the whole state of the dear fellow is a comfort to me. I met, two days ago or more, at an improvised luncheon given by Mrs Skirrow,[11] a *Miss* Skirrow[12] who was about to proceed to Shalstone: how *lush* and green your grass and leafage must be! No, I could not get to L^y^ Selborne's[13] either last week or the week before: I knew the rooms would be crowded, and supposed you would hardly stay late—I was dining with Ld Carnarvon,[14] and went home at once. Now, is not here a very gossip's letter? As the pseudo-Anacreon says—"I learn to tattle like a crow."[15] But the tattling goes into the kindest and most indulgent of ears—knows full well

Your affectionate RB.

Manuscript: Carl H. Pforzheimer Library, RB 48

1. See Letter 19, n. 5.
2. James Russell Lowell (1819–1891), who at this time was United States Minister to the Court of St. James (1880–1885).
3. Arthur Duke Coleridge (1830–1913), amateur musician and frequent host at

musical parties. He mentions another musicale in 1886, when "my poet [Browning] was as happy as he could be" (J. A. Fuller-Maitland, ed., *Reminiscences* [London, 1921], p. 171).

4. The Hon. Mary Georgiana Marjoribanks, daughter of Lord Tweedmouth, married Sir Matthew White Ridley (1842–1904), fifth baronet Ridley and later (1900) first Viscount Ridley.

5. Lady Catherine Lucy Wilhelmine (Stanhope) Primrose (1819–1901), daughter of Lord Stanhope, the historian, and wife of Harry, Duke of Cleveland. In 1869 Browning was her houseguest at Raby Castle (*Dearest Isa,* Letter 122, September 19, 1869), and during the London season she entertained much at Cleveland House in St. James's Square. She was one of Queen Victoria's bridesmaids, and G. W. E. Russell speaks of her as an accomplished artist and an admirable writer (*Portraits of the Seventies,* pp. 453–455).

6. George Macdonald (1824–1905), poet and novelist, who lectured in London on Shakespeare and other literary themes with great success. Among his friends he counted the Mount-Temples, the Carlyles, Tennyson, Dean Stanley, and Browning.

7. Alexander Strahan was Macdonald's publisher. Perhaps it was he who in 1867 offered Browning all the profits from *The Ring and the Book,* paid in advance, "for the incidental advantage" of the poet's name (*Dearest Isa,* Letter 98, April 23, 1867).

8. An idiom meaning "to promise wonders." Probably *e Toma* is a corruption of *et omnia* (Alfredo Panzini, *Dizionario Moderno delle Parole che non si trovano nei Dizionari comuni* [Roma, 1950]).

9. The owl picture when finished was called *Disturbed Life* (Letter 34, n. 4).

10. The Melbourne, Australia, International Exhibition, 1880–1881. The official catalogue lists 252 oil paintings and 150 water colors by British artists. Pen was represented by *A Stall in the Fish Market, Antwerp* and *The Unanswered Question.*

11. The wife of Charles Skirrow, Master in Chancery, and Browning's dear friend and correspondent (D&K, p. 190 and *passim*).

12. Presumably an unmarried sister of Charles Skirrow. FitzGerald diaries indicate friendship with the Skirrows as early as 1853, mentioning Charles, Walter, Stephen, and Marianne (MPFG). A memorial plaque in the church at Shalstone indicates that Stephen Tindall Skirrow died in London in 1864, aged forty-three.

13. Lady Laura Waldegrave (1821–1885), daughter of the eighth Earl Waldegrave, married (1848), the Rt. Hon. Sir Roundell Palmer (1812–1895), barrister, M.P., Attorney General, Lord Chancellor, created Baron Selborne (1872) and Earl of Selborne (1882). Their town house was at 20 Portland Place, near Mrs. FitzGerald. Lord Selborne abstained from voting for the destruction of the Irish church and thereby lost the woolsack. One day at Aldworth, Tennyson read his "Ode to the Duke of Wellington" to please Mrs. FitzGerald. When he came to the lines "And, as the greatest only are, In his simplicity sublime," he pointed to Lord Selborne and said, "To that man only in the present time do these lines apply" (*Memorials Part II. Personal and Political,* by Roundell Palmer . . . [London, 1898], II, 418).

14. Henry Howard Molyneux Herbert (1831–1890), statesman and fourth Earl

of Carnarvon (1849). Browning was his houseguest at Highclere Castle in 1873 (D&K, p. 221), and Lady St. Helier speaks of his remarkable literary ability and scholarship (*Memories of Fifty Years,* p. 265). He was High Steward of the University of Oxford from 1859 to 1890, and his verse translation of the *Agamemnon* appeared (1879) two years after Browning's.

15. Browning's father is said to have sung his infant son to sleep with the odes of Anacreon (*Catalogue . . . of the late R. W. B. Browning . . .* sold by James Tregaskis, London, June 9, 1913, p. 8); and Browning always kept his father's school-book copy of the *Odes* (Sotheby, no. 333, p. 69). Browning here refers to ΕΙΣ ΠΕΡΙΣΤΕΡΑΝ, "To a Dove" (no. 14 in the Hiller-Crusius edition of the *Anthologia Lyrica*), by one of Anacreon's many imitators. The poem, which is a dialogue between an interlocutor and a dove, ends with the impatient admonition, "Go away! Man, you've made me more talkative than even a crow."

Letter 21

19. Warwick Crescent. W.
July 13. '80.

Dear Friend, I was intending to write in a day or two: but I like to assure you at once that there is not a particle of truth in the article of "Truth." [1] I never met Swinburne at a Station, never "shook an umbrella at him," nor spoke to him after that foolish fashion: nor did he ever play the fool by calling here and going through such a piece of buffoonery with a camp-stool as is described in the paper —which I read by the merest chance on Saturday at the Club, while waiting till another journal should be replaced on the table beside me. There may be scores of such paragraphs in the "Society" pamp[h]lets, which I never happen to light upon. Fortunately the last person to believe in my gratification by this sort of nonsense would be Swinburne himself—a generous nature—and unlikely to suspect others of conniving at ungenerosity—and falsehood besides.

I received Mr Knox-Little's [2] Sermons some time ago, and felt greatly obliged and honored by the gift: it reached me however when I was in the thick of engagement and occupation, and I have waited till I could make the proper acknowledgement by reading the book attentively: as soon as I can do so, I will write to the kind giver, you may be sure. Your own fourth volume of Karr [3] came safely to hand, and I am busy with it: the others interested me—but I have a very mixed feeling for the author, and not too much belief in his veracity. The humours—he considers so exquisite—of his funny friend,—the practical jokes of which the success depends on lying, pure and simple,—these I think I compliment rather than insult the narrator by distrusting altogether. And the delectable "love"-adventure—that of Stephen,—who I suppose must be M. Alphonse—*that* I also disbelieve in—to the credit of the actor in it.

Here is poor Tom Taylor gone away from us abruptly enough! [4] I never knew him intimately,—but he was a good kindly fellow,—and by no means the worst critic in the world.

Ever affectionately yours
Robert Browning.

Manuscript: Carl H. Pforzheimer Library, RB 49

1. The weekly journal *Truth* for July 8, 1880, included an anonymous article (pp. 53–54) called "Anecdotal Photographs. Algernon Charles Swinburne," which reported that Browning once met Swinburne at a railway station, shook his umbrella at him, and exclaimed, "Ah, you foolish boy, why will you so degrade such splendid talent?" The article also stated that Browning's language on the occasion was too strong for print and that Swinburne once called at Warwick Crescent, carrying a camp stool so that he could sit at the feet of the elder poet.

2. The Rev. William John Knox-Little (1839–1918), one time (from 1870 to 1874?) rector of Turweston, about three miles from Shalstone; later (from 1875 to 1885) rector of St. Alban's Cheetwood, Manchester, and (1881) canon of Worcester. Between 1877 and 1891 he published nine volumes of sermons. Mrs. FitzGerald wrote in her copy of Mrs. Orr's *Handbook* (pp. 224 and 276–277) that Knox-Little set Browning's "One Way of Love" to music. When Knox-Little sang the song with

impromptu accompaniment at Mrs. FitzGerald's house, Browning said, "You are the organ, Sir. I only pull the bellows."

3. Jean Baptiste Alphonse Karr (1808–1890), French critic and novelist, whose *Le Livre de Bord, "souvenirs personnels,"* was published in four volumes in 1879. He was known as Alphonse Karr.

4. Tom Taylor (1817–1880), journalist, dramatist, and editor of *Punch* from 1874 to 1880, died on July 12, 1880. He knew Browning as early as 1858, when he called on him in Florence (*Letters to William Allingham*, ed. Mrs. Helen P. Allingham and E. B. Williams [London: Longmans, 1911], p. 100).

Letter 22

Hôtel Colomb, Lans, par Grenoble,
(Isère) France.[1]
Aug. 17. '80.

Dear Friend,

I shall write hurriedly enough, but perhaps sufficiently for my immediate purpose—which is to acquaint you with the place where you are engaged to acquaint *me* with your news of so many kinds. We had a very favorable passage and journey to Paris where, on arriving, we found ourselves literally in the arms of Milsand[2] & Dourlans:[3] after a couple of days, we left for Lyons & Grenoble—and were equally fortunate in our travelling. At Grenoble, on Saturday, we visited the Grande Chartreuse,[4]—a most interesting experience,—and on Monday—yesterday—started for Villard-de-Lans, a village beyond Lans pure & simple: it did not invite us however, and we at once returned to this little rural quiet unspoiled Lans where, in a minute country inn grandiloquently styled as above, we found exactly the accommodation we require: the simplest possible lodging—of perfect cleanliness and *sufficient* comfort—with a capital *cuisine bourgeoise*—more to our taste than Hotel-proper luxuries—and the kindest simplest people we ever met: the hamlet is a hamlet indeed—one only shop as yet discoverable—which may truly be called a "general dealer's"—and altogether "rough" to a degree intolerable to anybody but ourselves—except for the cleanliness—(which is a recognized advantage)—the fine air, the beautiful country, the grand mountains which frame in a wonderful vale or plain of pasturage and cornfields: the whole being peaceful to the desired degree. We hope to pass the great heats here—and then some Southward progress will be welcome. There is not much here, but enough—if you write according to pleasant promise: so, with my Sister's love, take that of

Yours affectionately ever
Robert Browning.

Manuscript: Carl H. Pforzheimer Library, RB 50

1. Browning's account book (BM) indicates that he purchased Baedeker's *Switzerland* on August 6 and that his holiday from August 10 to November 7 cost about £120. He and his sister spent "a couple of days" in Paris, were in Grenoble on August 14, and in Lans on August 16. They left Lans on September 20, slept at Grenoble and at Turin, spent a few days in Genoa, a day or two in Milan, and arrived in Venice on September 28. They left Venice on October 28, arriving back in London on November 7 (D&K, p. 256).

Since 1947 Lans has been called Lans-en-Vercors, a village with a population of 114, eight miles southeast of Grenoble.

2. Joseph Milsand (1817–1886), French Protestant, critic, and long-time friend of Browning. Almost every spring, he was Browning's house guest at Warwick Crescent.

3. Gustave Dourlans, French friend of Milsand and therefore of Browning.

4. *La Grande Chartreuse* in the mountains near Grenoble, founded by St. Bruno in 1086, until 1903 chief monastery of the Carthusian order. (See Letter 23.)

Letter 23

Hôtel Colomb, Lans, par Grenoble, (*Isère*).
Sept. 4. '80.

Thank you exceedingly, dear Friend, for the great pleasure your letter gave me. The enclosure was very welcome as furnishing the only precise account I have had of Pen's performances: he is always reticent, and never says more of a picture than that he hopes it turns out better than he expected: he did however give a little notion of "The Tanner's Garden,"[1] laying most stress on the difficulty he felt in painting it. We have nothing new to offer in return for your various doings of interest: this place continues the entirely satisfactory resort we found it nearly three weeks ago: we take long morning walks and—as yesterday's experience was—met not one peasant in the course of three hours: and, if we chose to clamber, I don't know what fresh wonders we might come upon every day. We are in no mind to leave yet, and indeed Italy would be insufferably hot just now. You bid me tell you something of the G[de] Chartreuse: I shall refer you to a "Guide to Grenoble" which, when you read the high-flown paragraphs, will excite expectations I cannot say were gratified. My Sister only dined in a quite distinct building, and was ministered to by Nuns: I—and too many other travelers by far—saw whatever was to be seen in the building. The acceptance of the Hospitality of the Convent means that you dine there at your own expence (very moderate indeed, but still exacted:) and the consequence is anything but a *conventual* behaviour on the part of the multifarious guests, who make merry as at an eating-house, in a mean-looking room: the lower classes, still more uproarious, getting their meal in a downright pot-house style. The fare,—all *meagre,* though you would hardly guess it,—is excellent, and the wine capital: the convent's single dole to a visitor, on his entry, is the traditional bumper of "Liqueur": after dinner, there is an extra charge for another, if you incline to it. Refection ended, an assistant, in secular clothes, takes the company somewhat hurriedly over the interior, explaining, to whoever keeps ahead of the rush, what this corridor is called, when that wing was built, and so forth. We inspected a cell which happened to be empty for the moment: a clean chamber of the size of this in which I write, with a compartment wherein is a bed—the covering for which is deposited on a shelf above it: a little oratory is contiguous to the cell, with a prie-dieu, crucifix and religious prints. Each monk has a little bit of garden,—not much cultivated, but with a flower or two. There is an under-cell, furnished with turning-lathe, and other implements of manual labour—"for they all *work*," said our Guide. I was surprised at the handsome library of 20,000 volumes "of all sorts," maps &c which are at the disposition of the brotherhood: all I can say is, my own Father [2] would never have desired better lodging, living, and occupation (all but the lathe-turning) nor—in *one* mood possible to my mind—should I. The burial-ground was impressive: an oblong square divided by a walk in the middle: on your left as you enter—the *Fathers*—distinguished by a cross of stone, with (I think) the name: on your right, the simple graves of the Brothers marked merely by a wooden cross. We were admitted to the tribune of the church—whence, according to accounts, there is presented a striking spectable as the monks prostrate themselves at the midnight mass. One may stay two days at the Convent and see this and more: I had not the least mind to do so. Had I arrived alone, three centuries ago,—been gratified by a crust & water, and shown the mysteries by an intelligent recluse,—well, who knows whether a wish for that vegetative life might not have arisen? As it is, I had no more "vocation" than a holiday explorer of the Tower has to turn Beef-Eater. Still, I shall not refuse so constantly as has been my wont a *petit-verre* of Chartreuse after coffee![3] The Monks all die early of the cold, and are prepared for their fate, I hear. Have you had enough of this?

No,—don't send the "Saturday"—I have seen it, as also the "Times," "Spectator" and other noticers of my poems.[4] The "Saturday" is, I fancy, an old friend of mine: certainly one and the same kind person writes the articles on me this long while—everyone of which contains a passage to the effect that "it is rash to disregard any of Mr B's writing, because, at its very worst, you may come unawares on something decidedly good—as in the four stanzas which follow the rubbish of 'Fifine.'" I have always detected my friend by this luminous warning. But what matters? Few things have given me more solid satisfaction than an assurance of intelligent George Smith,[5] my Publisher[,] that it made no sort of difference in the demand for a book of mine whether all the critics praised it or abused it. "You have a certain appreciable number of steady readers who will have what you write,—quite independently of what others write about it.["] So best! Here is an egotistic tirade! But you need no assurance, Dear Friend, that I rejoice in all the good points in your home-chronicle—the splendid weather, and harvest,—and the confidence in the improvement in your Son's health. Write as you kindly engage to do, and be sure, in all that you tell me, of the true sympathy of yours

affectionately ever *RB.*

Manuscript: Carl H. Pforzheimer Library, RB 51

1. In 1880 Pen showed *A Tan-Yard, Dinant* at the Royal Academy and in 1881 *The Tanner's Garden, Dinant* (Algernon Graves, *The Royal Academy of Arts* [London, 1905], I, 320). Browning here refers to the second picture, which Pen was painting in 1880.

2. Robert Browning, the poet's father, was born in Battersea on July 6, 1782, and died in Paris on June 14, 1866. He is always described as a man of simple tastes and a great bibliophile.

3. Browning himself preferred port, but he did put in some chartreuse, which he

served to Michael Field, when they called on him in 1888 (Sturgeon, *Michael Field,* p. 22).

4. Browning's *Dramatic Idyls, Second Series* was published on June 15, 1880, and received a poor press. *The Saturday Review* (or *"Saturday Reviler,"* as it was known to Liberals) was, as Browning would expect, unfriendly (August 21, pp. 237–238).

5. George Murray Smith (1824–1901), Browning's publisher after 1867.

Letter 24

Lans, (Isère,) France.
Sept. 13. '80.

Dear Friend,

I have received several newspapers & the "Academy," but no answer to my letter of Saturday week—one wherein I gave you the account you desired of the *Chartreuse*. This is to apprise you that we leave next Monday (the 20th) and therefore that any further favors should be directed to us at *Venice, poste restante,*—the next place we count upon stopping at. If all goes as we venture to hope, we shall sleep at Grenoble on Monday, at Turin on the 21st, at Genoa on the 22d and following day or two: thence, after a day or two at Milan, we shall reach Venice—we expect—not later than Oct. 1. and *there* have news of you, if none come meanwhile. The weather apparently "broke up" here, two days ago: but, despite of the storminess, we took our usual exercise, and continue to be more than satisfied with the rough primitive place and kind people. The scenery is exceedingly beautiful and still all but unexplored by us—so infinitely might we vary our walks were we adventurous and easily tired of old favorites. We leave our blessing on the place. It seems odd perhaps that I count *another week* as no time in which you can answer this letter: but there is some necessity of a letter from Lans going back to Villard-de-Lans there to rest all night:

and similarly a letter from London goes thither at once—and only gets to us next morning: so—write to Venice (I shall not enquire at any Post Office on the road) and tell me—as I hope may be the case—that the visit you had so much at heart has proved all you could desire: and meantime and ever believe me

Affectionately yours
Robert Browning.

(Belgravia [1]—Pig and all—received this morning. [)]

Manuscript: Carl H. Pforzheimer Library, RB 52

1. *Belgravia: an Illustrated London Magazine* published Katherine S. Macquoid's "The Heart of the Ardennes" in the issue for September 13, 1880 (pp. 280–298). One of the six illustrations was Pen's pig picture, *Watching* . . . (p. 289). Browning's postscript is written in the upper margin. See appendix for description.

Letter 25

Lans—Sept. 19. '80.

Dear Friend, a second letter, this morning, I did not expect: and all I can give in return for this and the other with the "Academy" and "Times" will be the last line I write from this place—whence, as I have already mentioned, we go to-morrow. You have kept up fully the old traditionary kindness, and the journals &c have been nearly all our bringers of news from England: for—this first time—I neglected to arrange that a paper should be sent regularly. I was glad of all your gladness in the fine harvest,—and *very* glad to hear of your escaping from that overflow which you describe.[1] Here the weather was admirable till a week ago—and has returned to its habits for the last two days: with snow on the mountain, the valley is even too warm this last morning of ours.

I shall be greatly interested in reading Guizot's Memoirs [2] when you lend them to me on my return. No doubt he had strong affections and they were answerably rewarded: but I confess to a thorough dislike of the man — whose great powers nobody could dispute. His appreciation — (as you quote it —) of his wife's "passion for truth" was sadly in abeyance during that abominable affair of the Spanish Marriages: [3] and our own Queen, — who, with foibles enough, was ever a brave truth-teller, — could rightly say she was proud such a course — and such excuses for it — came not from *her* or her minister. M. de Loménie may well say "the *entente-cordiale* was disturbed on this occasion." [4] It effectually destroyed all faith in the character of Louis Philippe, and was the main cause of his downfall. I remember the very words of Guizot in the French Chambers in excuse of his having told a direct falsehood on the subject to our Ambassador: "Quand je reçois un ministre je ne subis pas un interrogatoire" [5] — a good reason for holding the tongue but not for uttering a lie. Again, the strenuous protestant (I heard him say proudly in a speech "Protestant comme mes pères"[)] [6] — he was a vehement opposer of any attempt on the part of the Italians to get rid of the Pope's catholic rule. You are touched naturally by those assurances to his wife that all his efforts to distinguish himself were inspired by her influence: [7] but there is his past life to dispose of *that* assertion: he very properly strove to excel from the beginning. The publication of such letters is repugnant to me. Those are fine manly words of Carlyle in his "Life of Sterling" when, speaking of certain intimate letters of the actually dying friend's last moments, he says "These are of my own, and of the things belonging to no other" [8] — such is at least the sense of what I read so long ago. For my own part — I have intact the long series of letters addressed to me by my wife before our marriage — and *what* letters! I have never opened the box of my own letters [9] [of] which she wore the key round her neck: but one bitter-sweet experience awaits me when —at no very distant day—I shall—for the first and last time—reread them—and then destroy—hers and mine together.[10] However other people feel differently, and the destruction of such crowns and palm-branches will be hard to bear, no question—hence the postponement of it. *Poveri noi!*

I was much obliged to you for the incidental news of Pen contained in those two letters: his reticence is such that I hear less than I like of his doings: and his habitual depreciation of them would mislead me, were I not used to it. Why do you suppose he will join us at Venice—when he says he shall be detained all the Autumn at Dinant? A few days there would do little good, in an artistic point of view. I may induce him to spend next winter in Rome, if I go there:[11] he would have a studio and turn his visit to advantage. I saw what you wrote about the desirability of a young artist "imbuing himself with the works of the Great Masters": but did any "great"—or even "good master" really begin that way? Does not all mediocrity (educated mediocrity) come of a beginner's determining to look at nature through the eyes of his predecessors who assuredly began by looking for themselves? I should expect a genuine painter, aspiring to be "good" if not "great" to begin by ascertaining what he likes best to see in nature generally,—then master the means of expressing what he likes and sees,—and, *then only,* ask himself how others have gone through the same process and with what results—correcting no doubt in a multiplicity of cases his own views, but never wholly setting them aside. And the reason why this should come last is—that the characteristic of the greatest masters is *imaginativeness*—*not* technicality—in which the moderns have surpassed them. But before attempting to imagine an angel, one ought to be able to express a stone or a flower: and the humble labour at this first necessary stage is an earnest that the artist uses it with a view to turning his skill to better account eventually. I know a sad instance of a young man, a friend of mine, who took the contrary course. He had great imagination, and at once tried to draw things much above angels when he was unable really to properly draw apes: and I gave him introductions to Leighton,[12] Millais, Rossetti[13] & Watts:[14] I remember Millais said of his specimen-drawings "He begins where Michelagnolo never arrived"—the end is that he never now aspires to painting anything above an animal. Certainly whenever Pen "imagines"[,] he will not be now "put out" by an ignorance of the grammar of his art. He always told me on what subjects he would try his skill—when he possessed it: and if he painted an ambitious picture "to please me"—that only meant that, "to please me," he was venturing already a little beyond what he felt justified in doing. Anyhow, The Tannery Garden, with its three or four figures, and the "Girl with three dogs"[15] on which he is now engaged, show that he thinks he can rise above the "still-life" subjects which he wisely exercised himself upon years ago. I have just sent him a letter from an American lady,[16] unknown to us both, who offers him—what I am sure he will not accept—a commission to come to London this October to paint her portrait, on the strength of what she has heard of his powers: she enclosed 3. photographs that he might begin at once! But how I run on—with baggage to pack and matters to dispose of! Goodbye to Lans—goodbye, dear friend to you—from yours

affectionately ever RB.

Manuscript: Carl H. Pforzheimer Library, RB 53

1. At Shalstone extensive flooding could occur from the brook that runs at the bottom of the village street, also elsewhere, from the River Ouse. Mrs. Caroline (Tew) Greaves of Shalstone recalls that when she was about five years of age (1880) the floods were such that villagers living near the brook could occupy only their upper rooms, with food supplies handed in by men from a horse-drawn cart. At Hunt Mill by the Ouse, in an outlying part of the parish, the cottages were so badly damaged that they had to be demolished (MPFG).

2. François Pierre Guillaume Guizot (1787–1874), French historian and statesman, minister under Louis Philippe. His daughter, Madame Guizot de Witt, pub-

lished *Monsieur Guizot dans Sa Famille et avec Ses Amis,* an English translation of which appeared in 1880. He is mentioned in Browning's "Respectability."

3. On October 10, 1846, the two daughters of Queen Maria Isabella of Spain, Isabella and Fernanda, married, respectively, the Duke of Cadiz and the Duke of Montpensier, son of Louis Philippe of France. The marriages were preceded by great intrigue on the part of the French and English factions at the Court of Madrid.

4. Ch. de Loménie, in his review of the English translation of Madame Guizot's book (see n. 2) in *The Academy* for September 11, 1880 (pp. 181–182) made the statement that Browning quotes.

5. On September 1, 1846, Lord Normanby, the English ambassador, asked Guizot whether the marriages would take place simultaneously, and Guizot replied that they would not. Subsequently, the Queen Mother pressed for a double marriage, but Guizot did not inform Lord Normanby of the change in plans. On February 5, 1847, Guizot said in the French Chamber of Deputies, "Quand un ambassadeur me fait l'honneur de venir me voir et de m'addresser des questions, ce n'est pas un interrogatoire que je subis. Je ne dois dire que la vérité; mais je ne réponds qu'autant qu'il convient à l'intérêt de mon pays et de la politique que je soutiens de répondre" (Guizot, *Histoire Parlementaire de France: Recueil Complet des Discours Prononcés dans les Chambres de 1819 à 1848 par M. Guizot* [Paris, 1864], V, 368). At this point, the deputies exclaimed, "Très bien! très bien!"

6. We learn here that Browning was present at the ceremony on February 5, 1852, when Guizot delivered the *discours de réception* on the occasion of Charles Montalembert's reception into the French Academy. Guizot said, "Je suis resté fidèle à la foi protestante de mes pères" (*Discours de M. Guizot en Réponse Au Discours Prononcé par M. le Comte de Montalembert pour sa Réception à L'Académie Française Le 5 février 1852* [Paris, 1852]).

7. In his review, de Loménie quoted the words of Guizot to his wife, " 'Tis for thy sake that I will not willingly neglect any opportunity of distinguishing myself from other men" (see n. 4).

8. "And four days before his [Sterling's] death, there are some stanzas of verse for me, written as if in star-fire and immortal tears; which are among my sacred possessions, to be kept for myself alone" (Thomas Carlyle, *The Life of John Sterling* [London, 1851], p. 334).

9. The phrase "my own letters" is an addition. See appendix for description.

10. Browning's father preserved all his son's letters from the earliest days, and late in 1885 Browning spent more than a week in destroying them (*The Critic,* January 2, 1886, p. 11). Browning did not destroy the love letters, which Pen published in 1898 and which are now in the Wellesley College Library.

11. Browning never returned to Rome or to Florence.

12. Frederick Leighton (1830–1896), President of the Royal Academy of Art (*Dearest Isa,* p. 29).

13. Dante Gabriel Rossetti (1828–1882), whose twenty-year friendship with Browning ended in 1872 (*Dearest Isa,* p. 99).

14. George Frederick Watts, R.A. (1817–1904), whose portrait of Browning (1865) is in the National Portrait Gallery. Ronald Chapman says that Browning was always welcome at Watts's studio "but not much liked. He was found to be so very lacking in the monumental" (*The Laurel and the Thorn: a Study of G. F. Watts* [London, 1945], p. 75).

15. Pen appears not to have finished his *Girl with Three Dogs* because of difficulty with the model (Letter 26).

16. Perhaps Mrs. Moore, although she says she first met Browning in 1879 (Letter 42, n. 5).

Letter 26

Venice, Sept. 3[*0*]. *'80.*

Dear Friend,—with so much to say,—it perversely happens that I have so little time wherein to say it, unless I would lose another post: so, briefly,—first of all, however,—thank you most heartily for all your kindness. The dropping of *manna* in the shape of newspapers and periodicals has been incessant and ever welcome: and the letters are acknowledged even more gratefully. We did all we proposed to ourselves: left Lans for Grenoble, and Turin: saw the Exposition [1] there, and went on to Genoa, and, after a few days, to Milan—thence starting for Venice last Tuesday. There were some difficulties on arriving about the quarters we were to be established in—our friends the Storys having engaged rooms for us in another Hotel than the old one: we at last got settled in our customary lodgings at the "Universo." Our whole journey so far has been a success: the weather was and continues to be delightful—beyond any we remember on former visits to Venice. We shall—I hope—see nothing to prevent our staying two or three weeks longer—the place proving more attractive than ever: but you shall be duly informed of our projects when we turn our unwilling faces Northward. Do you know Shelley's "Julian & Maddalo"? [2]

"If I had been an unconnected man,
I, from that moment should have formed some plan
Never to leave Sweet Venice: for to me
It was delight to rove by the lone sea."

and so on — and so on — till there comes the inevitable —

"But I had friends in London too . . .
And so, next morning, urged by my affairs,
I left bright Venice" —

as we shall do: the "friends" — dear Friend — are the counterbalance even to the charm of Venice. Now of yourself — I hear with the natural mixed feeling of your hopes and fears — and hope — with as little fear as the circumstances admit — that your infinite patience and untired solicitude will have their deserved effect in the case of your Son. Some sustainment under much anxiety there must surely be in all these testimonies to your value in Shalstone: I read the paper just now with great sympathy: and shall of course preserve and return it, with the "Academy." I believe my friend & publisher Smith arrived here, according to his intention, last evening: I shall soon know. We were called on, two days ago, by Mr & Miss Robinson [3] — on the eve of their departure after a stay of certain weeks. Mrs Orr had preceded us here. Several acquaintances are in the town probably: but I am slow to hunt them out. It was a vexation however to find that Willy Bracken had gone the morning of the day when we called, — after five months' sojourn, too! Pen has not written for a fortnight, but soon may be expected to do so: he has finished his "Garden," but finds the little girl a bad sitter, and is inclined to postpone that picture till another year,[4] and utilize his remainder of country-life by "doing something in the open": I regret this, — but he knows best. S. will supplement this hasty scribble: there needs no supplement to the affection with which I am ever, dear Friend,

Yours Robert Browning.

Manuscript: Carl H. Pforzheimer Library, RB 54. The date of this letter was corrected in pencil by Mrs. FitzGerald. See appendix for description.

1. *Esposizione Nazionale di Belle Arti: Catalogo degli oggetti componenti la mostra di arte antica.* Torino, 1880.

2. Browning quotes, with some few errors, from P. B. Shelley's *Julian and Maddalo* (1818), lines 547–550, 564, and 582–583.

3. Perhaps Agnes Mary Frances Robinson (1857–1944), biographer, critic, poet, and the daughter of G. T. Robinson, an architect. She married (1888) James Darmesteter (died 1894), an Oriental scholar, and secondly Emile Duclaux (died 1904), director of the Pasteur Institute. She lived much in Italy and included among her friends Pater, Symonds, Gosse, and Vernon Lee (*Annual Register,* 1944, p. 429; *Times,* April 14, 1944, p. 86). She presented Browning with her *The Crowned Hippolytus* (1881) (Tregaskis, no. 653) and *The New Arcadia and Other Poems* (Sotheby, no. 1126, p. 133). Browning's address book (BM) lists a W. C. Robinson, 30 Russell Square. A Rev. W. Robinson and Mrs. Robinson were guests at Shalstone in 1884 (*Buckingham Express,* September 6, 1884)

4. See Letter 25, n. 15.

Letter 27

Albergo dell' Universo, Venice, Oct. 13. '80.

Dear Friend,—I should have written at once on the arrival of your very pleasant letter but that the need of attending to some friends who claimed an old promise that I would do the little I could for them broke in upon the morning hours: and though Shelley asserts that "one can *write* and read in gondolas by day and night (having the little brazen lamp alight)" [1] —*that* puzzles me to conceive, and in *gondolate* our long afternoons have been floated away. To-day I pass the hours in my room,—having spent the morning abroad,—and write to you with a feeling of relief. Here is your "Academy" too, for which due thanks! Now, why am I at home? Because in the evening S. and I are bound to see the "Barbiere di Siviglia" by—

Paesiello:[2] the original masterpiece, produced some hundred years ago at Petersburg, which was supposed to be sure of perpetual youth and popularity — till once on a time young Mr Rossini took on himself to ask its composer — then old and glorious — if he would object to a juvenile attempting the same subject under the enormous disadvantage &c &c. &c. Whereto the senior replied with a knowing chuckle that the novice was quite free to enter the lists with him: and so was ushered in the work we have never since been tired of — while Paesiello's performance was brought out here, "for one night only," as a musical curiosity — and a great delight I lost (as I thought) by having to dine out instead of being present: but I so stirred up the somewhat torpid enthusiasm of a moderately music-loving friend or two that application was made to the manager for a repetition — which he granted "though nobody had patronized the piece on the other occasion": so to-night somebody is to incline a studious and respectful ear to the "music old, nay, obsolete — which once was sweet, Oh, passing sweet Though now tis past away."[3] (Whose lines are those, my learned lady? *I* know, although I have not seen them for half a century: I spare your guessing and say — Kirke White's: only, my memory is at fault.[)]

The weather is warm, fine, characteristic: there are not many foreigners here, — nothing like the gaiety of the two last seasons: but the city is lovelier than ever. We are at this moment, — *we two,* — alone in the Hotel, save for the apparition at the dinner-table of a mysterious tall black-robed lady with four little dogs jingling at her footsteps who is said to fight with her maid and swear at her gondolier. All the huge palace otherwise — deserted! Mrs Orr preceded us and is gone again. The Storys are capital company, and friendly Americans abound. We have a jewel of a gondolier who understands our taste and takes us in and out the most recondite nooks and corners of the city while the sun is too fierce for boating in the open. The day before yesterday we were six hours out and away, — at Torcello, Burano, St Francesco, and other islets. My *fifth* visit to

Venice, by the way.[4] I will try for your "weed from the Rialto," be sure.

Pen sent us three photographs of his finished pictures, the Owls, the Still Life,[5] the Tan-Garden: he abandons for the present the girl's portrait, and gives the last day of a fast-breaking season to a landscape, — large as "Solitude."[6] He then takes a "lonely holiday" which he begins to need: The photographs give no notion of colour, of course, but show careful work. *Your* photograph of the Library was a great acquisition.[7] I have had it mounted here. You have been good indeed to William[8] — but he deserves something for his perfect behaviour, and is properly grateful, I am sure. Our doings are undecided upon as yet, — but you shall know when ourselves know: here, at any rate, we stay for some time longer. My friend George Smith, with his wife and daughters, are here, — and who knows how we shall feel when the whole *brigata* breaks up? I have written so lightly that I hardly like to speak of the deep satisfaction I feel at the[9] (in the main) good news in your letter. May all good continue to you & yours! Ever affectionately yours, R Browning.

Manuscript: Carl H. Pforzheimer Library, RB 55

1. *Julian and Maddalo,* lines 551–554.

2. Giovanni Paisiello (1740–1816), whose *Il Barbiere di Siviglia* is dated 1782. Mrs. Orr says (II, 484) that the performance was in the Rossini theater and that Wagner was in the audience. Gioacchino Rossini's *Barber* was first performed in 1816 in Rome.

3. "The most beloved on earth | Not long survives to-day; | So music past is obsolete, | And yet 'twas sweet, 'twas passing sweet, | But now 'tis gone away." Henry Kirke White (1785–1806), "On Disappointment," lines 49–53. The word "Oh" is a correction. See appendix for description.

4. During Browning's first Italian tour in 1838; then with his wife and son in 1851; then with his sister in 1878, 1879, and 1880.

5. See Letter 34, n. 4.

6. *Solitude,* which pictured a river, a boat, and distant hills in evening light, was shown in 1880 at the Royal Academy and then in Liverpool. (See Henriette Corkran,

Celebrities and I [London, 1902], p. 163.) Mrs. Moore bought the picture in 1882 (Letter 42, n. 5). Of Pen's several large landscapes, one (5′ x 7′6″) showed a hilly background, a river in the middle distance, and five nude females in the foreground (Sotheby, no. 30, p. 10).

7. Very likely a photograph of the library at Shalstone showing one of Pen's paintings over the fireplace (MPFG).

8. William Grove.

9. The remainder is cross-written. See appendix for description.

Letter 28

Venice, Oct. 23, '80.

Dear Friend,

This is to apprise you that we leave on our homeward journey next Thursday — the 28th, and to prevent your sending any letter or newspaper after this good bye to Venice reaches you. We had meant to stay till the absolute end of the month: but I have — wisely or rashly — accepted an invitation to the Ld Mayor's Dinner on the 9th [1] — and as we want to travel leisurely and stop a little at certain places on the road, we anticipate somewhat so as to leave a day or two at our disposal in case of any good reason for delay, — hoping to find ourselves in Warwick Crescent neither before nor after Saturday, Nov. 6. We proceed by Ferrara, Bologna, Ravenna, Parma — or Mantua, and so on to Turin and Paris. Your terrible account of the fog in London is confirmed by other letters and all the newspapers. Here, we have had uninterruptedly fine weather since our arrival on the 28th ult. Scirocco has prevailed, and dulled the customary brightness of Venice for the last week: but no rain till this morning — when a few minutes of dropping made a clearance for the sun which is blazing while I write, — while, in the shade even, the heat is almost oppressive. We have — strange to say — and contrary to all previous custom — "gone out" a good deal: there are, or have been, friends and acquaintances so hospitably disposed as to break through our habitude. The Mundellas[2]—always kind,—Americans, (of course!)—the Layards,[3] and others. Yesterday, I dined (*we,* that means) with an American family whose cook is—who but my old Ferdinando[4] of Florence, who married my wife's maid,[5] and was with us many years—up to the very last. The dear old fellow gave us a genuinely Tuscan dinner—having beaten his brains about its achievement for days before, and "twice changed his mind twice as to the appropriate pudding." To-morrow we dine with Layard—who showed us his house, the day before yesterday,—full of fine pictures and choice works of Art. Somehow, Venetian visiting is a quite different thing from the London laborious "dining-out"—the lulling influence of the sea makes itself felt through the palace walls—and it is helped by one's being waited on at table by gondoliers in their white livery with blue badge and sash. Dear Friend, I have twice investigated every stone of the Rialto and failed to find a blade of grass indicative of a root which I could obey you by transporting to Shalstone. I must find some trifle of about the same value—and you will take the will for the deed, I well know. Oh, I must tell you: M. Deschamps[6] is about to have a winter exhibition of English oil-paintings in that Bond Street Gallery where Makart's[7] picture was exhibited last year—and he writes to ask for Pen's "fine Picture" of the Inquisition:[8] I shall rejoice in its getting seen at last. And now—*A rivederci,* dear Friend! I am happy that all seems to be prosperous with regard to your Son: may you also regain the strength you must have taxed in helping on such a success! Ever affectionately yours *RB.*

Manuscript: Carl H. Pforzheimer Library, RB 56

1. The annual banquet celebrating the inauguration of the Lord Mayor of London was traditionally held on November 9. In 1880, at the inauguration of Sir William McArthur, Gladstone addressed more than one thousand guests, Browning among them (*Times,* November 10, 1880, p. 6a).

2. Anthony John Mundella (1825–1897), M.P., his wife Mary (Smith) Mundella, and their daughter Mary Teresa. His granddaughter Dorothea Lady Charnwood tells of the family's friendship with Browning in her *Call Back Yesterday* (London, 1937). Browning met the Mundellas in 1873, was their dinner guest on occasion, and in 1886, when Dorothea was ten, she and her mother spent a fortnight with Browning and his sister at the Hand Hotel in Llangolen, Wales (*Call Back Yesterday*, p. 219).

3. Sir Austen Henry Layard (1817–1894), excavator and diplomat, retired in 1880 to Venice, where he made his home in the Palazzo Capello.

4. Ferdinando Romagnoli, the Browning's manservant from 1853 to 1861 (*Dearest Isa*, p. 10).

5. Elizabeth (Wilson) Romagnoli, Mrs. Browning's maid. The records of the cemetery of Saint Anna in Asolo say that she was born in Rottemburg [*sic*], England, in 1820 and died at Asolo on April 6, 1902. (See *Dearest Isa*, p. 9.)

6. C. W. Deschamps, an art dealer connected with the Hanover Gallery, 47 New Bond Street.

7. Hans Makart (1840–1884), Austrian painter, whose *Entry of Charles V into Antwerp* and other paintings opened the first season of the Hanover Gallery in April 1880 (*The Academy*, May 1, 1880, pp. 328–329).

8. See Letter 29, n. 8.

Letter 29

19. Warwick Crescent. W.
Nov. 20. '80.

Dear Friend, I am happy that all seems going on tolerably well with you. It was an ungenial day when you left London, but worse weather followed: and probably you are safer in Shalstone now the passage is effected. Well, I have read, and burned, and herewith return — all according to your commands. I knew the Lowe epitaph [1] and translation of it. Lady Violet [2] is very good and indulgent. I *did* approve — as who could fail to do? — the version of Pepoli.[3] I never saw the man, but remember reading his little book of poems: he was the writer of the libretto of *I Puritani*. There is an echoing repetition of rhymes in this particular poem which is pleasant enough, and an example of what I do not recollect elsewhere in Italian poetry. He was very poor (of course) when in exile here: and I remember helping Forster [4] to write an article for the "Examiner" about the above mentioned book — F. being ignorant of Italian but desirous of doing a service.

I found two days ago the note of George Sand [5] in which she appoints the day for my wife to call on her: the letter is dated Feb. 13. '52: and the sonnets were *published* in '44, — eight years previously: yet the whipper-snapper of the memoir of Miss Blagden must make them the consequence of the meeting! [6] How characteristic a vulgarity is the absence of any care about truth! His other "fact" was just as easy to verify, and so he put down as complete a falsehood. Enough of him! I dined last evening with Lowell — to become acquainted with his wife: who is recovering from her illness which I heard was serious indeed. She walked (with much assistance) and presided at table, amiably enough. Lowell is an old acquaintance of mine, and very charming. On Wednesday I saw dear Carlyle — *not* so changed as I was led to expect. He is silent now, unless spoken to — but when he does speak all the old soul is in the little he says. "He much desires to be released from this world, if God please." He still goes out daily — and such a bracing sunny day as the present must be good for him. Tyndal [7] and his wife called while I was there.

Do you hear from Pen? The critics are not goodnatured to his picture, — see the "Times" of this morning,[8] — which finds there is no expression in any figure in the piece. Another critic [9] found that there was a doubt — faulty therefore — as to which feeling (of pity or sense of obligation) was predominant in the Magistrate's face: that is, Indecision ought to be Decision. But how harmless is all such criticism when a picture is once fairly hung up and open to view for the next month or more! In the case of a *book* — the ill word may possibly *shut up* its contents altogether from the reader of the criticism, if he believes it fair and good. Deschamps did wrong in letting the picture be seen at first *unvarnished* — spite of my entreaties: the operation was performed on Monday — to the benefit of the colouring. Good bye, dear friend, "I gossip like a crow" as Anacreon's pigeon confesses.[10]

Ever affectionately yours RB.

Manuscript: Carl H. Pforzheimer Library, RB 57

1. Robert Lowe "dallied on the epitaph 'Humilis Robertus'" (M. E. Grant Duff, *Notes from a Diary 1892–95* [London, 1904], II, 240). In June 1866 Lowe was responsible for the fall of Gladstone's Ministry. *The Owl* for July 11 (p. 6) published "An Epitaph By the Right Hon. W. E. Gladstone," a forty-eight line poem beginning, "Here lie the bones of ROBERT LOWE, | A shifty friend, a bitter foe" and concluding, "But if he's gone to lower level, | Let's all commiserate the devil."

2. Lady Beatrice Violet Greville. (See Letter 8, n. 9.)

3. Count Carlo Pepoli (1796–1881), Italian poet and patriot, the librettist of Bellini's *Norma* (1832) and *I Puritani* (1834). He was a friend of the Carlyles, a political exile in England (1849–1859), and professor of Italian literature at the University of London. Mary F. P. Fitzgerald, aged sixteen, translated his poem "Descrizione di Messina," and Mrs. FitzGerald was so pleased that she wrote on November 10, 1880: "Your translation quite surprizes me by its accuracy combined with the rhythmical arrangement of the words so much so that I shall like to shew it to Mr. Browning when he calls next Sunday and therefore do not return it at once" (MPFG).

4. John Forster (1812–1876), critic, historian, and early literary friend of Browning. The Forster collection in the Victoria and Albert Museum has *Prose e Versi di Carlo Pepoli* (Londra: P. Rolandi, 20 Berners Street. Presso l'autore, 65 Regent Quadrant, 1837). An unsigned review of this book appeared in *The Examiner* for September 4, 1836 (p. 568).

5. George Sand (1803–1876) wrote to Mrs. Browning on February 12, 1852, inviting the Brownings to her home "dimanche prochain" (Kenyon, II, 50). This letter seems to be the one Browning later gave to Mrs. Moore (*Lippincott's Monthly Magazine,* May 1890, p. 690).

6. Mrs. Browning included two sonnets addressed to George Sand in her *Poems* (1844), yet Alfred Austin in his introduction to *Poems by the Late Isa Blagden* (1873) said that the sonnets were "wrung" from Mrs. Browning by the interview in 1852 (p. xvi). He also said, erroneously, that Isa Blagden tended Mrs. Browning during her last illness (p. xiv).

7. John Tyndall (1820–1893), professor of natural history and superintendent of the Royal Institution.

8. Of Pen's *Delivery to the Secular Arm* (see Letter 19, n. 4) *The Times* (November 20, 1880, p. 11e) said: "None of the actors in the drama are moved one whit; the condemned girl, the condemning judges, and the attendant soldiers are all the merest puppets, and, indeed, we discover no merit of any kind in the picture except a somewhat careful and level execution of the technical portion of the painting." In 1881 Mrs. Moore presented the picture to the Pennsylvania Academy of Fine Arts, where it has been rolled up in a case since 1944.

9. *The Academy* (November 20, 1880, p. 373) said, "The face of the lean and withered chief inquisitor strikes us as admirable, but we cannot say as much for the other figures in the picture."

10. See Letter 20, n. 15.

Letter 30

19. Warwick Crescent. W.
Nov. 27. '80.

Dear Friend,

"Somewhat better" must pass, in default of more assurance, for good news; and I am glad indeed to hear it. Go on to "decidedly better" and "well," and my gladness will keep pace and proportion. I have forgotten being curious about Hanbury Williams [1] and his poetry: very likely I was induced to enquire about the latter by some circumstance equally forgotten: and my curiosity is again so far returned, that, whenever *you* return, if bringing the books with you be no undue trouble, I shall be grateful for a sight of them. There is a book of questionable propriety which was written by Lady William Russell's [2] relative—Hall Stevenson [3] (I think the name is) who was the original Yorick of Sterne: She had his portrait, and used to tantalize me by saying she possessed the work—"Crazy Tales"—praising its wit—and then refusing to lend it me "just then." Does it lurk in some back shelf of your enviable library? I have just finished my friend Trevelyan's "Fox" [4]—and cannot go with his glorification of that scapegrace's early days: he was as kindly as you please, and as clever,—but I should require far more decided proof than I find that there was one touch of principle from rank Toryism to furious Liberalism. Nor do I believe in his superlative taste for poetry: I thought, when I skimmed Rogers's recollections of his talk,[5] and the opinions recorded were shallow enough.

The blind old man was Captain Dommett, Alfred's Father,[6] who, at an exceedingly advanced age, was operated on successfully by Alexander[7] for cataract.

I had a letter from L[d] Wentworth[8] yesterday informing me of his approaching marriage with Miss Stuart-Wortley: a charming person in every way. When I spoke of her to him at Venice last Autumn,—in the presence of Miss Fletcher,[9]—he affected to have forgotten her,—thought she was married, &c. I am a *little* surprised in this case, at the efficacy of a title in actuality with another in prospect,—but *ainsi va le monde!* I shall call on the lady's mother[10] to day or to-morrow,—and shall, I suppose,—hear some sort of apology for the impressions of both—as they favoured me with them last January. S. tells me you are indignant (in your friendliness) at the notice of Pen's picture in the "Times":[11] WHY? The Art Critics are less qualified by acquirement—and no more by morality—than their brethren who pronounce upon literature: and the sooner Pen understands *that* the better. One such opinion as Alma Tadema[12] gave me, last Monday, is worth something. Oh, yes—you shall see George Sand's letter:[13] I would send it but that its size unfits it for enclosure in my squat envelopes. Goodbye, dear friend—

Ever affectionately yours RB.

Manuscript: Carl H. Pforzheimer Library, RB 58

1. Sir Charles Hanbury Williams (1708–1759), minor writer of sarcastic and social verse.

2. Elizabeth Anne (Rawdon) Russell (died 1874), wife of Lord George William

Russell (1790–1846), and one of the magnificent English women of the nineteenth century. Browning knew her in Rome in 1859 (D&K, p. 114) and remained a good friend thereafter.

3. John Hall Stevenson (1718–1785), country gentleman and poetaster, the original Eugenius of Laurence Sterne's *Tristram Shandy* (1760–1767). In his best known publication, *Crazy Tales* (1762), each of his friends at Crazy Castle entertains the group with a *fabliau.* In 1790 he published *Yorick's Sentimental Journey Continued by Eugenius.*

4. Sir George Otto Trevelyan (1838–1928), historian, statesman, and the nephew of Lord Macaulay. In his *Early History of Charles James Fox* (1880) he calls Fox "our first great statesman of the modern school."

5. *Recollections of the Table Talk of Samuel Rogers* (1856) included, in somewhat fragmentary form, many of the literary observations of Charles James Fox (1749–1806).

6. Alfred Domett (1811–1887), one of Browning's earliest friends, was the son of a naval officer who left the Royal Navy for the merchant service (Sir Frederic G. Kenyon, *Robert Browning and Alfred Domett* [London, 1906], pp. 5–6).

7. Not further identified than as an oculist.

8. Ralph Gordon Noel Milbanke (1839–1906), thirteenth Baron Wentworth (1862) and second Earl Lovelace (1893), married his second wife, Mary Caroline Stuart Wortley, on December 30, 1880. Lord Wentworth, who was Byron's grandson, had broken off his engagement with Miss Fletcher after learning that her parents were divorced (Marie Belloc Lowndes, *The Merry Wives of Westminster* [London, 1946], pp. 66–67).

9. Julia Constance Fletcher (1858–1938), American novelist and dramatist who wrote under the name of "George Fleming." She was born in the United States, the daughter of the Rev. James Coolie Fletcher, and Henrietta Malan, who was the daughter of the Rev. Dr. César Henri Malan of Geneva. Her parents separated when she was still a girl, and she went with her mother to live in Venice, although she spent much time in London. When she was eighteen, she achieved fame with her *A Nile Novel, or, Kismet* (1876), which has been dramatized in our day by Edward Knoblock and the dramatization made into a Broadway musical (1954). Her dramatization of *The Light that Failed* (1903) was successful, and her literary criticism for the *Times Literary Supplement,* from 1902 to 1910, was incisive. Her mother's second husband was Eugene Benson (1839–1908), an American painter. After 1913 she remained in Italy, where she lived in the Palazzo Capello, the setting of Henry James's *The Aspern Papers* (1888). Among her literary friends were Henley, James, Kipling, Pater, Wilde, and Browning, whom she once thought to be her "best friend" (see Letter 45, n. 3). (See her obituary in *The Times,* July 11, 1938, p. 14c; "Eugene Benson" in *DAB;* and Katherine L. Mix, *A Study in Yellow* [Lawrence, Kansas, 1960], p. 228).

10. Wife of the Rt. Hon. James Stuart Wortley.

11. See Letter 29, n. 8.

12. Sir Lawrence Alma-Tadema (1836–1912), painter, who was born in Holland, settled in London (1870), elected member of the Royal Academy (1879), and knighted (1899).

13. Very likely that of 12 février 1852 (see Letter 29, n. 5).

Letter 31

19. Warwick Crescent. W.

Jan. 2. '80 [for '81] [1] — Do you wonder, or reproach me, dear Friend? Or, as a dear friend should, believe there has been some intervention of circumstance to hinder the proper letter from reaching you on the proper day? *So* — rightly! for I was cheated out of the single quarter of an hour which I had counted upon through the whole of the most exacting day of a week which was an incessant demand on my time — and strength too. To go back no farther than sad Wednesday — I spent all the morning in following poor George Eliot to the grave: [2] I stood there, as need was, bareheaded in wind and rain, — and caught a cold which is even heavier on me now than the next day when, — under similar conditions, — I was present at Wentworth's wedding with my friend Miss Stuart Wortley: — of the "dinners" afterwards, and the talking with fits of sneezing between interesting passages, I say nothing. On Friday, — first, the long Grosvenor [3] business (what is to tell you thereon? people to see and pictures to turn the back upon!) and so forth till letter-writing day — Saturday: when — earliest came the visit to Pen's pictures,[4] arrived overnight (of which more hereafter) then the call upon Millais, a necessary piece of politeness: then the house-affairs — the notes and parcels requiring an immediate answer: then, the Academy with its Old Masters, — then the dinner (to which I could just drag my cold and myself) at old Lady Stanley's [5] — and at midnight nothing was done that should have been done but the making up the little parcel for Portland Place,—which parcel *should* have been preceded or accompanied by a word begging your acceptance of it. Now shall I make any amends for all this silence by bidding you believe that all the while there was a loud voice inside the aching head and obstructed breast urging [6] the need of thanking you, and putting into at least a word or two the warmest of wishes for the New Year? My Euripides makes Admetos say that if even a ghost appeared to him he would be glad "since a friend is dear whenever he may come": [7] so, even as late as this, comes your—"other myself—which is—a friend"—for *so* you must translate "ἀλλος εγω"—κ.τ.λ., [8] in your Greek exercise. Many words—one thought!—which is—all happiness to you, Dear friend, from

Yours affectionately ever *RB.*

Manuscript: Carl H. Pforzheimer Library, RB 46

1. The references to George Eliot's funeral and Miss Stuart Wortley's wedding show that Browning misdated.

2. George Eliot (1819–1880) died on December 22 and was buried on December 29, 1880, in Highgate Cemetery.

3. For a discussion of the Grosvenor Gallery, see Joseph Comyns Carr, *Some Eminent Victorians* (London, 1908), pp. 126–132; and *Grosvenor Notes with Facsimiles of Sketches by the Artists,* ed. Henry Blackburn (London, annually 1879–1889). Pen did not exhibit at the Grosvenor in 1880.

4. Pen's pictures, which were later exhibited at the Royal Academy and at the Grosvenor, had just arrived from his studio on the Continent (see Letter 33, n. 2).

5. Lady Stanley of Alderley "had been one of the great hostesses of her long day, and she had entertained all the famous Victorians" (Lowndes, *Merry Wives,* p. 39).

6. The word "urging" is a correction. See appendix for description.

7. "Were you to come in dreams you would have delighted me, for it is sweet to see friends even by night . . ." (Euripides, *Alcestis,* lines 354–356).

8. Under ἐγώ, Liddell and Scott's *Greek-English Lexicon* quotes "τι ἔστι φίλος; ἄλλος ἐγώ." "What is a friend? A second self."

Mrs. FitzGerald in her eighty-third year

Shalstone: The Manor House, showing the Virginia creeper on the south wall

Shalstone: The formal garden

Shalstone: The school built by Mrs. FitzGerald in 1852

Letter 32

19. Warwick Crescent. W.
Feb. 5. '81.

Dear Friend, I return the very clever & pretty *sestine*—I suppose, in more than enough honor, dedicated to your little piece of property. Such a dainty stepping backward and forward and either sideways is very appropriate to the trifle danced round,—and the lady's musical and suggestive name is another warrant for the courtliness of the measure.[1] So, you are coming to Town, and this will be my last of the scribblings you too much dignify in styling "letters": they are honest scribblings however as far as they go. You often speak of your own multitude of correspondents, but I presume they each and all have something special to say: my own are empty enough in the main of any reason for troubling me—as they certainly do. A few days ago Mr Halliwell-Phillips [2] must needs call on me to take the Director of the Shakespeare Society to task for some abuse of him in a publication of the Director's—not in any way warranted by the Society: I at once told him I was sorry but could do nothing in the case: whereupon last evening I get a portentous "publication of the correspondence"—including my own modest bit of sorrow and explanation. Had I guessed this consequence would come of my politeness I should have either said more or nothing whatever. Still, there are compensations in plenty when the post brings such a charming letter from Swinburne [3] as it did at the same time. He is a noble heart, I am sure, spite of some early eccentricities and perversenesses. He sends me his new book generously, for I have not sent him my things this long while. The pleasantest letter of yesterday however was from Pen—describing to me his picture now in progress—a subject very different from those of the canvasses you will see, I hope, soon after you arrive: though these are good, and satisfactory as showing progress. You will be in time for the Old Masters, the Grosvenor, and other delights: and I shall have mine in congratulating P[ortland] P[lace] on housing you again—next Sunday. Thank you much for George Sand's very characteristic letters:[4] the sudden change from "Casimir who is incapable of a falsehood" to Casimir the brute &c. &c. is very significant: and I suspect all signs of "motherliness" in George Sand. Maurice I remember as a "pas grande chose"—Solange as a handsome well-behaved woman.[5] George herself was exactly as I had long before expected she would be. And now, good bye, dear Friend: I hope the mild weather is removing all the ills it should in your case; and the change to Town will do the rest. Ever affectionately yours

Robert Browning.

Manuscript: Carl H. Pforzheimer Library, RB 59

1. The lady who wrote the sestine in praise of Shalstone remains unidentified.

2. James Orchard Halliwell-Phillips (1820–1889), noted Shakespearean and librarian of Jesus College, Cambridge. On March 12, 1879, Browning accepted the presidency of the New Shakspere Society (1873–1890) with the understanding that the post was purely honorary (*BSP,* I, 112). Swinburne had satirized the group in a skit (1876), and Dr. Furnivall, the founder, replied with some heat. He called Swinburne "Pigsbrook" (from the Anglo-Saxon *swin* and *burn*), and Swinburne called him "Brothels-dyke" (derived from the Latin *fornix* and *vallum*). When Swinburne dedicated his *Study of Shakespeare* (1880) to Halliwell-Phillips, the latter became eligible for Furnivall's venom and was attacked in the preface to the New Shakspere Society's facsimile edition of the second quarto of *Hamlet* (1881). On January 26, Halliwell-Phillips wrote a protest to Browning, who replied the next day (Hood, p. 192) with a civil refusal to be drawn into the controversy. Halliwell-Phillips sent another letter on January 31, and then, on February 14, published the whole *Correspondence with Robt. Browning . . .* (See Oscar Maurer, "Swinburne vs. Furnivall," *University of Texas Studies in English,* [1952], XXXI, 86–96.)

3. In 1863 Browning had been critical of Swinburne's poetry (D&K, p. 150), but he warmed toward the younger poet when Swinburne praised Browning in his *George Chapman* (1875). Browning sent him presentation copies of *Pacchiarotto* (1876), *Agamemnon* (1877), and *La Saisiaz* (1878) (Griffin and Minchin, *Life of Browning,* p. 258), and on January 26, 1881, Swinburne sent Browning a copy of his

Studies in Song (Cecil Lang, *The Swinburne Letters* [New Haven, 1960], IV, 187). Browning's kind words here are rendered ironic by an unhappy sequel. Furnivall published a pamphlet on February 8, *The "Co." of Pigsbrooke & Co.,* referring to the "drunken clown" and the "little sneak at school." Swinburne wrote furiously to Browning, concluding, ". . . it is obvious that in addressing the President of the 'New Shakespeare' Society [i.e., Browning] I could no longer without degradation subscribe myself as yours very sincerely. A. C. Swinburne" (*ibid.,* IV, 197). There seems to be no more correspondence between the two poets; but after Browning's death Swinburne composed a set of sonnets in his honor.

4. Mrs. FitzGerald may have lent Browning a copy of George Sand's *Correspondance* (six volumes, 1881–1886). Casimir Dudevant was George Sand's husband; Maurice her son; and Solange her daughter.

5. Remainder cross-written. See appendix for description.

Letter 33

19. Warwick Crescent, W.
Apr. 20. '81.

Dear Friend, Your letter reached me last evening, — too late for "an answer which you might find *to-day*" — if I understand your expectation. To-morrow will be time enough, however, for the receipt of such poor news as are mine to give. I congratulate you on being out of the bitter weather which came back on Monday. I felt it was oppressing me again, and have kept to the House all yesterday and this forlorn Tuesday — forlorn indeed with its notices of poor Lord Beaconsfield.[1] It was on the 18th March I sat by him at dinner and admired his vivacity and good nature: and, two months after, on the night of this 18th, he is gone. I always liked his works and had an interest in himself[.]

Well, — as to the Pictures: [2] only this day have I got anything like even an intimation concerning their fate: and even now, nothing is absolutely *sure:* but I hear from one of the Hangers that *two* are hung — I *suppose,* "The Tan-garden," and "Heresy": and this, apparently after a real battle, — the *size* of the works seeming to almost call for their exclusion, so piteous are the appeals of the painters of "thousands" of little pictures, which, — it is urged, — want so very small a space for exhibition. Very likely — and *I* shall urge on Pen to paint sometimes according to the Academy's requirements — and sometimes for the more liberal walls at Paris and Brussels. Observe, — one cannot be *sure* of the eventual hanging till this evening — when the Council & President make a formal inspection of the arrangement — after which, official notice is given. Next Monday is "Varnishing Day" — and I hope Pen will be with us by then. All this of ourselves: now of you somewhat, Dear Friend. It was good to hear you had enjoyed two pleasant days at Chobham [3] (a place I remember a little) — and you cannot fail to enjoy yourself where you now are. You must write from Shalstone, and I will write, — and what scraps of knowledge I arrive at, you shall have. Meantime and ever believe me,

Yours affectionately
Robert Browning.

My Sister is better, — thanks you and sends her kind love. Pretty cards, too! [4]

Manuscript: Carl H. Pforzheimer Library, RB 60

1. Benjamin Disraeli (1804–1881), Earl of Beaconsfield (1876), died on April 19, 1881. Browning had dined with him at Lady Airlie's on February 18 (D&K, p. 261). In spite of Browning's kind words here, the two men did not admire each other.
For Mrs. FitzGerald's correction see appendix.

2. In 1881 Pen showed two pictures at the Royal Academy and then in Manchester: *The Tanner's Garden* and *Heresy*. He was also represented the same year by two pictures at the Grosvenor (Letter 34, n. 4).

3. A residential town in northwest Surrey. Probably Mrs. FitzGerald had been visiting the Vicarage of Valley End, a small parish near Cobham. Dr. Edward Huntingford (1831–1905), the vicar, had been her friend since 1851. Two of her sons

(Henry and Alfred) had been his pupils at Eagle House School, Hammersmith, during Dr. Huntingford's headmastership, from 1848 to 1874 (MPFG; *Alumni Oxoniensis*).

4. The postscript is in the upper margin. See appendix.

Letter 34

19. Warwick Crescent, W.
July 23. '81.

Dear Friend, you judge very justly of the feelings I entertained for the Dean.[1] I was to have met him this day week at the Archbishop's,[2] it appears. He was then supposed to have passed out of the principal danger. I go to the Funeral on Monday. The last time I saw him was at Lady Martin's,[3] not three weeks ago—when his health seemed perfect. He had been at the Grosvenor Gallery and was greatly taken with Pen's "Owls"[4]—"the single picture he would care to have." I was unable to go to either of his Garden Parties—at the last of which he caught the cold which ended as we know. Pen liked him much—as who did not? Well,—what shall I lighten up this letter with? Yesterday I called on Mrs Baden Powell[5]—when a youngish foreign looking man came and addressed me—"You don't remember me? Stuart!" I certainly did not—having never seen him since he was a boy twenty years ago or more—but I was glad to renew acquaintance with the author of "Il Marchese del Cigno."[6] He is here on some Statistical business.

How does the change in the weather affect you? I am *cold*—at this moment. Pen writes that he had been completely disabled by the heat, but is better now and at work again. I have at last got the authentic list of lucky ones at the Melbourne Exhibition, and find him duly set down for the Golden Medal for his "Fishmarket" and "Unanswered Question"—quite an unexpected honor.[7] He writes that the son of his "Tanner in the White Shirt"—in the picture at the R[oyal] A[cademy] has just been drowned. The little book you mention, "Odes & Addresses &c," was the *coup d'essai* of Hood.[8] I never read it, however. There is a capital life of Landor just come out in one little volume—by Sidney Colvin.[9] Adieu, dear friend—I am ever affectionately yours

R Browning.

Manuscript: Carl H. Pforzheimer Library, RB 61

1. Dean Stanley died on July 18, 1881, and was buried in Westminster Abbey on July 25.

2. The Most Rev. Archibald Campbell Tait (1811–1882), Archbishop of Canterbury (1869).

3. Helena Saville Faucit (1817–1898), the actress, married (1851) Sir Theodore Martin and was Browning's friend for many decades. (See Theodore Martin, *Helena Faucit* [London, 1900].)

4. In 1881 Pen showed two pictures first at the Grosvenor and then in Manchester: *Disturbed Life,* a picture of owls, and *Still Life, Dinant,* a picture of sunflowers and a tray with peaches and melons (Sotheby, nos. 24 and 25, p. 9). *The Academy* (May 14, 1881, p. 362) referred to "Mr. R. Barrett Browning's wonderful owls and scarcely less wonderful copper pan . . ."

5. Henriett Grace Smyth (1826–1914), daughter of Vice Admiral William Henry Smyth, became in 1846 the third wife of the Rev. Baden Powell (1796–1860) and the mother of ten children. Among her friends were Jowett, Dean Stanley, Ruskin, Browning, and Thackeray. (See Ernest E. Reynolds' biography of her son, *Baden-Powell: A Biography of Lord Baden-Powell of Gilwell* [London, 1943 and 1957].)

6. Roberto Stuart, *Il Marchese del Cigno: Romanzo,* 2 vols. (Milano, Treves, 1875). He was very likely the son of James Montgomery Stuart, with whom Browning had been friendly "twenty years ago or more" in Italy (*Dearest Isa,* p. 186).

7. Yet the *Art Journal* does not include Pen in its list of gold medalists at the Melbourne Exhibition (XLIV, 1881, p. 255).

8. Thomas Hood's *Odes and Addresses to Great People* (1825). Frederick Locker's copy of the first edition, in half morocco, was in Browning's library (Tregaskis, no. 431, p. 48).

9. Sidney Colvin (1845–1927), Slade Professor of Fine Art at Cambridge from 1873 to 1885, published his *Walter Savage Landor* (English Men of Letters Series) in 1881 and thanked Browning in the preface for kind help.

Letter 35

19. Warwick Crescent, W.
July 30. '81.

Dear Friend, I must briefly thank you for your letters — (two, including the newspaper — which I mean to examine and duly return) — and these poor pomegranate flowers — which, for all your care, arrive much as a live baby would after a journey in a box: *one* sprig, however, seems recoverable and has been attended to. Yes, it has been a sad enough week: not the least mournful incident being the death of poor little Bice Trollope[1] — married a year ago to Charles Stuart Wortley: she bore him an infant — a girl — and is dead in consequence. It seems so lately ago that I was waliking [*sic*] her & Pen on their ponies at Florence, frisking like two butterflies. She was just of Pen's age — and I can well believe what he writes this morning, that "he is sorry indeed — remembering her so well in old days." The Dean, too, was very good to him. Well, — I am glad your eyes are no worse, if no better. I wish the news of your Son's health were more encouraging, but the great comfort is the absence of suffering — such, I gather from your letter at least, is the case. I believe our work here is as good as done, — and we may go when we please — which may as well be soon. I have despatched all four of Pen's pictures,[2] — those at the Grosvenor as well as at the Academy, — to Manchester, in compliance with the request of the Council: so that he will be well represented there — and I hope Mr Knox Little may see them, and like them — as his kind way is. I saw Mr Keane[3] at the Ship Dinner[4] — but was a long way divided from his end of the table: my white face and Sala's[5] crimson visage were in striking contrast, I dare say. My main amusement was in an Italian Gentleman[6] on my right hand

—very *naïf* and talkative. It was the Skirrows' goodbye dinner: I shall see no more of them till next season,—if we reach one.

It is rainy and cold: I suppose I need a change—not having moved from this place,—save for a day to Oxford,[7]—since I returned to it ten months ago. But I am sleepy and should prefer to doze away a month or two over a few books. You forget, by the bye, that I myself take in the "Athenaeum," and you [need] never send it me. But I shall write again and more to the purpose. Meanwhile and ever, dear friend, believe me

Affectionately yours RB.

Manuscript: Carl H. Pforzheimer Library, RB 62

1. Beatrice Trollope (1853–1881), the daughter of Thomas Adolphus Trollope, was born in Florence and married (1880) the Rt. Hon. Charles Stuart-Wortley.

2. See Letter 33, n. 2.

3. Perhaps Thomas Keane FitzGerald, Mrs. FitzGerald's eldest son, who was on another occasion a guest of the Skirrows (Letter 65, n. 1).

4. From this letter and others (D&K, pp. 290 and 307) one deduces that the Skirrows gave an annual large dinner party at the Ship Hotel in Greenwich at the close of the London season. The Ship was a famous Victorian eating place built on the site now occupied by the *Cutty Sark*.

5. George Augustus Henry Sala (1828–1896), journalist and prolific writer of books. He was on the staff of *The Daily Telegraph* and edited *Temple Bar* from 1860 to 1866.

6. A year later, Mrs. FitzGerald entertained at Shalstone the Italian Count who is here as the Skirrows' dinner guest, and she was "full of praises" of him (D&K, p. 290). MPFG recalls with pleasure the visits of Count Cassini. He was entertained at 22 Portland Place and by the Purefoy FitzGeralds at Preston Candover (MPFG).

7. In 1881 Browning went to Oxford on June 18 (account book in BM) and returned to London on June 20 (D&K, p. 263).

Letter 36

19. Warwick Crescent, W.
Aug. 6. '81

Dear Friend, I am grieved that my last letter in London — the Saturday's Tribute — is only one of great sympathy with you under your apprehensions. I hope that your own health will not give way: but you must know all I hope, — and I shall do you no good by saying more on the subject: I would rather divert you from it for a moment, if it were possible. Thank you for the monstrous paper-clip:[1] I fail to recognize any face I am familiar with: whom do you take it to resemble? I think the pinch of the beak will befit bills rather than friendly letters.

We count upon starting on Tuesday — and, next evening, we proceed on our search after a second Lans — we even fancy we have found one, near Grenoble, but on the other side. When we settle — there or elsewhere — you shall be immediately apprised, and thither you will address the accounts of all happening at Shalstone — for which I shall look anxiously. And thither you may send too, if your goodness incline you, the "Academy": which, you are not aware, has for the last three weeks (not counting to-day's number, which I have not yet seen) — given as many paragraphs, of formidable size, to the proceedings of a "Browning Society"[2] — for the elucidation of the more obscure works of that author! They meet in October, read addresses, and are printing a "Bibliography" of your much-enduring friend. The founder[3] applied to my Sister for "names of friends who might wish to join" — but she resolutely refused to give any information of the kind — saying that I had kept free of all attempts to help myself to a reputation, except by writing books. Therefore, as the Academy[4] devotes itself especially to your friend, I should be glad to see it, while away from London. I shall receive the "Athenaeum" and "Pall Mall Gazette"—and Nineteenth Century & Contemporary Reviews. After France, we go to Italy—I suppose, Venice: and thence to friends (the Balls) [5] who have a Villa near Bassano—*in sight of Asolo:* there we think of staying for a few days. What we shall do after *that*—is too uncertain just now: but you shall always be informed of our doings when they are determined upon. It is rather curious that I feel so little interest in traveling now: if I had your Shalstone—or a cottage in half an acre of garden—I should never move, I am convinced. I always had the faculty "de m'amuser sur place." I have *this moment* (since writing the last end of the page) desired a gardener to set the little patch of wretchedness called "our garden" in something like decent order: I put my foot in it this morning for the first time this more than twelve months—ghastliness of the realization of the "Sluggard's Garden" [6] struck me: so that by the time of our return it will be re-ordered, gravelled, and,—above all,—stocked with shrubs—plenty of green, with me, compensating for any absence of flowers—if one must choose an absence. So much for my projected husbandry. I began by too entirely despising this little house, which has behaved well enough by me for nearly twenty years: I never condescended to consider it as other than a makeshift: but now I ask myself "what better I deserve"—as Coleridge did, when his tea got cold: [7] and I daresay I shall die here. It is clear now that Pen's preference is for a Continental life,—and as he thrives there,—which he never did in England,—thrives morally, I mean, in his love of work,—there is little good in wishing him transplanted: I by myself—or with my Sister, which is the same thing—want nothing for ourselves, now, but a continuance of God's goodness,—and so may it be!

I expected to hear from Mr Natorp,[8]—a friend of ours, who is gone to Dinant to paint along with Pen,—he being an amateur only, but zealous: he was to tell me about Pen & his pictures: his letter may come later.

I return the old newspaper — with many thanks to your Son: the argument of Erskine[9] is very interesting: — and — what if I enclose the prospectus of that same redoubtable "B. Society?"[10] Don't return it, but deposit it with your archives. And now — seriously, goodbye, and God bless you & all dear to you, dear friend! S. will write, I know. Give my kind regards to Miss Smith.[11] I went to say farewell to the Speddings[12] on Thursday, — saw Mr Lawrence[13] & others.

Ever affectionately yours
Robert Browning

Manuscript: Carl H. Pforzheimer Library, RB 63

1. MPFG still has a large brass paper clip representing a duck with colored stone eyes and a beak to act as clip. Other such Victorian clips were decorated with profiles of famous personages, such as Prince Albert.

2. In 1881 Dr. F. J. Furnivall and Miss Emily Hickey (see Letter 46, n. 3) conceived the idea of a Browning Society while on their way to pay a call on the poet. On July 27 they sent out a prospectus announcing the purpose of the society and the membership fee of one guinea a year. The first meeting was held at University College on Friday, October 28, at 8 p.m. From that date until June 26, 1891, the society held eighty-four monthly meetings, not including July, August, and December of each year.

The Society published Browning's "Essay on Shelley" (1881), a bibliography of his work and criticism thereof (1881), a facsimile edition of *Pauline* (1886), many of the papers read at the monthly meetings, and a regular column of notes and queries on Browning's life and work. It also presented an annual entertainment at which Browning's poems were read and, after they had been set to music, sung; dramatic presentations of *In a Balcony* (1884), *A Blot in the 'Scutcheon* (1885 and 1888), *Colombe's Birthday* (1885), *Strafford* (1886); and dramatic readings of *Luria* (1888) and *Colombe's Birthday* (1890).

The first meeting was attended by 300 persons, 70 of them being members. There were 152 members by the end of the first year; and by 1886, 238, more than one-third of whom were Americans (*Academy,* June 26, 1886, p. 450). The members often referred to themselves as "apostles" and were proud that by 1884 there were twenty-two Browning societies in such places as Graz, Port Elizabeth, and Copenhagen. The membership began to decrease after 1886, and thrice in 1890 Dr. Furnivall had to improvise remarks when the expected speaker failed to appear. At the tenth annual meeting on June 26, 1891, it was resolved to make the coming session the last.

Browning was delighted with the attention of the Society, not only because of the resultant increase in the sale of his books, but also because of the "evident annoyance" it gave to his critics (Hood, p. 207). He was touchy about even the slightest criticism of the Society.

In 1877 at Cornell University in New York, four years before the founding of the Browning Society in London, Professor Hiram Corson had founded the first Browning Club. Many others were subsequently founded in the United States, where there are fourteen still active. One American Browning Society held a unique meeting, which featured the color brown: in the curtains, table cloths, bread, sugar, and members' costumes (*BSP*). See Letter 46, n. 6.

3. Dr. Frederick James Furnivall (1825–1910), Chaucerian, Shakespearean, oarsman, and tireless founder of societies: Early English Text (1864), Chaucer (1868), Ballad (1868), New Shakspere (1873), Browning (1881), Wyclif (1882), and Shelley (1886) (*Frederick J. Furnivall: A Volume of Personal Record* [London, 1911]).

4. Dr. Furnivall contributed to *The Academy,* which therefore paid a great deal of attention to Browning.

5. John Ball (1818–1889), botanist, traveler, and politician; first president of the Alpine Club (Austen H. Layard, *Autobiography* . . . [New York, 1903], I, 226).

6. "I pass'd by his Garden, and saw the wild Brier, | The Thorn and the Thistle grow broader and higher" (Isaac Watts, "The Sluggard" from *Divine Songs,* 1720).

7. Thomas Carlyle, *Life of John Sterling* (1851), p. 75.

8. Gustav Natorp was born in Hamburg in 1836, emigrated to the United States in 1854, retired from his successful business in 1875, and devoted himself to art. In November 1881, he became Rodin's first pupil (Frederick Lawton, *The Life and Work of Auguste Rodin* [New York, 1907], pp. 241–244). Between 1879 and 1889, Browning wrote him at least sixty-one letters, "chiefly on Pen's art work" (Broughton, Northup, and Pearsall, *Robert Browning: A Bibliography,* D2053, p. 387).

9. Very likely Thomas Erskine of Linlathen (1788–1870), a lay writer on theology and the friend of Carlyle and Dean Stanley. His doctrines on intuition and the inner witness of the heart would be congenial to Browning (*Cambridge History of English Literature,* XII, 314–315).

10. MPFG still has the prospectus (see n. 2).

11. Laura Bullen Smith, the daughter of Bullen Smith, who was for twenty-two years a leading merchant in Calcutta, head of the firm of Jardine, Skinner, and Co. (from a newspaper clipping quoting the *Calcutta Englishman* with penciled date 1877—MPFG). Mrs. FitzGerald wrote in her diary of October 7, 1892, "Laura Smith came to Shalstone in 1852 where she stayed some years and greatly endeared herself to my precious Mary, and my husband had a great regard for her and improved her much in her education . . . She . . . came up direct from Scotland quite young and travelled down here with Mr. Pierrepont of Evenly, my great friend

who encouraged her to think she would be happy with me. She has continued all these years to be a devoted friend."

12. Mrs. John Spedding and Miss Spedding of 80 Westbourne Terrace (*London Post Office Directory* for 1881). Mrs. Spedding was the sister-in-law of James Spedding, editor of Bacon's *Works,* who made his home with her and who had died on March 9, 1881, as a result of a carriage accident (*DNB*). Mrs. FitzGerald was engaged to dine with Spedding at a large literary party on the day of his accident. His niece, Sarah Frances Spedding, who wrote under the name of "Susan Morley," was a dear friend and frequent houseguest at Shalstone (MPFG).

13. Samuel Laurence (1812–1884), portrait painter, whose "most intimate friend" was James Spedding. In the winter of 1874, an artist named Laurence gave drawing lessons at 22 Portland Place to Geraldine Mary FitzGerald. She and her sisters were taken to his studio to see his paintings (MPFG). His portrait of Browning (1866) is now at Baylor University (Wilson, *Robert Browning's Portraits, Photographs, and Other Likenesses,* p. 83). Both a correction and an annotation appear here. See appendix for description.

Letter 37

Hôtel Virard, St Pierre de Chartreuse, Isère.[1]
Sept. 6. '81.

Dear Friend, I delayed writing to you for a day or two, in consequence of a project we had of making a visit to the Convent this morning — & passing the night there — a little event to chronicle for your possible amusement: but there was rain and no tramping for us — so, though the weather is cleared again, I shall delay our ordinary walk to say a word or two. Your last account (to speak of what most presses) seemed favourable, — though one dares not expect absolute recovery now. May every alleviation assist you both, — since no more can be hoped.[2]

The general news from England is dark indeed.[3] Here, we have many bright days, and do our best to turn them to account. I walk before as well as after breakfast — the latter being never less than a little under a four hours trudge: and then we take two hours to conclude the day's work. The beauty of the country continues to attract us greatly. Such air, too—I don't know my own red face in the glass. We shall stay here till the end of next week,—completing five weeks of a life funnily contrasting with that of your friends, the two letter-writers: [4] though they too have a reason in their choice of places. I can assure you, however, that if unfortunately Geneva had been quite in the way, I should have never turned more than—perhaps—my head in the direction of that ill-omened "La Saziaz" [*sic*]: it, and all connected with it, are painful to me, and I have fitter ways of affectionately bringing poor Miss S.[mith] to mind than by visiting her grave: My friend, Dourlans, did so, however, this year—at least, he saw the Chalet, I know, and climbed the Salève—spraining his foot in the achievement, from which he suffers yet. Let me remember, by the bye, that the first snow fell on the mountains here on the night of the 1st Sept. It is melted to-day apparently. Pen wrote yesterday that the rain with him was incessant and unmatched within people's remembrance. Let me thank you for the "Academy" and other papers. We have a good stock just now—the "Contemporary" and "XIX Century" coming together. I don't know what Mr Sotheran [5] means by the "B. Society"s being "only mooted." Of course its first meeting cannot take place before the time originally appointed for it: but if it "has not yet come to any definite existence," I suppose that it has been by spontaneous generation that I have on the table here the proofs of a "Bibliography of R. B." [6] "published for the B. Society by Trübner & Co"—containing the most extraordinary list of every one of my works, from the biggest to the least,—with the minutest description of the same—mentioning every variation in any edition of every line and word that has been altered at any time,—illustrations from letters &c—and yet, at page 32 (as far as the proofs go) only getting to "Dramatis Personae" published in 1864. I should have thought it would have taken months to get all the work done: whether it be worth doing at all, is another matter. It makes me feel as I look at the thing, as if I were dead and *begun* with, after half a century. The fact is, I never got much help from any but individuals—none to mention from Reviews: the secret being, I suppose, that, not writing for any, and never being able to do a good turn for a friend who would repay it in kind, when *he* took pen in hand, I was just the person to conveniently let alone or even abuse—to give a little relief from the necessary eulogistic tone when Greek meets Greek in the tug of—amicality. What does it matter? One fine day, we find that all the wonderful Novels, Travels, Poems, are "puffed" into congenial air,—but enough of it. I am very glad for your sake, Dear friend, that you never "wrote a book"—as you certainly might have done,—far more to the purpose than much of the weekly turn-out of Mudie-ism.[7] But here my Sister brings me a letter to put in my envelope, and you shall be relieved from my nonsense. Have no "panic that good (sense) is troublesome"! no indeed! And, be sure if that pleasure should remain for me, I will even yet "rummage" your books for a whole morning. I never read Hazlitt's memoirs,[8] and should greatly like to do so: he was always an interesting person to me—very much so. Ever yours affectionately

R Browning.

I find, by a card I received two days ago, that the Manchester Exhibition opens to-morrow—the Private View being to-day. If you hear anything from that kind & good Mr Knox-Little about Pen's four pictures[9]—which they asked for—I should be glad to know how they are hung & what is thought about them.

Manuscript: Carl H. Pforzheimer Library, RB 64

1. In 1881 Browning and his sister spent their holiday in France and Italy. They left London on August 8, arriving at St. Pierre de Chartreuse on August 11 (Hood, p. 197). They left St. Pierre on September 18, stopped at Chambéry and at Turin, and arrived in Venice on September 21. They left Venice on October 31 (D&K,

p. 268) and arrived back in London on November 4. On the holiday, Browning "spent less than £100" (account book in BM).

2. Browning refers to the final illness of Robert FitzGerald, who died on October 28, 1881, at Charleywood, Herts.

3. Dark news from England included the wreck of a mail steamer (*Times,* September 3, p. 5), a great fire in Cheapside (*ibid.,* p. 10), and an armament race involving Germany, France, Russia, Italy, and Austria (*ibid.,* September 5, p. 9c).

4. Not identified.

5. Very likely Henry Sotheran, the bookseller, of H. Sotheran and Co., 49 Cross Street, Manchester.

6. *A Bibliography of Robert Browning, from 1833 to 1881.* Compiled by Frederick J. Furnivall. Publisht for The Browning Society by N. Trübner . . . London, 1881.

7. Charles Mudie's Select Library in New Oxford Street and Museum Street circulated current books to its clients, who paid a fee of one guinea per annum (*DNB*).

8. William Hazlitt's *Literary Remains* (1836).

9. See Letter 33, n. 2.

Letter 38

Albergo dell' Universo, Venezia, Italia.
Sept. 24. '81

Dear Friend, on arriving here I found your letter to my great satisfaction—and yesterday brought the "Sat^y Review"—for which, many thanks. We left our strange but lovely place on the 18th reaching Chambéry at evening,—stayed the next day there,—walking, among other diversions, to "Les Charmettes," the famous abode of Rousseau—kept much as when he left it: I visited it with my wife perhaps twenty five years ago,[1] and played so much of "Rousseau's Dream"[2] as could be effected on his antique harpsichord: this time I attempted the same feat, but only two notes or thereabouts out of the octave would answer the touch. Next morning we proceeded to Turin, and on Wednesday got here, in the middle of the last night of the Congress Carnival,[3]—rowing up the Canal to our Albergo through a dazzling blaze of lights and throng of boats, — there being, if we are told truly, 50,000 strangers in the City. Rooms had been secured for us, however: and the festivities are at an end, to my great joy, — for Venice is resuming its old quiet aspect — the only one I value at all. Our American friends [4] wanted to take us in their gondola to see the principal illuminations *after* the "Serenade," which was not over before midnight: but I was contented with *that* — being tired and indisposed for talking, and, having seen & heard quite enough from our own balcony, went to bed: S. having betaken her to her own room long before. Next day, we "took stock" of our acquaintances, — found that the Storys, on whom we had counted for company, were at Vallombrosa, though the two sons [5] have a studio here: other friends are in sufficient number however: and last evening we began our visits by a very classical one — to the Countess Mocenigo,[6] in her palace which Byron occupied: she is a charming widow since two years — young, pretty and of the prettiest manners: she showed us all the rooms Byron had lived in, — and I wrote my name in her album *on* the desk himself wrote the last Canto of Ch. Harold, and Beppo upon. There was a small party: we were taken & introduced by the Layards who are kind as ever, and I met old friends — Ld Aberdare,[7] Charles Bowen, and others. While I write comes a deliciously fresh *bouquet* from Mrs Bronson,[8] an American lady, — in short, we shall find a week or two amusing enough: though — where are the pine-woods, mountains and torrents, and wonderful air? Venice is under a cloud, — dull and threatening — though we were apprehensive of the heat, arriving, as we did, ten days earlier than last year. And what do you think befell us in this abode of peace and innocence? Our journey was delayed for three hours in consequence of the one mule of the village being requisitioned by the *Juge d'Instruction* from Grenoble, come to enquire into a murder committed two days before. My Sister & I used once a day to walk for a couple of hours up a mountain-road of the most lovely description, and stop at the summit whence we looked down upon the minute hamlet of S^t^

Pierre d'Entremont,—even more secluded than our own: then we got back, in an hour, to our own aforesaid. And in this Paradisiac place, they found, yesterday week, a murdered man—frightfully mutilated—who had been caught apparently in the act of stealing potatoes in a field: such a crime had never occurred within the memory of the oldest of our folk. Who was the murderer is the mystery: whether the field's owner—in his irritation at discovering the robber,—or one of a band of similar *charbonniers*[9] (for they suppose the man to be a Piedmontese of that occupation) remains to be proved: they began by imprisoning the owner, who denies his guilt energetically. Now the odd thing is, that, either the day of, or after the murder,—as I & S. were looking at the utter solitude, I had the fancy "What should I do if I suddenly came upon a dead body in this field? Go and proclaim it—and subject myself to all the vexations inflicted by the French way of procedure (which begins by assuming that *you* may be the criminal)—or neglect an obvious duty, and return silently?" I, of course, saw that the former was the only proper course, whatever the annoyance involved. And, all the while, there was just about to be the very same incident for the trouble of somebody. But my ***

Manuscript: Carl H. Pforzheimer Library, RB 65. The letter is incomplete.

1. In 1858 (Kenyon, II, 293).

2. Rousseau wrote both words and music for this simple pastoral dance-tune for his drama *Le Devin du Village* (1752).

3. The Geographical Congress (*Academy,* November 19, 1881, p. 390) was holding sittings in Venice. The city was illuminated, and the festivities included a great barge carrying singers and musicians on the Grand Canal (Horatio F. Brown, *In and Around Venice* [New York, 1905], pp. 136–143).

4. Daniel Sargent Curtis (1825–1908) and his wife, Ariana Randolph (Wormeley) Curtis (1833–1922), Bostonians and the authors of *Three Plays* (Boston, 1868). (See *Recollections of Ralph Randolph Wormeley* [New York, 1879].) In Boston he was known as "pinch-nose Curtis" from his having gone to jail rather than pay damages after having pinched the nose of a man who trod on his foot in the streetcar. In Venice they lived at Barbier's before purchasing the Palazzo Barbaro. In 1879 or

1880, W. W. Story introduced them to the Brownings on the Lido, and Curtis kept a record (MS at Baylor University) of his conversations with Browning, including Browning's comments favorable toward Jews and unfavorable toward Carlyle. (See also Wilson, *Robert Browning's Portraits, Photographs, and Other Likenesses,* p. 114; and Broughton, Northup, and Pearsall, *Robert Browning: A Bibliography,* D1382, p. 371.)

5. Thomas Waldo Story, a sculptor; and Julian Russell Story (1857–1919), a painter.

6. In 1819 Byron took a three-year lease on the Palazzo Mocenigo, which is illustrated in Henry James, *Italian Hours* (Boston, 1909), p. 64.

7. Henry Austin Bruce-Pryce (1815–1895), first Baron Aberdare (1873), F. R. S. (1876).

8. Katherine Colman (DeKay) Bronson (1834–1901), the daughter of Captain George Colman DeKay, was born in Bloomingdale, New York City. In 1855 she married Arthur Bronson (died 1885) of New York at Grace Church and lived in "Castle Hill," the house he built in Newport, Rhode Island, until the family moved abroad in 1875. Henry James and Anthony Trollope were also on the *Bothnia* when the Bronsons crossed (*Selected Letters of Henry James,* ed. Leon Edel [New York, 1955], pp. 47–48). Casa Alvisi, their house in Venice, extended its hospitality to a large circle of distinguished friends, Browning especially. Among Mrs. Bronson's many gifts to the poet was an 1848 coin of the Venetian Republic, which he wore on his watch chain with his wife's ring. Browning corresponded with her from 1881 to the time of his death and dedicated his *Asolando* (1889) to her. She wrote "Browning in Asolo" (1900) and "Browning in Venice" (1902) for the *Century Magazine.* After her daughter's marriage (1895; see Letter 59, n. 5) she moved to Florence, where she lived in the Villa Mercede on Bellosguardo, and became a Catholic. (See her obituary in the New York *Evening Post,* October 2, 1901; Henry James, *Italian Hours,* p. 112; and Broughton's index. For much of the information in this note, I am indebted to Mrs. John Hall Wheelock, Mrs. Bronson's niece.)

9. Charcoal burners.

Letter 39

19. Warwick Crescent, W.
Nov. 5. '81.

Dear Friend, your letter to my sister *did* reach us just before our departure. I was packing, and troubled with many distractions but sat down to say a word at least of what was in my mind,—but I was suddenly called away: my Sister supposed I had written,—but not one free moment was mine till the Post-hour had gone by. There was a strike of the gondolas, and threatened impossibility of our departure: I had to get my luggage conveyed to the station overnight, and *walk* thither next morning—as we *did:* and the Post goes out at 4. p. m.! I supposed you would be in the country, and only on arriving last evening found your letter—*letters*—and a clear way open to our intercourse.

I shall not think you unreasonably affected by this merciful release of the poor sufferer from his sorrows.[1] What *life*—in the true sense—has ended,—or rather, what true life has not begun? The grief was appropriate to the beginning of the affliction: its close—if our weak ways of feeling cannot resolve to call it *joyful*—yet they may acquiesce in this break of a better morning on what has been a long twilight at best. The absence of pain,—the unremitting solace of your affection,—the comfort of what you describe as an ignorance of any sort of doubt, in these days when doubts settle on the most confiding souls,—all these are more than alleviations, surely. Of your own part in helping your child through the darkness, I need not speak: it cannot be other than its own reward. Bunyan's weary pilgrim whose last words are "Farewell, Night—Welcome, Day!" were never more appropriate than in this case: May they be as befitting in the mouths of us all "who needs must pass the river."[2]

Dear friend,—I am overpowered by all your goodness to the garden, and to me, and wherever it could display itself: "overpowered," I truly say.[3] Let me say vocally what little I can when I see you as you promise so kindly. Come to our quietest of dinners on Wednesday at 7. We will talk or be silent as you please,—though there is much to talk about. My sister will speak for herself, I believe. Dear friend, I am ever affectionately yours. I had intended to see you to-morrow at P[ortland] P[lace]: but the present arrangement is the right one. God bless you. Robert Browning.

Manuscript: Carl H. Pforzheimer Library, RB 66

1. See Letter 37, n. 2.

2. At the end of Pilgrim's Progress, Part II (1684), Mr. Despondency says, "Farewell night; welcome, day!" as he enters the River of Death, which separates the pilgrims from the Celestial City.

3. On August 6 Browning wrote (Letter 36, n. 6) that he had engaged a gardener to put his garden into something like order. One deduces from the present letter that Mrs. FitzGerald and perhaps her gardeners assisted in the restoration of the garden while the Brownings were on the Continent (see Letter 42, n. 2).

Letter 40

19. Warwick Crescent, W.
Dec. 10. '81.

My dear Friend, I am sorry indeed to find you have written a letter to my Sister "in low spirits": No doubt the various kinds of strain on them, as well as your indisposition, must try you, body and soul. I trust however that, with the removal of many of these causes of anxiety, and considerable physical suffering, you may again become "prosperous even as your soul prospers"—if I do not misquote the pretty and touching words of the Apostle.[1] I was glad to hear Horne say,[2]—an old acquaintance of mine whom I met, after a long absence, two days ago,—that, though in a month or two he would be eighty,—"he did not feel it in any way." Poor fellow, with a real and rare genius he has played the game of life—as far as his own card-dealing was concerned—but scurvily enough: yet he looks happy, and indeed talks just as he did forty years ago and more. Did you ever read his "Orion"—or his fine "Death of Marlowe"? This last prevented me from writing a play on the same subject—a matter I had somewhat at heart once. His hair is white now, but no thinner than when I first saw him. By the bye, did you notice the portraiture of poor "little but compact" R. B. in this week's "World"? [3] It delighted my Tailor, whose comment on it was "well-dressed you *are,* Sir,—but "almost a dandy"—*no!"* He seemed a little more careful in his measurement than usual—so can fame impose!

They have sent me the proofs of the paper you missed at the *first* meeting of the Society—by Mr Kirkman [4]—whom I never saw in my life, though I have been aware of his kind feeling for my poems: you will receive it in good time: I feel a poor sinner indeed when such praises are given me: the bracing effect always came of the blame—when I knew it to be ignorant or malicious merely. Well, one must look neither to the right hand or the left, but keep as straightly one [*sic*] as one's means allow. Goodbye, dear Friend whom I shall miss the sight of to-morrow: [5] take this hand-shake over the distance with the best wishes of yours affectionately ever

Robert Browning.

You saw the account, at the sale, of the [6] Cranmer Bible [7]—(black letter)—I have a copy, but wanting the title, and a leaf or two at the end, I believe: it was my Father's purchase, of course.

Manuscript: Carl H. Pforzheimer Library, RB 67

1. See Letter 3, n. 1.

2. Richard Hengist Horne (1803–1884), whose correspondence with Mrs. Browning was published in 1876. Presentation copies of his tragedy *The Death of Marlowe,* (1837) and his epic *Orion* (1872) were in Browning's library (Sotheby, no. 764, p. 104; and no. 710, p. 100).

3. "Imagine their surprise on discovering that the crabbed and mystical poet [Browning] is identical with the possessor of the compact little figure, the urbane and genial bearing, the well-made clothes; and that this gentleman, who is as far a dandy as a sensible man can be, is the author of poems, some of which have given universal and unrivalled pleasure . . ." ("Poets in Private Life," *The World,* December 7, 1881, p. 7).

4. The Rev. J. Kirkman, M.A., read his "Introductory Address to the Browning Society" at the first meeting on October 28, 1881 (*BSP,* I, 171–190).

5. Had Mrs. FitzGerald been in London, Browning would have paid his customary Sunday call.

6. The remainder is in crosswriting. See appendix for description.

7. *The Byble in Englyshe of the Largest and Greatest Volume . . .* [Archbishop Cranmer's or "The Great Bible"] large folio, printed by Edward Witchurch . . . 1541. "A perfect and generally sound and clean copy of this rare edition" (*Sale Catalogue . . . of the Sunderland or Blenheim Library*. December 1–12, 1881). The *Times* for December 8 (p. 8a) reported that the Bible had been sold at auction to Leighton for £115. The Sotheby catalogue of the Browning collections does not list a Cranmer Bible.

Letter 41

19. Warwick Crescent, W.
Jan. 14. '82

Dear Friend, you are alone[1] as I am—Pen having left on Thursday evening. With your note this morning came a postcard announcing a "safe arrival after a very pleasant voyage"—this is the more satisfactory as he had been slightly unwell the day before. He will go at once to Dinant to inspect and give directions about his pictures—and then leave for Paris without delay: he is absorbed in his new projects of work in as new a style—and, as I always hoped and indeed believed would be the case—these projects are of an imaginative order. He has altogether proved a dear good considerate fellow during his stay here, and I feel it hard to part with him—even for his good as it promises to be. He will get your "World" at Dinant, no doubt. You too are satisfied with your juvenile party, and the studies of the young ladies must go to your heart—which has been set upon such.[2] Have you indeed "more than 10.000 books"? You know Pryor's pretty verses beginning "All in a lonely Study—Where books are in great plenty"[3]—*that* was the Bishop of St David's[4] notion of an Earthly Paradise—and not very far from mine. I bless my lot whenever I can, as last night, find myself at home for the hours between dinner and bed-time,—book in hand, lamp at elbow, and fire at not too far from footstool. . When we leave this house, there must be a sifting of worthless from worthy—the former being mainly presentation copies of Poetry! The remainder I shall send to be rebound in a few cases—cobbled in many,—and so consign them to posterity until arises some descendant who has a soul above Elzevirs [5] though not above shillings and pence. These ignoble nobles! [6] But I remember that some five & thirty years ago a man in my service possessed a curious document,[7] —signed & attested by Charles II. and sundry ministers,—conferring high dignity on the founder of the family: I recommended him to submit it to the present owner of the Title—(an Earl)—who returned it as [8] "of no interest to him." *You* will "find interest" in the piece of writing I return—which indeed is of interest to everybody. It was at the Lady's Réunion that Ld Byron first met the Guiccioli.[9] The character is not at all like my Father's—whose penmanship I will show you some day. Yes—Tauchnitz [10] sent me the book—which of course you may see whenever you please—as well as Domett's very clever poem [11] and all else belonging to yours affectionately ever R Browning.

Manuscript: Carl H. Pforzheimer Library, RB 68

1. This may refer to the departure of a large party of grandchildren who had spent Christmas at Shalstone. The "juvenile party"—as Browning terms it below—was a memorable occasion and much enjoyed (MPFG).

2. Mrs. FitzGerald took an especial interest in the education of her granddaughters, the children of Richard Purefoy FitzGerald.

3. Not identified.

4. The Rev. Connop Thirlwall (1797–1875), historian and Bishop of St. David's from 1840 to 1874. "He rarely quitted 'Chaos,' as he called his library, unless compelled by business" (*DNB*). On St. David's day in 1867 he wrote "One of the persons I met last night was the poet Browning. I was amused to find that he has a pet owl who is inseparable from him" (*Letters to a Friend* by Connop Thirlwall, ed.

A. P. Stanley [London, 1881], p. 98). In her copy of James Fotheringham's *Studies in the Poetry of Robert Browning* (London, 1887, p. 34) Mrs. FitzGerald wrote "Thirlwall" beside the words "a learned bishop, who read everything and read 'The Ring and the Book' through."

5. A reader has inserted a question mark after "Elzevirs." Louis Elzevir and his descendants were distinguished seventeenth-century Dutch printers. Browning's library contained at least four of their books, dated 1628, 1633, 1635, and 1662 (Tregaskis, nos. 328–331, p. 37).

6. Browning may be criticizing noblemen who auction off their libraries (see Letter 40, n. 6).

7. On September 6, 1651, Col. William Carlos (d. 1689) hid with Charles II in an oak tree of Boscobel Wood. By royal patent he was granted an elaborate coat of arms (*DNB*). Browning's document consisted of eight pages, octavo, bound in red, with a transcript of the Latin grant and an English translation: ". . . since by the protection of a poor cottage and the top of a spreading oak-tree, he concealed us for some days and nights, the enemy all the while being hotly in search of us . . ." (Sotheby's *Catalogue . . . Joseph Hornstein,* February 25, 1918, p. 212).

8. Remainder in cross-writing. See appendix for description.

9. Byron's first significant meeting with Countess Teresa Guiccioli, his "last attachment," was at Countess Benzoni's *conversazione* early in April of 1819 (Leslie Marchand, *Byron* [New York, 1957], II 773).

10. Christian Bernhard, Freiherr von Tauchnitz (1816–1895) published Continental editions of British and American authors. After 1872 his list included the Brownings.

11. Alfred Dommett's published verse includes *Venice* (1839), *Ranolf and Amohia* (1872), and *Flotsam and Jetsam* (1877).

Letter 42

19. Warwick Crescent, W.
June 3. '82.

So, you don't come up to Town, Dear Friend,—and though I am glad that you have let your house, since you wished to do that, I do not forget that I have the less chance of seeing you: though probably some opportunity will present itself. I wish you could see our little glory of a garden: I never thought that so much display could come out of shrubs planted a few months ago. Well, "blessings" do indeed "brighten when they take their flight,"[1]—and it is amusing to hear S. and myself agree that we shall miss nothing so much in any new abode as that garden which, for so many years, we ignored the possibility of getting any good out of. I repeat—not one shrub shall be left behind,[2] wherever we go. Thank you,—and thank the clever and dear young lady[3]—for the honor you have done my poems by illustrating what flowers my ignorance allowed me to mention in them: they are very nicely drawn,—while *your* diligence is surprising:[4] the book was returned to your servant yesterday: so, take again my true thanks—and bear the proper part in them to your young artist, pray!

We are lonely here again. Milsand left us on Wednesday: Pen was to leave Paris last Tuesday, and I have no news of his arrival. Yesterday Mrs Moore[5] bought his two Landscapes, "Bonvignes" and "Solitude," and ordered a copy of his Bust:[6] but always remember what he & I never forget that his first & most precious patronage came from Shalstone.[7] His Statuette[8] has at last arrived—having been intelligently directed to "Bariet Warwick, Paddington"—and even "Paddington" was a mistake for it was found at Charing Cross. The figure is very clever,—in a difficult attitude imposed on Pen by his Master,[9]—not, therefore, likely to please anybody but a *connoisseur* in difficulties surmounted: still, as a "study" it is very satisfactory,—proving the power he has obtained in so short a time. Mrs Moore is going to give him an order for a bust of R. B—who, again, is going to sit for a bust to Miss Montalba[10]—the order of Mrs Bronson. All these incentives to vanity go to the right person, fortunately,—one who is tolerably proof against all such illusions. Dear Friend, tell me how you are, and what you do. I am enjoying the prospect of a week's rest: but the weather is cold and—to-day—storm-boding. Farewell, dear Friend—I am ever affectionately yours

Robert Browning.

Manuscript: Carl H. Pforzheimer Library, RB 69

1. "How blessings brighten as they take their flight," Edward Young, *Night Thoughts* (1742), II, 600.

2. Mrs. FitzGerald interlined "plants from Shalstone." See appendix for this and for note 3 below.

3. Mrs. FitzGerald interlined "Geraldine."

4. MPFG has the album (10″ x 7″) of sixteen watercolors by Geraldine FitzGerald, illustrating flowers mentioned in Browning's poetry. Opposite each illustration Mrs. FitzGerald transcribed the appropriate verse.

5. Clara Sophia Jessup (1824–1899), the daughter of Augustus E. Jessup, scientist and "extensive manufacturer of paper," married (1842) Bloomfield Moore of Philadelphia, who associated himself with her father in the paper firm of Jessup & Moore. She wrote several volumes of fiction and of poetry (sometimes under the name of Mrs. Clara Moreton) as well as books of etiquette (under the name of Mrs. H. O. Ward); and she was philanthropically active during the American Civil War. Her parents left her an immense fortune, and, after the death of her husband (1878), who left her a second fortune of more than $5,000,000, she moved to England, where she legally added a hyphen to her name, becoming Mrs. Bloomfield-Moore.

Immediately she established with Browning what she called "the closest and dearest friendship" of her life; and he told her, she said, "Remember, wherever you are, if you need me send for me. I would go to the ends of the earth to serve you." She purchased several of Pen's pictures, some of which she presented to museums in Philadelphia, Boston, and New York; and she made many other, significant gifts to Philadelphia museums. She also rescued from bankruptcy John Ernst Keely (in *DAB*), the celebrated impostor of the Keely Motor Company. (The Pennsylvania Historical Society has recently acquired his letters to her.) Browning thought she was mad to be giving her money to Keely and was somewhat piqued when she reneged on buying one of Pen's pictures (Hood, pp. 273, 276, 283, and 321).

Her daughter Ella married the Swedish Count Carl Gustave von Rosen, and her daughter Mary married the Baron Carl von Bildt, who was premier of Sweden in 1890. Her son, Clarence, who continued his father's business, brought suit against her, maintaining that she was certifiable and obligated to distribute the fortune among her children. The suit was settled amicably. (See obituary in New York *Times,* January 6, 1899, p. 6f–g; Philadelphia *Public Ledger* for January 6 and Philadelphia *Evening Bulletin* also for January 6; C. J. B–M, "Robert Browning," *Lippincott's Monthly Magazine,* May 1890, pp. 683–691; *BSP,* III, 110*–117*; DeVane, pp. 482 and 487; and "Ancestry of Clarence Bloomfield Moore of Philadelphia," *National Genealogical Society Quarterly,* March 1940, pp. 1–7.)

6. A 21½″ bronze bust of an Italian model, with head turned to her right, signed R. B. B., 1882 (Sotheby, no. 1273, p. 149).

7. Over the mantelpiece in the morning room at Shalstone hung a self-portrait of Pen showing the young artist seated at an easel observed by a man and woman in

Belgian (?) costume. The painting is now in the Browning Settlement, a Fellowship House on Browning Street, London, S. E. 17.

8. Pen's first *Dryope,* a 38-inch bronze statuette, is signed R. B. B. and dated 1882 (Sotheby, no. 1272, p. 149).

9. Auguste Rodin (1840–1917). On January 2, 1883, he wrote to Browning that he was "honoré de pouvoir donner quelques conseils de sculpture au fils du Grand Poète Anglais . . ." (ALs, Sotheby, no. 265, p. 57), and Browning replied on January 4 (Lawton, *Rodin,* p. 243). The Browning Collections included Rodin's *L'homme au nez cassé,* a bronze mask (Sotheby, no. 1274, p. 149).

10. Henrietta Skerrett Montalba (1856–1893), a London-born sculptress who lived in Venice. Her terra-cotta bust of Browning was exhibited at the Grosvenor in 1883; and another, bronze bust (1889) of the poet in academic robes is at Oxford (Wilson, *Browning's Portraits,* p. 179).

Letter 43

19. Warwick Crescent, W.
June 10. '82.

Dear Friend—if my *eighth* letter,—seven having preceded it in succession,—prove a dull one, you will not wonder but forgive. (A final *ninth* has to be yet indited to Pen.) Yes,—your kindness is as great as the journey seems easy,—and yet, for all that, it cannot be—as I return on Thursday morning to keep a dinner engagement in the evening: how could one of mere flesh and blood make Shalstone episodic between Oxford & London? It must be for another and easier time—which may happen sooner than you suppose—though not than I wish. Why do *you* not go to the Commemoration? [1] it would *pair* with your visit to Cambridge.

It was very good of you to invite Mr Furnivall "like an idle goose, from his pen broke loose, to taste the country air" [2]—and I am sure he enjoyed his taste. I wish Mrs Orr could get a similar escape from London, with all my heart—she needs it still more:

but her Father [3] is old, and misses his *Bezique* and other comforts. F[urnivall] conveyed your invitation in as pretty a form as possible, and she was highly pleased with your care about her. I quite agree with you in abominating the Phonetic Spelling, root and branch, theory and practice. Landor's attempt was exactly in the opposite and scholarly direction,—to restore the true forms, and show the relation to the *root* of each word when possible [4]—a thing avoided by the phonetic *farnetici*.[5]

Did Miss Ogilvy's [6] marriage really get accomplished? I have seen and heard nothing about it,—nor had Miss Graham [7] whom she called a great friend of hers.

Even this poor letter has been interrupted and the ending I tack on will be the worse for it. Oh, Shalstone—there need no explanations and assurances when one has to say one cannot go and be quiet with a dear friend in a lovely place! Be happy there, Dear friend, & believe me ever

Affectionately yours
R Browning.

Manuscript: Carl H. Pforzheimer Library, RB 70

1. On June 14, 1882, Oxford conferred the honorary D.C.L. on Browning, who had just completed his seventieth year. His account book (BM) for June 13 lists his expenses for cab, tickets, and hire of gowns, concluding "Total Oxford 'Doctorate'" £3.19.

2. Not identified.

3. After her husband's death (1858), Mrs. Orr rejoined her father, Frederic Septimus Leighton, M.D. (1800–1892). He gave up his practice in 1843 and lived thereafter in Bath, Scarborough, and (after 1869) in London (*DNB* sub Orr).

4. Walter Savage Landor was especially interested in spelling reform, preferring for example, *lookt* to *look'd*. (See "orthography" in the index to R. H. Super's *Walter Savage Landor* [New York, 1954]; and D&K, pp. 272–273.)

5. "Frenetics."

6. On June 5, 1882, the Hon. Patrick Greville-Nugent, son of the first Baron Greville, married Emma Ermengarde, only daughter of the late Augustus Ogilvy of Cove, Dumfriesshire (*Times,* June 13, 1882, p. 1a).

7. Not identified.

Letter 44

[*19. Warwick Crescent, W.*
June 17, 1882][1]

*** You are far too hard on the very harmless drolleries of the young men, licensed as they are, moreover, by immemorial usage.[2] Indeed there used to be a regularly appointed jester, *Filius Terrae*,[3] as he was called, whose business it was to jibe and jeer at the honored ones, by way of reminder that all human glories are merely gilded bubbles and must not be fancied metal. You saw that the Reverend Dons escaped no more than the poor poet—or rather I should say than myself the poor poet—for I was pleased to observe with what attention they listened to the Newdigate[4] ***

Ever affectionately yours,
R. Browning.

Text: Orr, II, 453. The letter is incomplete.

1. The date is that of the first Saturday after the Oxford Commemoration (Letter 43, n. 1). MPFG has a portion of this letter on a half sheet.

2. Victorian undergraduates continued the tradition of insulting recipients of honorary degrees. Often the insult took the form of pained groans at allegedly faulty Latin constructions in the encomium. Conversely, the students were prepared to show their approval of felicitous phrasing, as they did during Joachim's investiture by throwing bronze coins at the feet of the public orator (*Times*, March 9, 1877, p. 10a–b). When Browning received the D.C.L., a red cotton nightcap dangled from the gallery rested on the head of the Professor of Divinity and was skillfully transferred to the head of the poet (*ibid.*, June 15, 1882, p. 8d).

3. *Terrae-Filius; Or, The Secret History of the University of Oxford, in Several Essays* . . . by N. Amhurst, of St. John's College. London: R. Franklin, 1721.

4. Compounding their abuse of the adults, the students traditionally paid rapt attention to the Newdigate Prize Poem, which was composed and declaimed by a student. Browning missed the point of their exaggerated attention. In 1882 the Newdigate, on "The Fall of Carthage," was delivered by Dugald Sutherland MacColl of Lincoln College.

Letter 45

19. Warwick Crescent, W.
July 15. '82.

Dear Friend, I am heartily glad that you are better, or no worse at least, and cheerful certainly. I always had the bad habit of being angry with people being ill if I could discern a cause for the illness in their own conduct—and if I loved them enough. I liken any carelessness in such persons as to their health to a foolish dancing one's heart over a precipice—and the only hard words my wife ever got from me were just on that account,—when she would run risks, be forgetful of taking meals, allow herself to be talked half-dead by inconsiderate visitors, and so on: I remember two such women who on one occasion "were each determined to sit the other out"—in my absence, you may be sure—for I used to grow brutal when Her poor face began to show suffering.[1] Enough! Don't go, for the future, to Browning or other Societies on foot thro' a cold night, and you shall not need fear me.[2] I was touched by what you told me in Monday's letter of Miss Fletcher's calling me, at that time of her distress, "her very best friend."[3] I never was *that,* but certainly no sort of enemy of hers, then or now. Her "story" admits of being told two ways only if it be cut in half, and the beginning or the end taken as the whole. Both parties were to blame,—she, in pouncing unscrupulously on a goose,—he,[4] in disingaging [*sic*] himself from the fox for no reason at all when he had foolishly rushed into the foxes [*sic*] mouth—which having secured him was not meaning to bite the prize. If it is the part of "a friend" to tell the unpleasant truth, I performed a friend's part in the correspondence I had with her—and we might have continued on a good footing had not Mrs Procter[5] thought it necessary to volunteer the information that I thought ill of Miss F[letcher]'s mother — so it would be advisable for Miss F. not to dedicate her book to me as she was about to do — a very unnecessary piece of meddling of which Mrs P. informed me herself. Very ill of the lady, I *did* think — on sufficient information, — but Mrs P. might have kept to herself, what was never meant for anybody else. My intimacy has all along been with *Barry Cornwall,* — my *habitude* with his wife grew out of that, and is a quite distinct matter. Were I to see Miss F. again I should use the liberty of good fellowship — as when one youngster tells another " Come, you know you were tipsy and talked nonsense: not that I myself am pretending to be your betters."

F. K's memoirs [6] I have skimmed for the anecdotes — knowing most of the people she mentions. Hardly one anecdote but was old in my memory, — many, relating to herself, might be supplemented to advantage if you wished to have the right and complete knowledge of the matter. I met her much oftener than is set down, in those days — but she hardly noticed me; though I always liked her extremely. As for my *poetry* — she told me this year she had been reading it with entire surprise — confessing she never cared about it — that is, examined it at all. I became first intimate with her in Rome some twenty five years ago — and then she liked me, I know, — as a generally sympathetic person, not without poetic sympathies. At last comes the examination, and then, — so many years too late, — the "surprise." It is like the lady's avowal in the last page of "Democracy" [7] — "I never understood a word of B. — so I never tried!" Nor did I wish Fanny K. "to try": none of the kind things she says now can move me like a word of hers in the Campagna "You are the only man I ever knew who behaved like a Christian to his wife" [8] — and this simply because, on an excursion, that wife being unable to follow the party to some ***

Manuscript: Carl H. Pforzheimer Library, RB 71. The letter is incomplete; see appendix.

1. Isabella Blagden and Sophia Eckley outdid each other in their attempts to be first in the affections of Mrs. Browning (*Dearest Isa,* p. 31).

2. Although the poet refused to supply the Browning Society with the names of his friends who might wish to join, he did send Mrs. FitzGerald a copy of the prospectus for her archives (Letter 36, n. 10). See Introduction, p. 17.

3. We learn here that Julia Constance Fletcher had intended to dedicate her novel *The Head of Medusa* (1880) to Browning but did not do so after being told that Browning had gossiped about her mother. The actual dedication (dated from Queen Anne's Mansions, August 1880) read: "I dedicate this book to my dear mother; begging her to accept it from me as one more proof — where surely no proof is needed — of my deep love for her, my admiration, and my profound respect."

4. Baron Wentworth (Letter 30, n. 8).

5. Anne (Skepper) Procter (1799–1888), the wife of Bryan Waller Procter (1787–1874), who wrote under the name of "Barry Cornwall." She was reputed to have a taste for gossip and bitter comment.

6. Frances Anne Kemble (1809–1893), actress and author, published her *Records of Later Life* in 1882. The book contains but two slight references to Browning as having been present at dinner parties.

7. *Democracy: An American Novel* (New York, 1880) was published anonymously but is now known to have been written by Henry Adams (*DAB*). It was a best seller in its day, and it concludes with a letter from Sybil Ross to a Washington lawyer in which she says, "I read Mr. Browning's 'Last Ride Together,' as you told me; I think it's beautiful and perfectly easy, all but a little. I never could understand a word of him before — so I never tried" (p. 373).

8. At a picnic in the Roman Campagna in 1854, Mrs. Browning was too tired to accompany the other picnickers on a walk after luncheon. Browning volunteered to remain with her and elicited from Fanny Kemble this often-quoted remark (Orr, 1, 291).

Letter 46

[19, Warwick Crescent, W.
July 22? 1882.][1]

*** They always treat me gently in "Punch"[2] — why don't you do the same by the Browning Society? I see you emphasize Miss

Hickey's[3] acknowledgment of defects in time and want of rehearsal: but I look for no great perfection in a number of kindly disposed strangers to me personally, who try to interest people in my poems by singing and reading them.[4] They give their time for nothing, offer their little entertainment for nothing, and certainly get next to nothing in the way of thanks—unless from myself who feel grateful to the faces I shall never see, the voices I shall never hear. The kindest notices I have had, or at all events those that have given me most pleasure, have been educed by this Society—A. Sidgwick's paper,[5] that of Professor Corson,[6] Miss Lewis's[7] article in this month's "Macmillan"—and I feel grateful for it all, for my part—and none the less for a little amusement at the wonder of some of my friends that I do not jump up and denounce the practices which must annoy me so much. Oh! my "gentle Shakespeare," how well you felt and said—"never anything can be amiss when simpleness and duty tender it."[8] So, dear Lady, here is my duty and simplicity tendering itself to you, with all affection besides, and I being ever yours,

R. Browning.

Text: Orr, II, 503–504.

1. The date is determined by the *Punch* portrait (n. 2) and the Browning Society's entertainment (n. 4).

2. "Punch's Fancy Portraits.—No. 93. Robert Browning, D.C.L." (*Punch,* July 22, 1882, p. 34).

3. Emily Henrietta Hickey (1845–1924), poet, lecturer on English language and literature in the London Collegiate School, and cofounder of the Browning Society. Her father and grandfather were Irish parsons, the latter an author who wrote under the name of "Martin Doyle" (*DNB* sub William Hickey). She wrote articles on Browning, edited his *Strafford* with notes and preface (1884), and is recognizable in Max Beerbohm's cartoon of the Browning Society. In 1901 she became a Catholic and thereafter was active in the Catholic Truth Society. (See Enid Maud Dinnis, *Emily Hickey: Poet, Essayist, Pilgrim* [London, 1927].)

4. The Browning Society gave its first annual "Entertainment" at University Col-

lege, Gower Street, on Friday, June 30, 1882 (*Academy,* July 8, 1882, p. 29). The program consisted of readings and songs from Browning's poems, concluding with a solo and chorus of "Cavalier Tunes" set to music by C. Villiers Stanford.

5. Arthur Sidgwick, tutor at Corpus Christi College, Oxford, read his "On the Love Poems of Browning" to the Oxford Browning Society and published it in the *Journal of Education* (May 1, 1882, pp. 139–143; Henry John Newbolt, *My World as in My Times* [London, 1932], p. 88–91).

6. Hiram Corson (1828–1911), professor of literature at Cornell University (1870–1903), read his paper "The Idea of Personality, As Embodied in Robert Browning's Poetry" at the eighth meeting of the Browning Society on June 23, 1882 (*BSP,* I, 293–321). He was the only American charter member of the London Browning Society, and later founded many Browning Clubs throughout America (see Letter 36, n. 2).

7. Mary A. Lewis read her paper to the Browning Society on January 27, 1882, and then published it in *Macmillan's Magazine* (July 1882, pp. 205–214). The article, "Some Thoughts on Browning," concludes, "The best wish we can offer to the remaining years of the nineteenth century is that future historians may be able to say of it that whereas Clough and Matthew Arnold embodied the philosophical and religious thought of its central period, Robert Browning became the representative man of its close."

8. *Midsummer Night's Dream,* V, i, 82–83.

Letter 47

Hôtel Virard, St Pierre de Chartreuse,
Isère, France.
Aug. 16. '82.[1]

Dear Friend, all was pleasant to read in your letter except the remark that "most of my own letters during the last year had been *kind*": they were very untrue to the spirit which dictated them if they were not *all* so: what can there have been to be *"unkind"* about? I may observe perhaps on any matter in which we think diversely—where would be the use of writing at all if it were confined to expressing agreement on points whereon we agree, and letting all the others go unnoticed? The contrary way is an assurance that we *do* happily agree when there is no disagreement expressed. I used to particularly dislike a trick which a poor friend of mine [2] had,—along with many better practices,—of letting unpleasant matters—which herself had brought forward—pass in silence when I put them in their true light—as if *that* were the respect due to truth. For instance,—she once wrote to inform me what a worthless person was somebody who had done such and such a bad thing—precisely stated. I inquired into the circumstances and found, beyond the possibility of a mistake, that the real culprit was quite another person, utterly unknown to the person accused,—the blunder having arisen from just the fact that one name was confounded with another, Eccles—with Eckley: all which I set duly down,—and the reply contained no allusion to the blunder or its rectification,—as if nothing more needed be said on the subject! So did not *I* think—nor my correspondent find, I assure you! I have never had occasion to do more than perhaps object to what struck me as—well, really, there has been *nothing* worthy of objecting to, and if I was over-particular I was to blame, and you must forgive me. I don't know if you did *last* night however: for, what do you think, I had a strangely distinct dream of acting as you shall hear. I thought I was in charge of two not very large sums of money destined to—or belonging to—W. S. Landor [3] and—yourself—and, for some good reason as it seemed, I neglected to pay you as I was bound to do: whereupon I heard that you had been seriously inconvenienced—and I was in great distress, and doubtful how to excuse myself—by letter or by word of mouth: when, lo, on searching my pockets for the money (in gold) I was about to restore, I found it was inextricably mingled with the money belonging to Landor—and that a certain *rouleau* of napoleons was missing—in the distress about which—I woke! There, interpret if you please! Would a Daniel explain that the owing gold was—golden opinions, unrighteously with[h]eld on some occasion? Or, as "morning dreams go by contraries," and this night dream was ended at 5. this morning, have *you* been my niggard or neglectful paymaster?

Did I ever tell you of what happened to me on the last day of my stay here last year? [4] That as I, & my Sister, were taking our farewell of a solitary field at some little distance, of great beauty and peacefulness — the odd thought presented itself to me — "Suppose in the midst of this green quiet there were concealed a corpse, which you came suddenly upon: would you, — knowing the practice of the authorities here to forthwith *arrest* the unlucky discoverer as presumably the murderer, — think it your duty to proclaim the discovery?" I believe I made up my mind that the risk should be run. Next day, we found that a murder *had* been committed, and that the body of the victim *had* been found in that very field, and that the field's owner had been arrested on suspicion: indeed, we were much inconvenienced by the fact, for our journey to Chambery was delayed through the mule, which should carry our luggage, being put in requisition by the Juge d'Instruction from Grenoble, who rode over to enquire into the case: This morning, in the course of my walk I entered into conversation with two persons of whom I made enquiry myself. They said the accused man, a simple person, had been locked up in a high chamber, — protesting his innocence strongly, — and, troubled in his mind by the affair altogether and the turn it was taking, had profited by the gens d'armes negligence, and thrown himself out of window — and so died, continuing to the last to protest as before. My presentiment of what such a person might have to undergo was justified, you see: tho' I should not have in any case taken *that* way of getting out of a difficulty. The man added "It was not he who committed the murder, but the companions of the man, an Italian charcoal-burner, who owed him a grudge, killed him, and dragged him to the field, — filling his sack with potatoes as if stolen, to give a likelihood that the field's owner had caught him stealing and killed him, — so M. Perrier, the greffier [5] told me." Enough of this grim story. I am very sorry to hear

Miss Barnfather has suffered so much — give her my true sympathy & every wish for her complete recovery. Yes, the Book Stand[6] is very pretty, and was a kind thought, which I greatly value. Have you read Prof. Corson's paper? — *that* again is a testimony I feel abundantly grateful for — and if Furnivall's Society had only produced *that* as its result I — for my own part — should thank it warmly. The poem you quote from is a *translation* from the old latin [*sic*] poem of Walter de Mapes, Author of the *Roman de la Rose:*[7] the whole of the stanza from which you give a grotesque rhyme runs thus "Mysterious truths and rites divine | I never could unfold 'em | Without a flaggon of good wine | And a slice of cold ham." But a far better version ***[8]

My sister was anxious to know exactly where the body was found: '*Vous savez la croix au sommet de la colline? A cette distance de cela!*' That is precisely where I was standing when the thought came over me.

Manuscript: Carl H. Pforzheimer Library, RB 72

1. Browning's account book (BM) indicates that his 1882 holiday lasted from August 1 to October 1, the expense amounting to "say" £80. He and his sister arrived at St. Pierre de Chartreuse about August 7 (D&K, p. 278). They had intended to accept an invitation to Ischia, but the accidental death of a house-guest there thwarted their plans (Letter 48, n. 1). They left St. Pierre for Venice on September 18, but on the way floods at Bologna and Browning's lameness prevented them (D&K, p. 278), and they returned directly to London.

2. Isa Blagden had confused Mrs. Eccles and Mrs. Eckley thirteen years previously (*Dearest Isa,* Letter 118, May 16, 1869).

3. Browning had been Landor's guardian from 1859 to 1864 and as such had been entrusted with funds. Landor's brothers allowed him £200 a year, which Browning administered (G&M, p. 288).

4. See Letter 38.

5. Registrar.

6. Dr. Furnivall got up a subscription and on May 7, 1882, Browning's seventieth birthday, sent the poet his own works bound in green morocco in an oak case carved with bells and pomegranates (*Pall Mall Budget,* December 19, 1889, p. 1626).

The case is illustrated in Sotheran's catalogue number 737 (1913, p. 69). On May 8 Browning wrote to Furnivall, "I never was so honored, so gratified by any action of any approach to a similar nature, that ever happened to me in the course of my life" (MS in Huntington Library).

7. Walter Maps or Mapes (*fl.* 1200), archdeacon and author of a satirical miscellany *De Nugis Curialium,* but not the author of the *Roman de la Rose.* The translation Browning quotes seems to be a free rendering of the sixteenth stanza of "The Confession of Golias" (included in the Camden Society's *Latin Poems Commonly Attributed to Walter Mapes,* 1841), which Helen Waddell attributes to the Archpoet and calls "the greatest drinking song in the world" (*Mediaeval Latin Lyrics* [Harmondsworth, 1952], p. 339). The stanza begins, "Mihi nunquam spiritus poetrie datur, nisi prius fuerit venter bene satur . . ."

8. Remainder from Orr, II, 489.

Letter 48

Hôtel Virard, St Pierre de Chartreuse
Isère, France. Aug. 23. '82.

My dear Friend, I see by the extract you append to the "Academy" that you are aware of the sad accident at Ischia. It happened on the 12th and Cholmondeley wrote to me a few days after that poor Miss Wade [1] "went out by herself up the mountain of Epomeo" (which is at the back of his house) "a splendid but frightfully dangerous place — to see the sunset and make some sketches: as she did not return, her two brothers & plenty of men went out to look for her, and after two hours search she was found in a ravine where she must have fallen 100 feet over a nearby precipitous rock. She was not dead but insensible: doctors were at hand and every remedy was applied, but she never recovered consciousness and died on the following day at 7.30. a.m. I went to Naples on Monday to meet her father & mother who came from the Engadine, and the poor girl was buried at sunrise on Wednesday." He then goes on very kindly to say that, though he is forced to go to England in a fortnight—as otherwise Arthur Wade would refuse the journey—still his house is at our disposal till May, and he urges us to go there all the same—as assuredly we shall not dream of doing,—our visit having been intended for *him*. It is useless to observe on the strange carelessness of everybody concerned—two brothers who let a stranger to the place go out unaccompanied to sketch at sunset on a "frightfully dangerous" mountain. It causes the sort of *anger* one cannot help feeling in spite of all the pity possible,—such imprudence that simply entails a life-long misery which two moments of conscientious thought would have spared. Apart from the sorrow we feel for the cause of it, the change in our own plans is of no importance whatever: we shall continue our stay here as long as we can, and then proceed quietly on the line to Venice, stopping at towns we have not previously visited—such as Bergamo and Vicenza. I [2] all along had a repugnance to the journey which would necessitate passing by Florence and Rome—my own desire to escape which, might have been overborne by the wish that S. should enjoy what to me would be the reverse of enjoyment. Meantime, the weather is magnificent, and I do not believe that any place in the world would suit either of us better than this—for the next month, at least.

I was much pleased with the version of "Hervé Riel," [3] and the kind—if too complimentary notice of the translator. There were but a very few faults—which I pointed out to Mr Furnivall who sent me the paper—as did M. Milsand. *"Still* the north wind," should be "Toujours ce vent du Nord" the reverse of "Le vent s'apaise": it was wanted to help in the ships. Then, "belle chevauchées" points to riding on horseback—not "riding at anchor": "Fresh and strong the breeze is blowing While yon ship at anchor *rides"*—Finally "sure as Fate" applies to the coming up of the English in pursuit—not to the action of Hervé Riel: apart from those minute mistakes, the translation is very good & spirited. Of course I had read all the authorities — which I am glad to see reproduced. I have desired Mr F.[urnivall] to thank the author, if he has occasion, for the great pleasure he has given me — but I never myself on any occasion thank a critic for his criticism, — judging by my own feeling, that seeks no such repayment for what he honestly thinks and says.

I suppose you sent Sotheran's Catalogue that I might see the Shakespeare Book-Stand: my own [4] shows more sympathy with the subjects of my poems, — being made for love not lucre, — fifty guineas rewarding the one — and my gratitude the other artificer.

By a new regulation, we got yesterday's newspaper *to-day:* this is a comfort in these stirring times. I know certain of the warriors in Egypt, — Garnet Wolseley [5] in particular. I had an imploring letter from my nephew [6] to use any influence I have "to get an order countermanded ["] by which he, of the 2^d^ division of the Black Watch, was stopped at Edinburgh from proceeding with the 1st. He is a fine young fellow just returned from two years service in India — whence the *reserve* of his regiment. I could do nothing, of course. Ever affectionately yours

Robert Browning.

Manuscript: Carl H. Pforzheimer Library, RB 73

1. The daughter of the Rev. Nugent Wade (1845–1891), consular chaplain at Elsinore, rector of St. Anne's Soho from 1846 to 1890, and canon of Bristol (1872). (See John Henry Cardwell, *Men and Women of Soho Famous and Infamous* [London, 1903?], pp. 156–179.) Her accidental death was reported in *The Times* (August 26, 1882, p. 6b).

2. The "I" following "Vicenza" is obscured. See appendix for description.

3. Browning's "Hervé Riel" (1871) appeared in a French translation by James Darmesteter in *Le Parlement* for August 15, 1882.

4. In 1913 Sotheran asked £120 for the Browning bookstand (Letter 47, n. 6).

5. Sir Garnet Wolseley (1833–1913), field marshal and author of *The Soldier's Pocketbook* (1869). On August 15 he left England to quell a rebellion of the Egyptian army, and on September 13 he routed the Arabic force in a night attack. He was rewarded with £30,000, promoted to major general, created Baron Wolseley,

and later the first Viscount (*DNB*). On December 17, 1882, Browning wrote to Mrs. Bronson, "Last Monday, we gave our genial little hero, Wolseley, a dinner—we of the Cosmopolitan Club" (unpublished letter in the collection of the Count Rucellai).

6. H. G. Hart's *New Annual Army List* for 1882 (p. 286) lists Lieutenant Charles Graham Moulton-Barrett as a member of the Black Watch, the first battalion of which was stationed in Edinburgh.

Letter 49

[*St Pierre de Chartreuse, Isère, France*]
September 3, 1882.

*** No, I attribute no sort of supernaturalism to my fancy about the thing that was really about to take place.[1] By a law of the association of ideas—*contraries* come into the mind as often as *similarities*—and the peace and solitude readily called up the notion of what would most jar with them. I have often thought of the trouble that might have befallen me if poor Miss Smith's death had happened the night before, when we were on the mountain alone together—or next morning when we were on the proposed excursion—only *then* we should have had companions. . .

This is the fifth magnificent day—like magnificence, unfit for turning to much account, for we cannot walk till sunset. I had two hours' walk, or nearly, before breakfast, however. It is the loveliest country I ever had experience of, and we shall prolong our stay, perhaps. Apart from the concern for poor Cholmondeley and his friends, I should be glad to apprehend no long journey—besides the annoyance of having to pass Florence and Rome unvisited, for S.'s sake I mean: even Naples would have been with its wonderful environs a tantalizing impracticality.

Your 'Academy' came and was welcomed. The newspaper is like an electric eel, as one touches it and expects a shock. I am very anxious about the Archbishop,[2] who has always been strangely kind to me.***

Text: Orr, II, 489–490

1. See Letters 38 and 47.

2. The Rev. Archibald Campbell Tait (1811–1882), Archbishop of Canterbury (1869), died on December 1, 1882.

Letter 50

St. Pierre de Chartreuse, Isère, F.
Sept. 16. '82

My dear Friend, I would have written to you before this, but that there was some uncertainty about our plans: the present will find you at Bitterne,[1] and, I sincerely hope, at ease respecting your poor young Lady,[2] whose kindness and geniality, as well as her talents, I well remember. We leave this place next Monday, the 18th, for Chambéry, — intending to sleep next night at Turin, and thence go to Bergamo, and Vicenza, — so as to arrive at Venice on Monday, Sept. 25: our friend Mrs Curtis has taken rooms there for us, our old "Universo" being disposed of, and no longer an Hôtel: you will please to direct to us "Venice, Poste restante": on arriving, a word at the office will get letters forwarded at once. It will be a delight to find ourselves in a warm country: the fine weather broke up suddenly, — with a fall of 10. degrees in one night, and the sudden spread of snow on the mountains was magnificent, — but rain followed, — and worse, — the ways became impassable in parts, or nearly. To day is promising however,—I climbed my little mountain before breakfast as usual—and only stop from accompanying my sister on her longer walk in order to make sure of saying this word to you—as it would be too sad to have any of *your* words go astray. Our friends never realize how much out of the way we are—"suppose we can telegraph" &c—and one telegram *was* sent to us a fortnight ago—and never has reached us. I shall give every order about transmitting what may come after our departure—but as letters have to leave the country—one cannot be sure of the people of the next post town taking the trouble. By the bye—you always make *St. Pierre*—that anomalous thing a female Carthusian,—*la Chartreuse,*—whereas he is simply the St. Pierre *of* Chartreuse—this being the veritable and ancient *Cartusia* which gave its name to the adjacent monastery: it is no old place, however, having been burned altogether some sixty years ago, and rebuilt by the Monks in its actual humble way. We have, both of us, got much good out of its pure air and simple life, but the rainy days affright one. I have nothing to read but newspapers—and Homer—eighteen books of whose Iliad I have digested. The papers are "palpitating with interest" as the French say, and I am all one rejoicing at the success of our army in Egypt—and as full of disgust at the critics at home who have been "impatient at Sir G[arnet] W[olseley]'s inaction": such wiseacres would have urged poor Miss Wade to get on faster, as she climbed an unknown precipice,—themselves being safe at its foot. Party spirit seems to extinguish every spark of patriotism now-a-days. Well—I hope you will not forget that Pen never had the "pen of a ready-writer." He writes regularly but briefly to me—speaking about his work as little as possible, though I gather that he has been much occupied with it: if your friends have anything to report, I shall be only too glad to hear it. He has been unwell, and poisoned with mussels—literally—but was better when I heard last. He has taken a Studio at Paris for six months and, I believe, will proceed there in Octo[ber] [3]:

perhaps a letter (belated, I don't know why) may arrive this day, in which case, if a word of news be to add, you shall have it. S. will also say something on her return. Dear Friend, I am always affectionately yours

Robert Browning

Very clever & prettily designed — the Hands & Torch! [4]

Manuscript: Carl H. Pforzheimer Library, RB 74

1. Eastfield Lodge, Bitterne (a northeastern suburb of Southampton) was the residence of T. Keane FitzGerald (MPFG).

2. Geraldine Mary FitzGerald became ill with rheumatic fever, which affected her heart for the remainder of her life (MPFG).

3. There is a tear in the paper here.

4. Perhaps Mrs. FitzGerald had sent one of her granddaughter's drawings.

Letter 51

19. Warwick Crescent, W.
March 17. '83.

Dear Friend, I see with great pleasure that the day is very fine and suitable for your journey — which I wish may benefit you — what remains to be benefitted, rather, for you struck me as quite yourself again — well, I wish you quite that self with all my heart. I should myself be better for a change — but my laziness stops anything like the first step to it. I had a kind invitation from the Mount-Temples to go to Broadlands,[1] which place I never saw, BUT — the repugnance to move was invincible. I return you the young lady's letter.[2] In the former of the two letters I got this week, you vexed me by speaking disparagingly of your "brain-pace" &c May I venture to say that all its fault is in the exercise of industry in a wrong direction—so far as regards my poems, at least. If you would—when you please to give them your attention—to confine it to the poems and nothing else, no extraneous matter at all,—I cannot but think you would find little difficulty: but your first business seems to be an inquiry into what will give no sort of help. You say "You cannot get over the two wives, for if Adam be a modern instance what business had he to have two?"[3] Now, read the poem and tell me where is the least word about two *"wives"?* Had you let the Title alone and gone on to the subject you would have seen the story is simply that a man once knew a woman who, while she loved him, pretended that she did not—which pretence, like a man and a fool, he believed, so of course was not married to her—but to a woman who did *not* love him but another though she said she did love him—which, like a man and a fool—he believed: one day as they sat together, each, on a sudden impulse, told him the truth—which, like a man and a fool, he disbelieved. Surely there is nothing so difficult here: but because of the fantastic title, you keep *that* in your head and turn from all the modern allusions to the marriage, priest, love-making &c which show it to be just a modern instance—like Rossetti's "Lilith"[4] who wears aesthetic costume, hardly befitting the "mother of all the daemons." So, with "Jochanan":[5] there was no need to "know *d'avance* all the Talmudic stories"—which,—such of them as I referred to, are all sufficiently explained in the poem itself—indeed every allusion needing explanation is explained. But you begin by asking of a friend "Who Jochanan was": why, *nobody*. "John" (as the name is in English) was no more the "John" mentioned by your friend than he was St. John of the Gospels: the poem *tells* you *who* he was, what he was, where he lived, and why he was about to die: what more do you want? I know there *was a* Saint Jochanan—but he was not *Ben Sabbathai*—a name expressly added to prevent *that* mistake. *Hakkadosh* is explained in the text, and so is *Ruach*—more at length than in your friend's letter: all the other stories are told at just as much length as is requisite for the purpose, and years of study of dictionaries and the like would make the student learned enough in another direction but not one bit more in the limited direction of the poem itself. I say all this because you imagine that with more learning you would "understand" more about my poetry—and as if you would somewhere find it already written—only waiting to be translated into English and my verses: whereas I should consider such an use of learning to be absolutely contemptible: for poetry, if it is to deserve the name, ought to create—or re-animate something—not merely reproduce *raw* fact taken from somebody else's book. If you will only concern yourself with what is set down,—regarding a name as a name that explains itself, and a passing allusion to just an allusion and no more, you will find no difficulty but what is a fault *in the writer:* and it is *not* a fault in him that if he says "Isaeus loved Chariclea and married her though she was in love with Euphorion who preferred—Ione"—you say—"I cannot understand this till I have learned the whole history of these personages and what marriage is in question." I am so anxious to stand well in your eyes that I talk thus plainly: and so much attached to you that I cannot bear to hear you say "The fault is in *me*—in my want of learning, and I must apply to my friend Miss little Anybody." [6] You will be glad to know there is a great sale for the book. Ever affectionately yours

Robert Browning.

Written in immense haste, which forgive!

Manuscript: Carl H. Pforzheimer Library, RB 75

1. William Cowper (1811–1888) inherited the state of Broadlands in Hampshire (1869) and was created Baron Mount Temple (1880). His beautiful wife, Georgina Tellemache, was one of the three vice-presidents of the Browning Society at its founding. (See Russell, *Portraits of the Seventies,* pp. 273–284.)

2. Mrs. FitzGerald had appealed to a friend for help in the interpretation of some

of the poems in Browning's *Jocoseria,* published on March 9, 1883. She then sent the friend's reply on to Browning. The knowledge of Hebrew displayed in the reply suggests that the friend was Emily Harris.

3. "Adam, Lilith, and Eve" was the sixth poem in *Jocoseria.*

4. D. G. Rossetti showed his *Lady Lilith* at the Royal Academy Exhibition of 1868, and the *Notes* included his sonnet on the subject (W. M. Rossetti, *Bibliography of the Works of Dante Gabriel Rossetti* [London, 1905], pp. 14–15). An illustration of the Rossetti painting faces page 90 of H. C. Marillier's *Dante Gabriel Rossetti* (London, 1904).

5. "Jochanan Hakkadosh" was the eighth and longest poem in *Jocoseria.*

6. See n. 2.

Letter 52

19. Warwick Crescent, W.
March 24. '83

Dear Friend,—all is well, then, and, once directing your intelligence the simple and straight way—to the substance of whatever poem you do me the honor to read, and not the quite extraneous matter of what—besides the substance—may be found touching upon it elsewhere,—I shall be sure of your understanding—however I may be uncertain of your liking what I write: my faults, as a writer, are many, I well know: but, as a poet, I do not let my imagination lie so idle as to versify what other writers have already invented. So enough of preaching & teaching! "Shushan's flower"[1] is the flower of Shushan—i.e. the lily, שׁוֹשַׁן. You see, when you call a housemaid Susan—you call her "lily." By the way, what do you suppose is the meaning of Pen's name—Penini—in Hebrew? פְּנִינַי, why, letter for letter "My rubies": the word is without a singular number: if it had one (it may have, out of the Bible) it would be even nearer by the last vowel-point—פְּנִינִי—that is, Penin*i* for Penin*ai!* Of all the wise wonderers as to what the name could mean,[2] nobody had learning enough to hit upon this pretty meaning — which, of course, was far from the thought of both the boy and ourselves when he began mispronouncing the true word. What a fine sunny cold day! I have been invited, amongst perhaps a dozen other pleasant proposals, to go to Leveson Gower's [3] to meet no less than Gladstone — who is just gone there: but I am constant to hearth & home! May I leave off somewhat abruptly, Dear Friend? My whole morning has gone to letter-writing, and here is luncheon! Enjoy yourself, and you will add to the enjoyment of your *Pambo alter* [4]

RB.

Manuscript: Carl H. Pforzheimer Library, RB 76

1. "And slowly woke, — like Shushan's flower besought" ("Jochanan Hakkadosh," line 670).

2. The child Pen gave himself the nickname Penini, which he meant for Wiedemann (Kenyon, II, 24). Among the "wise wonderers" as to the meaning of the nickname was Nathaniel Hawthorne, who thought it a diminutive of Apennino (*French and Italian Notebooks* [Boston, 1871], pp. 293–294).

3. Frederick Leveson-Gower (1819–1907), son of the first Earl Granville and liberal M.P. For many years Gladstone delighted in the hospitality of his house, Holmbury (John Morley, *The Life of William Ewart Gladstone* [New York, 1932], II, 459n.).

4. "Pambo" was the last poem in Browning's *Jocoseria* (1883).

Letter 53

19. Warwick Crescent, W.
Apr. 14. '83.

Dear Friend, — this will of necessity be a short and hurried letter — seeing that presently I give a luncheon to Mr Cholmondeley who comes by his own appointment — and there is still so much to do!

I owe and would pay you, however, real thanks for the news that you are at home again, and very well again, — no doubt, the stay at that exceedingly interesting Chequers' Court [1] has done you a world of good. Yes — I have read the new Letters [2] — with so much pain and indeed disgust that I willingly say just *that* and no more.[3] I can scarcely conceive that Froude's intention in publishing them was to bring the couple into contempt: and yet there are some points otherwise hardly to be accounted for. Thus, — the mistaken charge of Carlyle (in the Reminiscences) against the other "Thomas C." [4] as filching his reputation and, on the credit of the theft, getting civilities at Berlin — was amply disproved in letters to the "Athenaeum",[5] which showed that the Thomas C. in question had quite distinct and sufficient claims of his own to be so treated in Germany where he was no stranger: yet this story is repeated by Mrs C.,[6] — endorsed by C. himself, — and left without a word of explanation much less apology, to continue the false charge it has been shown to be. I believe there was nothing the matter with the unwise "creatures" (as they style everybody else) but too much leisure to study their own stomachs and cultivate disorder of the nerves. There is also something disagreeably like "snobbishness" in C[arlyle]'s protestation, as Lord Ashburton's [7] death was drawing near, "that he should lose the only friend he had" — — while Forster, — for one, — had been for years ready to cut off his right hand for — what he thought — his friend's sake: — sacrifices which pass for nothing by the side of the gift of a horse and an invitation to "the Grange".[8]

Just so, Allingham's [9] name occurs neither in the Will nor the Reminiscences, — if I remember as to the latter: yet for years he had been at C[arlyle]'s beck & call — giving him two hours' daily companionship in his walk — and those out of a poor man's bread-winning time.

> "Who would not smile if such a man there be?
> Who would not weep if Atticus were he?"

Pope originally wrote, in the second line, "laugh": what an immense improvement in the direction of the fitness of things is in the correction![10] Farewell, dear Friend, till next Saturday. The weather is dolefully grey and un-Spring-like: but we must un-Carlylize ourselves and put up with it!

Ever affectionately yours
Robert Browning.

Manuscript: Carl H. Pforzheimer Library, RB 77

1. Rosalind Alicia (Frankland-Russell) Astley (died 1900), the widow (1866) of Lt. Col. Francis L'Estrange Astley, resided with her son, Bertram Basil, at Chequers Court, which Lord and Lady Lee of Fareham presented to the nation (1921) as a country residence for the prime minister.

2. In 1883 James Anthony Froude, Carlyles' literary executor, published *Letters and Memorials of Jane Welsh Carlyle,* which had been preceded by his edition of Carlyle's *Reminiscences* (1881) and *The Early Life of Carlyle* (1882). Froude included the Carlyles' biting judgments and wounding statements, offending many and causing acquaintances to look forward to future publications with apprehension.

3. Mrs. FitzGerald underlined the words "no more" and added, "Yet I think he *does* say something more?" See appendix.

4. Thomas Carlyle (1803–1855), apostle of the Catholic Apostolic Church, was given (1838) North Germany as his province, where he was well recieved (*DNB*). To prevent confusion with the writer, he called himslf T. Carlyle, Advocate. Yet the writer complained of him as a "double-goer," dining with some ambassador at Berlin "in my stead" (*Reminiscences,* I, 313).

5. H. G. Graham clarified the situation in his "The Two Carlyles" (*Athenaeum,* May 14, 1881, p. 654).

6. *Letters and Memorials,* I, 204.

7. William Bingham Baring (1799–1864), second Baron Ashburton (1848). He and his first and second wives were intimate with the Carlyles. (See Iris Origo, "The Carlyles and the Ashburtons," in *A Measure of Love* [London, 1957], pp. 117–188.)

8. The Grange, W. Alresford, was the Ashburtons' great country house in Hampshire.

9. William Allingham (1824–1889), Irish poet and editor of *Fraser's Magazine* from 1874 to 1879.

10. In *An Epistle to Dr. Arbuthnot* (1735) Pope wrote, "Who but must laugh, if such a man there be | Who would not weep, if Atticus were he?" (lines 213–214). No edition I have consulted says "smile."

Letter 54

19. Warwick Crescent, W.
Apr. 28. '83

My dear Friend,

I am again pushed up into a very corner of time, but can say that I am indeed glad that so pleasant an utterance of a true feeling can give you the satisfaction you are good enough to acknowledge.[1]

I go on Wednesday to Oxford, on the occasion of the affair you may have seen mentioned in the papers: [2] but — true to my profession — I shall return in the evening, in spite of proffered hospitality.

I am called — forgive me the brief word — for the sake of yet one more in conclusion, — that I am ever affectionately yours,

R Browning.

Manuscript: Carl H. Pforzheimer Library, RB 78

1. Mrs. FitzGerald may have acknowledged the satisfaction she felt from the contents of Browning's missing letter of April 21.

2. The *Times* for April 28, 1883 (p. 12c) announced a forthcoming luncheon in Balliol Hall honoring the Prince of Wales. Among the guests were Lord Salisbury (Chancellor of Oxford) and the Duke of Buckingham and Chandos (*ibid.*, May 4, 1883, p. 10e).

Letter 55

19. Warwick Crescent, W.
May 5. '83.

Thank you, Dear Friend, for the card, and its Hebrew series of blessings. I suppose they are the contribution of your Jewish young lady friend.[1] I get more and more attached to that grand language.

Yes, there is engagement of every kind for this end of the week: Whitsuntide may bring some relief. The Oxford ceremony was very interesting:[2] I would however give no more than a day to it—returning in the evening. Your plan of the country does indeed put Shalstone into near communication with Oxford. I had a kind, somewhat pressing invitation from L^y Salisbury[3] to spend the holidays with them, but nothing shall tempt me from home—and I pleaded Milsand's presence. I sat just opposite and near to your Duke,[4] by the bye.

The picture-shows were interesting. At the *last* moment—literally—I sent Pen's portrait of myself—that he might not be wholly unrepresented at the Grosvenor:[5] they took the picture in late in the evening of Friday—next day being the private-view—so that no name appears in the catalogue which was already in print. At the R[oyal] A[cademy] Pen's bust attracts notice and is in a good place.[6] I go to the Dinner this afternoon, and shall see the Gallery under better conditions. Some portraits are admirable, and many pictures very good. To my mind, the very best is the Piazza di S. Marco by Logsdail[7]—quite fit to make the painter an Academician. Some of Millais' work is superb—Hall[8] too is in great force & Leighton hardly so good as usual. Herbert[9] miraculously absurd.

Here is the sun—but where is the warmth? I seem as if I never should feel it again—till there comes too much of it, and the journey of deliverance follows. "Never the time and place and comfort altogether!"[10]

Thank you again and again for your kindness and benediction: I am sure I return the latter fervently.

Ever yours affectionately
Robert Browning.

I treated myself lately to the Jewish Family Bible[11] published by Rider: a noble book. You must one day bring me acquainted with that Jewish lady,[12] if she please to permit me the great pleasure.

I hear Logsdail's capital picture was purchased for £1000: it is worth twice as much.

Manuscript: Carl H. Pforzheimer Library, RB 79

1. Emily Marion Harris (originally von Hirsch — *BSP,* III, 79*; obituary in *Times,* December 8, 1900, p. 13e). Her friendship with Mrs. FitzGerald began during her girlhood (see Introduction, p. 14). Later, at Mrs. FitzGerald's request, she wrote a Hebrew good wish on the back of a greeting card to be sent to Browning, choosing the Blessing of the Cohanim, "The Lord bless thee and keep thee, etc." Browning thereafter kept the card on his mantelpiece ("The Late Mrs. FitzGerald" by Emily Marion Harris, *The Jewish Chronicle,* August 4, 1899, p. 20).

2. See Letter 54, n. 2.

3. Georgiana Caroline Alderson (died 1890) married (1857) Robert Arthur Talbot Cecil (1830–1903), third Marquis of Salisbury, Chancellor of Oxford University (1869), and prime minister from 1885 to 1902.

4. Richard Plantagenet Grenville (1823–1889), third Duke of Buckingham and Chandos, whose principal residence, Stowe House (now Stowe School) was near Shalstone.

5. Pen painted several portraits of his father. Baylor University has fourteen, and recently one was discovered in The Black Bull in Sussex (*Times,* November 13, 1961, p. 12f). Of the two known to have been done in 1882, one shows the poet in academic dress (Letter 71, n. 4) the other, a portrait-bust, was presented to Reginald Smith of Smith, Elder and Company, the poet's publishers (Wilson, p. 133).

6. In 1883 the Royal Academy showed Pen's *Adelia Abbruzzesi,* a bronze bust of a Velletri girl, of which Emily Pattison said that it looked "as if it had the small pox" (*Academy,* May 26, 1883, p. 373). Browning was more pleased with the comment of Professor Alphonse Legros, "C'est étonnant" (Landis, p. 304).

7. William Logsdail began exhibiting at the Royal Academy in 1877 and exhibited almost annually thereafter. In 1883 he showed his *The Piazza* (Algernon Graves, *The Royal Academy of Arts* [London, 1905], V, 82).

8. Lindsay Bernard Hall showed *The Trysting Place,* and William Henry Hall showed *A Devonshire Village* (*ibid.*).

9. John Rogers Herbert, R.A. (1810–1890) showed four pictures at the Royal Academy in 1883, among them *A Mortally Wounded Bandit Chief Exhorting His Comrades to Return to an Honest Living* (*ibid.,* IV, 78). Although Browning found his work "miraculously absurd," it was "preposterously successful" and sold far and wide (*DNB*).

10. "Never the Time and the Place" is the ninth poem in Browning's *Jocoseria* (1883).

11. Browning's account book for 1883 (BM) shows that on January 23, he pur-

chased a "Hebrew Grammar" for five and six, and on May 1, a "Bible & Lexicon (Hebrew)" for four and nine. (See Sotheby, no. 389, p. 73.)

12. Mrs. FitzGerald introduced Miss Harris to the poet. Some twenty-five of his letters to her are at Baylor University.

Letter 56

19. Warwick Crescent, W.
June 23, '83.

Dear Friend, Here is another week gone by, and I only seem to breathe on this last day of it when—blessings on it—I dine at home. I can't tell you how my soul has been stirred by a card that reached me with particulars of a cottage to be sold "with a detached studio," for a price which I could pay, and easily! To be away and out of reach! Perhaps I should tire of it sooner than I imagine. Pen is at Dinant and full of projects as to pictures: his snake [1] is to be made useful in one of them. Don't let me forget to say that your translation was right in all but the beginning. ἤν με τάχ Ιλιόνη καλάγης is not "bring Ilione" but "bring me (the dog) to Ilione,—and the greek verb in the prose-bit comes from ὀλλυμί—with the preposition.[2]

Come by all means on the Thursday unless you like Tuesday better, for any reason. My sister tells me you have had a gay and gratifying time with your friends,—which is all as it should be. To day is turning out (1½ p.m) bright and warm,—it began otherwise. I have *never* seen the foliage so luxuriant as this year,—in London, that is. I had a sufficiently pressing invitation to go to Knebworth [3] next week, to meet friends of mine, but I was obdurate—which I mention that you may remember I am promised first to Shalstone. Peace and quiet!

I met at dinner last evening my old friend Odo Russell [4] "that was." He told me — what I knew — that his Uncle Lord Russell had written a play "Don Carlos" [5] — but added — what I was ignorant of — that he said, to the end of his life, that he would prefer being the author of a good play to attaining any other distinction in the world! It is well he contented himself with the easier "distinctions" for his ability extended to deserving them. Here is a visitor — and here is the end of my scrawly nothing-in-the-way-of-a-letter — but your goodness will accept it from yours ever affectionately

Robert Browning.

Manuscript: Carl H. Pforzheimer Library, RB 80

1. Pen paid £16 for a ten-foot python from Senegal that had been in the Antwerp Museum of Natural History. He kept it in his room, and his Italian model posed for hours with the snake twined around her while Pen worked on his statue *Dryope*. Visitors to the studio were apprehensive about the girl, but she outlived the python (*BSP*, I, 99*).

2. Perhaps the Greek is from an exercise book. Mrs. FitzGerald began the study of Greek when she was seventy using Joseph B. Mayor's *Greek for Beginners* (London, 1879), which is in two parts. At the end of Part I she wrote "Jubilate."

3. Robert Lytton (1831–1891) inherited Knebworth House, Hertfordshire, upon the death of his father in 1873. In 1880 Lytton retired there after returning from India, where he had been Viceroy (Aurelia B. Harlan, *Owen Meredith* [New York, 1946], p. 225).

4. Odo Leopold Russell (1829–1884), diplomat, son of Browning's friend Lady William Russell, nephew of Lord John Russell, and (1881) first Baron Ampthill.

5. Lord John Russell (1792–1878), prime minister from 1846 to 1852, first Earl Russell (1861), published his five-act verse tragedy *Don Carlos; or Persecution* in 1822, in which year there were five editions.

Letter 57

Palazzo Giustinian Recanato,
Oct. 9. '83.[1]

but the address by which my letters will best reach me is simply *Poste-restante*. Thus I begin, dear Friend, by a wise taking for granted that you will continue to write to me, though I am less inexcusably behind-hand in writing to you than usual. Though I arrived some days ago, I have found it hard to steal a minute for that employment of my "pen" — (I see it is declared to be busy" —) which I am so much bound to — for I have received some three or four letters since my own shabby bit of correspondence. Your goodness, however, is not easily turned back on its course, and you may rely on it, that if I have not done my duty by you, no one else has profited by the omission — the word to Pen being a necessity — as he expects to leave Dinant in a day or two for Paris. You are to know, then, that we left dear Gressoney last Monday — walking thence to Pont St Martin in seven continuous hours without stopping for a minute: next early morning we left for Ivrea — and got to Vicenza in the evening: on Thursday we started for Venice, were met at the Station by our Hostess [2] and her gondoliers, and were installed in this apartment, — furnished in all respects so as to make us perfectly comfortable. The weather was bad, — for the *first* time, on the day of our arrival, but has continued superlatively fine ever since: I believe the present to be the most enjoyable month in Venice, — clear fresh and bracing mornings, sunny noontides, and the most wonderful sunsets I remember. Last afternoon, S. and I rowed to the Lido, and returned between two *blazes* of gold and crimson, — the sky and its reflection in the sea. We try to keep up our walking, and are just returned from a stroll of some hours. I daresay we shall be home at the end of this October, notwithstanding the witchery of the place and the kindness of our Hostess — but (as Shelley said on a like occasion) "I have friends in London too." [3] There seem to be not so many friends — or indeed, strangers — in Venice as usual: the fear of cholera is said to have deterred the bold Britons from their customary visit. The Layards are here, — we dine with them to-night, — The Master of the Rolls,[4] Stopford Brooke,[5] and a few others known and unknown to me. Venice itself is more bright and beautiful than ever, — except for one deed of unutterable barbarism which has been perpetrated in my absence,—the destruction of the exquisite little island of St Helena,—all one garden with a solitary church, two years ago—now—a treeless yard built over by an iron foundry—the most hideous object imaginable: yet the whole island might have been bought for some few hundred pounds. Well,—one must bear it! Farewell, dear Friend,—with true thanks for your many favours. Would I could send you a stripe of the blue sky above me, at the open window where I sit. *That* would[6] be something like a proper gift from yours affectionately ever, Robert Browning.

Manuscript: Carl H. Pforzheimer Library, RB 81

1. In 1883 Browning and his sister spent their holiday in the Italian Alps and Venice. They left London on August 13, proceeded to Turin and Ivrea, and arrived at Gressoney St. Jean on August 22 (Hood, p. 221). On October 1 they left Gressoney for Venice, where they arrived on October 4. They left Venice on December 8, visited Pen in Paris for a day or two, and returned to London on December 13 (account book, BM).

2. In Venice the Brownings stayed in the Palazzo Giustiniani, which was attached to Mrs. Bronson's Casa Alvisi and which she had annexed as a guest house (Henry James, *Italian Hours,* [Boston, 1909], p. 112).

3. See Letter 26, n. 2.

4. Sir George Jessel (1824–1883) was Master of the Rolls from 1873 to 1883.

5. Stopford Augustus Brooke (1832–1916), divine and man of letters. His many publications include *The Poetry of Robert Browning* (London, 1902).

6. The remainder is cross-written. See appendix for description, and for a small correction in the first paragraph.

Letter 58

Venice, Oct 22. '83.

My dear Friend, by my reckoning I ought to have had an answer to my letter (of last week but one) some days ago,—but, unless a mysterious "Grazie" appended to a paragraph in the "Academy" was meant for an answer, none has arrived. Perhaps you expected an acknowledgement of another letter which came after mine had been dispatched: but I thought the understanding between us was that letter should be followed by letter—and my "last" is the one for which a reply is due. Anyhow, I shall be very glad to have the "grazie" made real and practical by news from Shalstone,—so, pray "thank" me in the way I like best!

As to the "Anthology." no, your "Selection" is a mere Selection: my "flowers" are comprised in three closely-printed volumes, whereof *two* only are with me: the verses you copied are well-known, and pretty enough—by a certain ΡΟΥΦΙΝΟΣ who has contributed to my Edition far more questionable matter than is likely to figure in a copy for general use.[1]

To-day, for the first time since our arrival, it *rains*—or, as the Venetians would say—in face of their dried-up wells, and parched gardens—the plague of drought has ceased. We have had wonderful weather,—and such sunsets as I never remember. I suppose our visit ought to be drawing to an end,—but it is hard to extricate oneself from the all-embracing kindness of our Hostess here.

Have you noticed that Pen's picture at the Fisheries' Exhibition has obtained a Gold Medal,[2]—the only one awarded to its class "Still Life"? I never dreamed—nor, I am sure, did he,—that any reward was obtainable for pictures, and am nearly as surprised as gratified that he has got—what, after all, are his deserts: but "it seems a story from the land of spirits, If any man obtain the thing he merits, And any merits that which he obtains."[3] Pen is in Paris now,—at a small but good Hotel immediately opposite his Studio—for economy's sake (in time as well as money)—and is about to superintend the casting of his statue,[4]—and to begin another. Well,—the rain is already over and gone. Pray write at once—if you have not anticipated my reminder, as I hope: but this morning's post brought nothing — and so, you get at once my complaints and my best regards.

Ever affectionately yours
Robert Browning

Manuscript: Carl H. Pforzheimer Library, RB 82

1. Rufinus, a Byzantine poet of unknown dates, contributed thirty-eight epistles to the *Greek Anthology*. They are of a light, amatory character.

2. See Letter 18, n. 8. The exhibition was held at the Gardens of the Royal Horticultural Society, South Kensington, from May 13 to November 1, 1883, under the patronage of the Queen (*International Fisheries Exhibition Official Catalogue* [London, 1883].)

3. "It sounds like stories from the land of spirits | If any man obtain that which he merits | Or any merit that which he obtains" (S. T. Coleridge, "The Good, Great Man," 1802).

4. See Letter 63, n. 4.

Letter 59

Venice, Oct. 29. '83,

Dear Friend, it is very pleasant to find that you care so much for my letters, and I am very sorry that I disappointed you by waiting for an answer to my *last* and not acknowledging the two or three that followed on your *first* which, — as has been always the case, — I replied to at once. Yes, I got the largely written one, as well as the others: but it did not seem necessary to assure you that in whatever character you choose to write, the result is always gratefully received. The "notice" in the "Academy" came from no "Miss Hickey" — with whom I have no correspondence except on a business matter or so — but from Mr Furnivall,[1] to whom I wrote concerning a letter he forwarded from Professor Dowden,[2] — and the "Mopsa" is no historical personage but the shepherdess of the "Winter's Tale" who tells Autolycus that she "loves a story in print, for then we know it is true": [3] I don't wonder that you failed to find her out in the Classical Dictionaries. So, this little matter settled between us, I shall beg a letter in return for the present at — Athens! [4] for, would you believe what I can hardly believe myself, I really go there with my Sister next Thursday or the first day afterward that suits for the boat from Brindisi. There happens a wonderfully advantageous opportunity of helping me to the realization of a dream I have had all my life, and began to despair of finding other than a dream. The perfect weather seems to continue on purpose: I write at an open window, with a cloudless sky and brilliant sun, — having just returned from a two hours' walk under a June or rather June-and-May influence. This journey was only decided on two days ago, and though fixed for Thursday[,] is contingent, as I have said, on the power of catching a good boat from Brindisi to Corfù, whence we get to Athens "through the Isles": to this indulgence I have been persuaded by our Hostess and her Daughter [5] — who would not undertake it except in our company — for of course my sister goes with me. This will hardly prolong our absence unduly — as I stipulated for leaving at once — and the time spent in Athens would probably have been passed in Venice, to which we shall not return, but, from Bologna, go home by Turin and Paris. Direct, — if your goodness impels you, to the *Hotel des Etrangers,* Athens.

Your translation, I remember, was right in the main but a little out at the end, — the merely "absent" being taken by you for the "Dead." I twice tried to find the original in my foolish book that has no index — for its hundreds of little six-line poems — but failed to discover this one.[6] Farewell for (I trust) but a few days: I am happy that all *is* well with you, as your letter indicates. My Sister (who wrote when I did) sends her kindest love. Ever affectionately yours

R Browning

Manuscript: Carl H. Pforzheimer Library, RB 83

1. On October 15, 1883, Browning wrote to Furnivall, "We arrived eleven days ago, eleven perfect days have we had, yet I see that Venice is 'drenched with rain'—that is, in the newspaper" (Hood, p. 225). A paragraph in *The Academy* for October 20 (p. 263) repeated Browning's observation, adding "as that is in print, 'we are sure,' as Mopsa says, that it is true . . ."

2. Edward Dowden (1843–1913), after 1867 Professor of English at Trinity College, Dublin. While working on his biography of Shelley, he corresponded with Browning regarding the letters of the first Mrs. Shelley (Hood, pp. 222–224 and notes).

3. "I love a ballad in print, a-life, for then we are sure they are true" (*Winter's Tale,* IV, iii, 262).

4. Browning did not go to Athens (see Letter 60, n. 1), although *The Academy* for November 3 reported that he did.

5. Edith Bronson (July 3, 1861–November 28, 1956) was born in Newport, Rhode Island, and lived abroad with her parents after 1875 (see Letter 38, n. 8). On June 26, 1895, she married Capitano di Fregata Cosimo Rucellai, R. N. (1864–1930), the ceremony being performed in the Patriarchate of Venice, by the Patriarch, later Pope Pius X. After her marriage she lived in the Palazzo Rucellai, Florence. (Her portrait faces page 257 of Betty Miller's *Robert Browning* [New York, 1952]. Her son, the present Count Rucellai, has the letters Browning wrote to her mother.)

6. There are hundreds of sepulchral epigrams in the *Greek Anthology* containing references to the absent or the dead.

Letter 60

Palazzo Giustinian-Recanati,
Venice, Nov. 8. '83.

Dear Friend,—broken at last is our beautiful weather, to the great delight of the Venetians whose wells are all dry, and water has to be purchased. Only yesterday, did the change come, and from the 4th of October, when we arrived, to the 6th of this month, was an uninterrupted stretch of blue sunny days: as for warmth, yesterday I was forced to take off a slight over-coat I had put on. The roses and other flowers are still in bloom, and butterflies abound in the Public

Gardens: this morning, for the first time, we kept home instead of taking our usual two hours' walk,—and already the sun has been out, and we shall presently follow his example. This is said to excuse, or rather explain, our lingering on and unwillingness to return to the fog and cold of which we hear sufficiently. As for the projected journey [1]—*that* we did well to forego. The first arrangements tempted us—and properly,—but they proved altogether incompatible with the powers of locomotion in the case of our intended companion: it would have been absurd to sail—or "steam" rather—directly from Venice to Athens—just see it—and then, as wearisomely return, all the rest of adjacent Greece unvisited: but the "cherry" vainly "bobbed at" this year, may be bitten and swallowed next time, if circumstances permit—and by our two selves we may effect twice or thrice as much in half the number of days. Meanwhile, our pleasures here continue unexhausted. Our "social enjoyments" which you refer to, are curious enough: we had a dinner the other day at which the only guests beside our own party, were Don Carlos [2] (the legitimate King of France as well as Spain) Princess of Montenegro [3] (whose husband was murdered, and whose daughter, a nice young clever lady, would be the actual Prince were she but a boy!)—Prince & Pss. Iturbide [4] son of the Emperor, and adopted, as such, for his successor by poor Maximilian,[5]—all deposed and all as gay as grigs! And our party, two days ago, had deposed potentates of a sort in Pr. & Pss Metternich—son of him who called Italy "a geographical expression." [6] D. Carlos passed the evening here a day or two ago, (our Hostess "receives" every evening) and I took the opportunity of asking him, *coi dovuti riguardi,* if he knew the secret of the "Man in the Iron Mask"—known to be transmitted from sire to son by the Royal family of France: [7] he said he did not—neither did his uncle Chambord: [8] the secret died with the little Dauphin [9] in the Temple: D. Carlos' aunt, the Dss. d'Angoulême [10] told him that, on one of the visits she was allowed to pay her poor brother when under the cruel care of

Simon,[11] she enquired if he knew—and the answer was "Yes, I have been told, and will tell nobody!"—This is worth remembering, I think.

That was indeed a narrow and most fortunate escape of your Son's:[12] I am indeed happy that you have no dreadful accident to deplore, as might so easily have been the case. By the bye, two eccentricities of a very different kind one from the other, have been exciting Venice last week: our second gondolier, Domenico, disappeared at dinner in consequence of his wife's indisposition, and returned the richer (?) by three boys at a birth,[13] completing his "quiverful"[14] to sixteen: and, as if to redress the overbalance of males,—but this is no laughing matter,—within the week, three sisters unaccountably drowned themselves with the most deliberate coolness at the Lido: the eldest some 26 years old,—in good circumstances, and the cause quite unknown. I must leave off: goodbye, Dear Friend,—tell dear Miss Harris that I hear of every one of her actions with great interest, and shall be delighted to read her paper on the Jewish trumpet.[15] Don't continue to write "Mopsa"[16] against bits of letters I send to Mr F.[urnivall] although he may please to print them. If ever I *do* write to Miss Hickey, be sure I will enquire who *can* have been the historical personage you confound with the "Mopsa" of the "Winter's Tale." I will cut out a bit from yesterday's newspaper. Ever affectionately yours

Robert Browning.

Manuscript: Carl H. Pforzheimer Library, RB 84

1. See Letter 59, n. 4.

2. Don Carlos Maria de Los Dolores (1848–1909), prince of Bourbon, claimant, as Don Carlos VII, to the throne of Spain.

3. Danilo II of Montenegro was assassinated in 1860 and was succeeded by his nephew, Nicholas (1860–1918).

4. Augustin, son of the Augustin de Iturbide (1783–1824) who was emperor of Mexico from May 1822 to March 1823.

5. Ferdinand Maximilian (1832–1867), emperor of Mexico from 1864 until his execution in 1867.

6. Clemens Wenzeslaus, Prince Metternich (1773–1859), first minister of Austria (1809–1848). His second son, Prince Paul (1834–1906), and Paul's wife, the Princess Mélanie, were friends of Mrs. Bronson ("Browning in Venice," *Cornhill Magazine* [February, 1902], p. 155).

7. The "Man in the Iron Mask" was a state prisoner in the reign of Louis XIV. He wore a mask covered with black velvet, which successfully concealed his identity. Browning's library contained G. A. Ellis's *True History of the State Prisoner, commonly called The Iron Mask,* 1827 (Sotheby, no. 1100, p. 131).

8. Henri Charles, Comte de Chambord (1820–1883), the "King Henry V" of the French legitimists. He was a nephew of the Duc d'Angoulême.

9. Charles Louis (1785–1795?), second son of Louis XVI and Marie Antionette. In 1792 the Royal Family was imprisoned in the Temple.

10. Marie Thérèse Charlotte (1778–1851), daughter of Louis XVI.

11. On July 3, 1793, the Committee of General Security named a cobbler Simon guardian of the Dauphin.

12. "This must refer to Mrs. FitzGerald's third son Richard Purefoy's escape from being killed in a bad accident that occurred at a road junction on a very dark night when driving home in a dogcart from Alresford to North Hall, Preston Candover, Hants" (MPFG).

13. With royal graciousness, Don Carlos called on the mother, congratulated her, gave her some money — and was at once suspected of having fathered the triplets (D&K, p. 293).

14. Mr. Quiverful in Trollope's *Barchester Towers* had fourteen children. "Happy is the man that hath his quiver full of them" (Psalm 127:5).

15. Not found.

16. See Letter 59, n. 3.

Letter 61

22, Portland Place. W.
Dec. 13. '83.

Yes, dear Friend of friends, I am in "your house" indeed, and under your immediate influence as I feel most thoroughly.[1] You have always been as kind to me as kind could be, — but, this time, under the peculiar circumstances, never was kindness so opportune. I was ordered to "go into lodgings" — to me, the extreme of discomfort: your offer at once relieved me of the necessity of waiting in Paris till some place for the sole of my foot could be found, — indeed till I get *complete* information about the state of things at W[arwick] Crescent, as I hope to do to day, I can decide on nothing — for the various telegrams and even letters are not sufficiently instructive. As it is, all is easy: I have to do a deal of little business necessary after four calendar months' absence this very day: and on Monday I am forced to go for a few days to Hatfield [2] to meet the D & Dss of Albany: [3] I say, "forced" — because, by an accident, I really am so. Last year, L^y^ Salisbury invited me to spend Easter there: and (*pray believe me*) I refused on the ground that I had not accepted an invitation which must be obeyed before I engaged myself afresh; that invitation being your own to Shalstone: I suppose I expressed myself awkwardly: for when I next saw L^y^ S. she asked "If I had any particular reason for refusing" — meaning (I fancied) — because of my politics (!) disagreeing considerably with those in vogue at Hatfield.[4] I at once said "Certainly not, — only what I told you, and if you care to ask me again, be sure I will gladly accept": so, she takes me at my unwise word, you see. Be also sure, that the next time *you* please to invite me to S[halstone] I will *most* gladly accept your goodness. I write this just before starting on my town-travels, and before I *know* anything worth communicating — as I *may* know before post-time: but I can add a line: if not, thus much goes to thank you heartily for this timely help. We had an *awful* passage: I was on deck, when we "shipped a sea" which sent every thing swimming — and threw up two great fishes! Bitterly cold too — hence, — think of the warmth and comfort of this house. *"My house"* you say: I am glad that it is not yours in the sense that it is allowable for you to give it away — so that I may tell you that of all the houses I ever saw it is the one I most envy — the fittest to be***

Manuscript: Carl H. Pforzheimer Library, RB 85

1. Browning returned to London from the Continent on December 13, going not to his own home but to Mrs. FitzGerald's town house, 22 Portland Place, she being at Shalstone perhaps. On December 24, he noted in his account book (BM) that "Home expenses" were extraordinary, "occasioned by illness of E. Guilliam." There is another entry for the hospital bill of E. Guilliam, and, on January 12, 1884, a payment of £7.7.6 for "Mrs. Guilliam." One concludes that Browning and his sister could not occupy their own house because Mrs. Guilliam was there with a contagious disease and that Browning paid the expenses. After his death, his housekeeper said, "When any of us were ill we had rest and medicine and the best medical advice, just like any of the family" (*Pall Mall Budget,* December 19, 1889, p. 1625).

2. Hatfield House, Hertfordshire, the seat of Lord Salisbury.

3. Leopold George Duncan Albert (1853–1884), the youngest son of Queen Victoria, created Duke of Albany (1881) married (1882) Hélène Frederica Augusta, Princess of Waldeck-Pyrmont.

4. Lord Salisbury's guests might be expected to be Tories.

Letter 62

22. Portland Place, Dec. 17. '83.

Dear Friend, I shall not leave your house, as I am presently obliged to do, without once more thanking you for all the kindness we have experienced in it. Nothing could be more perfect than all the arrangements made for our comfort: how differently should we have been circumstanced had we "gone into lodgings" at haphazard as we must have done if your hospitality had not interfered. My sister will tell you how satisfactorily things are going on at Warwick C^s and that there is no sort of danger to be apprehended on her return to-morrow.[1] I sincerely wish I could accompany her, and if I had been able to divine some weeks ago the misfortune that has befallen us I should certainly have refused the Hatfield invitation: but, once accepted, the refusal would be difficult; and least trouble to everybody will be given by my keeping my engagement. I see the invitation runs "for a few days": if the Ball is given on Thursday,[2] as I seem to have a notion it will be, I may probably stay *that* over — to avoid the ungracious appearance of running away from a bore "at my years," — at all counts, I trust the end of the week will find me at home. Pen will in all likelihood be there by that time. Poor fellow, he was quite prepared to start with us last Wednesday: he must want a respite from his really wonderful quantity of work.

You hope we don't "find Keane[3] in the way": our grievance is that he is always — or too much — out of it: I have had the great pleasure of more than one good substantial talk with him, — so has my Sister, — and we both agree, — as who could help agreeing?, — that nobody could be more kindly, gentlemanly, and all that a son of yours should be. He is at Brighton since yesterday, so that I cannot bid him the cordial good bye I would gladly do: you must be my spokesman: for aught I know, he may return before S. departs to-morrow. On my return — Saturday will assuredly find me at home — I will write and tell you what I remember of the sayings and doings — or at least persons and things at Hatfield. Your friends the Selbournes are likely to be there, — apparently the rejoicings being for the marriage: at all events, the young couple are expected.[4]

The day has been uncertain, — now sunny, now tearful, — but seems resolving to "hold up" and become fine for the afternoon. It is but a half-hour's expedition to Hatfield. When I last went there, I had for my companions Arthur Russell[5] & Grant Duff,[6] — pleasant ones indeed.

That Goldoni trifle is in print here,[7] but I have not seen it: another still more trifling *quatrain* has been printed with a complete mis-[s]tatement of the facts — such as they are. I wrote it on the spot for Moscheles who asked me to translate the lines that he might hang them over his piano as an admonition to all refractory singers. There was no "lady," nor "album" in the case.[8]

Farewell, dear Friend—all love and thanks to you, yet once again from yours

Affectionately ever
Robert Browning.

Manuscript: Carl H. Pforzheimer Library, RB 86

1. See Letter 61, n. 1.

2. The *Times* for Thursday, December 20, 1883 (p. 10d) includes Browning in its list of thirty houseguests staying with Lady Salisbury at Hatfield House, mentioning the "County Ball tonight."

3. Mrs. FitzGerald's eldest son.

4. Lord and Lady Wolmer were among the house guests staying with Lady Salisbury. Lord Wolmer was Lord Selborne's son, William Waldegrave Palmer, who married Lady Maud Cecil, Lord Salisbury's daughter, on October 27, 1883 (Roundell Palmer, *Memorials,* II, 89).

See appendix concerning deletion.

5. One of the three sons of Lady William Russell. On February 19, 1863, Browning wrote that he was to dine with Lady William that evening and go to Lady Salisbury's the next day (*Dearest Isa,* Letter 59, Feb. 19, 1863).

6. Mountstuart Elphinstone Grant Duff (1829–1906), statesman, colonial administrator, and author.

7. Browning wrote his sonnet "Goldoni" on November 27, 1883, at the request of the committee in Venice that was erecting a statue of Carlo Goldoni, the dramatist. Browning sent proofs to Furnivall, and the sonnet appeared in the *Pall Mall Gazette* (December 8, p. 2b; *BSP* I, 98*; and Hood, pp. 225–226).

8. "On Singers," Browning's impromptu translation of a Horatian satire, was composed on July 10, 1883, not for a lady's album but at the request of Felix Moscheles, the painter, and was published in the *Pall Mall Gazette* for December 13, 1883.

Letter 63

19. Warwick Crescent, W.
Apr. 26. '84.

Dear Friend, I am sure I wished you many happy returns of your Birthday [1] with all my heart. I had got a little book ready, and, at the last moment, could not lay my hands on it: forgive me, and expect (with moderation) the trifle. I enclose Miss Hickey's Poems, which amused me—especially the "Church Mice."[2] As to the rhyme for Folkestone, I am forced to say there is an *l.* in that word which sounds in the ear and should appear to the eye,—and it is absent from "joke's tone": my example would therefore run thus—

There was a sky-painter at Folkestone
Whose tone for the sky was egg-yolk's tone:
  This fanciful fellow
  Mistook blue for yellow
So—small was his fame out of Folkestone!

I am glad you were kept informed by the "Scotsman" of the feasting and revelry at Edinburgh.[3] I never met with such hospitality, and kindness from everybody. The "speechmaking" on my part was involuntary enough—indeed, I had no notion that the sudden uproar related to myself till the people behind me on the platform pushed and set me on my legs, while a benevolent person was in the very act of assuring the Lord Rector that nothing would get me off my seat. But "une fois n'est pas coutume"—and I shall . . . yet, don't let me be over-confident as I *was,* too truly!

Pen arrived on Tuesday night: he has been very wholly occupied since then: there was the great business of transferring the Statue from the Academy to the Grosvenor[4]—where it occupies the place of honour, and has been greeted most warmly. Milsand is still with us. Both would send you their kindest regards could I go to fetch them.

I am very glad you are coming up to Town again. I would not accept your "goodbye—perhaps for ever!"—you know: let us never anticipate such endings, come—no doubt—they will. Meanwhile and ever know

me for yours very affectionately
Robert Browning.

Manuscript: Carl H. Pforzheimer Library, RB 87

1. On April 25.

2. Miss Hickey's "Church Mice" appeared in her *Verse Tales* (1889). The MS still exists (MPFG).

3. On August 17, 1884, on the occasion of its tercentenary, the University of Edinburgh conferred the honorary LL.D. on 123 distinguished persons, including Browning and Tennyson, on which occasion Browning was surprised into thanking the audience in the only public speech he ever made. (See Flora Masson, *Victorians All* [London, 1931], pp. 230–238.)

4. Pen's 6′4″ bronze statue of *Dryope Fascinated by Apollo in the Form of a Serpent* was rejected by the Royal Academy and then accepted by the Grosvenor Gallery because tears were rolling down the poet's cheeks as he made his request (Charles E. Hallé, *Notes from a Painter's Life* [London, 1909], pp. 189–190).

Letter 64

Villa Berry, St Moritz, Engadin. Swd
Sept. 9. '84.[1]

Dear Friend, I seem behindhand in writing to you but we have been in considerable uncertainty as to what our arrangements might be. Mrs Moore was summoned to London and America on a sudden,—with quite sufficient reason, as she explained the case to us, but altogether against her strong inclination to stay: there was a great deal of telegraphing and receiving telegraphs, and all ended in her leaving a week ago. She would not hear of our own departure after just a fortnights [*sic*] stay,—less indeed,—and we are still, to all intents, her guests here and cared for most effectually. But another complication has arisen,—I have not time to explain it at length,—and it *may* so happen that she is on her way back again—spite of the passage on board the "Servia"[2] which was obtained with difficulty for next Saturday. Our going to Italy was—or appeared to be—out of the question, as the quarantine was rigidly enforced: we now hear that it is dispensed with—as well it may be when the Cholera is worse inside the guarded territory than out of it. We shall, however, certainly not go to Venice this year—as our friend [3] to whose hospitality we should have recourse is to be in Paris and perhaps London this autumn. I have more than one invitation from Italy: but mean to be content with a few weeks more of this delightful air—which has quite restored S. to her old health and strength,—and acts upon myself most advantageously. We walk for some two hours and a half on the mountain,—walk as long after luncheon, and are favoured by the finest weather possible. Everybody is leaving the place, and we are all but as much our own masters as at Gressoney. Should Mrs M. return, however,—in consequence of an ill-judged telegram sent yesterday by the attendant of her poor daughter,[4]—we might prolong our visit—as the least we could do in return for the pains she has taken to make us comfortable: otherwise we shall be in London at the beginning of October. And now—thanks for your Academy and the Buckingham account of the doings at Shalstone.[5] We are by no means so liberally supplied with books here, or newspapers, as you imagine: the Hotels probably are furnished with them, but we don't go there. Your cousins [6] have been very kind and attentive, and books of their lending lie on the table at present. Yes, "Obiter Dicta" [7] was sent to me before I left London,—I never saw, nor heard of the Author before—a Lawyer, whose note accompanied the book. I was much pleased with what he said about my poems: though anybody who cared for them might spare a "joke" at the expence of the Browning Society which has done so much to make other people care. For many a year I have had plenty of professed admirers—very like such in good faith—who "admired" at a great rate, and were extremely uncommunicative of their "admiration"—not by omitting to found and carry on a "Society" but, if they were Editors of Reviews, as some were, they told me to my face,—as George Lewis [8] did, — that they had *such* a difficulty in keeping out reviews of my works! — I being the exceptional person who was to prefer waiting till the next generation for any proof that I had been appreciated at all — while in the same breath he would desire me to "write what I could of her work to Mrs. L.[9] — who was so inspirited by a little encouragement!"

What else? That capital *"mot"* about Ld D^e^ Ros [10] was attributed at the time to Ld Alvanley,[11] I well remember: and as his I conceive it to be. I am glad to hear of Salvini's well-being: it is pleasant to think of him as in port after such troublous theatrical waters. Pen has been to see his Statue at Brussels: they have given it a capital place "where it can be seen all round": the Committee of selection, some twenty five in number, were Artists elected by Artists, and two thirds had to pronounce in favour of a work to ensure its acceptance — which, in this case, was "unanimous." Then, the proper time for sending in works ended on the 25th of July: and his permission to send — granted on the strength of the Photographs (all four) allowed him to do so a fortnight after. All this is in considerable contrast to the doings of the R[oyal] Academy.[12] I am not sure that we shall not return by way of Brussels in order to see Dryope done justice to.[13]

I fear this may not reach you at Cromer [14] after all: and that it will be safer to send it to Shalstone — for there is some delay in either the coming or going of the Post here — which I do not understand. I hope that my final proofs of "Ferishtah's Fancies," [15] which I despatched yesterday, will go straight to the Printers'. As it is a "dish of all sorts" you may find some more or less palatable morsel, I hope. There were several things I thought right to say — and said they are, with whatever success. I must end this scribbling, with the usual but never conventional assurance that I keep all your kindnesses in my memory and the author of them in my heart. S.[arianna] (by my side) sends her true love to you. I can hardly fancy a finer afternoon than this which is calling us out—and both of us wish you were here to enjoy it—as you would. Good bye & God bless you.

Ever affectionately yours
Robert Browning

Manuscript: Carl H. Pforzheimer Library, RB 88

1. In 1884 Browning and his sister spent their holiday at St. Moritz as houseguests of Mrs. Moore (Clara Sophia Jessup Moore; see Letter 42, n. 5), who had rented the Villa Berry there. They left London about August 18 (Hood, p. 231) and returned on October 3 (D&K, p. 309), having changed their original plan of spending an additional six or seven weeks in Venice, because of an Italian quarantine.

2. The *Servia* (commissioned 1881) was the first steel Cunard liner, the largest (7,392 tons) and fastest then in commission (*Britannica*).

3. Mrs. Bronson.

4. Mrs. Moore's daughter Mary married the Swedish Baron Carl von Bildt, who separated from her and confined her in an insane asylum in Austria. Mrs. Moore sought custody of her daughter but was refused on the ground that she was herself insane. She submitted to examination in Paris, was judged sane, and granted custody ("Noted Woman Dead," Philadelphia *Public Ledger,* January 6, 1899.)

5. "The annual village exhibition of flowers, fruits, and vegetables, took place on Friday, August 29th . . ." (*Buckingham Express,* September 6, 1884).

6. Perhaps Mrs. FitzGerald's Irish cousins, the Misses Richardson. Other Irish cousins, the Misses Story, lived much in Italy (MPFG).

7. Augustine Birrell (1850–1933), author and statesman, whose *Obiter Dicta* (1884) contains an appreciative essay "On the Alleged Obscurity of Mr. Browning's Poetry" (pp. 55–95). By way of joke, he says, "[The reader] comes up gasping, and more than ever persuaded that Browning's poetry is a mass of inconglomerate nonsense, which nobody understands—least of all members of the Browning Society" (p. 76).

8. George Henry Lewes (1817–1878), miscellaneous writer, the "husband" of George Eliot. He was connected editorially with *The Leader* in 1850 and *The Fortnightly Review* from 1865 to 1866 and contributed to *The Pall Mall Gazette.*

9. George Eliot.

10. Henry William FitzGerald (1793–1839), nineteenth Baron de Ros, grandson of the first Duke of Leinster, and a cunning roisterer. Browning's *The Inn Album* (1875) was based upon an episode in his life (DeVane, p. 386).

11. William Arden (1789–1849), second Baron Alvanley. He is said to have been as droll, witty, and clever as Lord de Ros (Charles Greville, *Memoirs* [London, 1874], III, 334).

12. See Letter 63, n. 4.
13. They did not (D&K, p. 309).
14. A fashionable seaside resort on the North Sea.
15. Published on November 21, 1884.

Letter 65

19. Warwick Crescent, W.
Nov. 4. '84.

My dear Friend,

Yes, I met your Son[1] very unexpectedly at dinner on Thursday: I called on Mrs Skirrow that afternoon for a few minutes, and, while sitting there, a telegram arrived to excuse the appearance of somebody at a dinner she was going to give in the evening: whereupon she said it would be a real kindness if, on so short notice, I consented to be stop-gap,—which I cheerfully did,—though I try all I can to keep at home just now, and had dined out for the first time the day before. I much fear poor Mrs Skirrow will be a long while yet confined to the sofa: she was carried up & down stairs, of course.

If you "wince" at every little instance of spite at "Browning's" very existence, it is well you did not know that personage nearly half a century ago, as you sometimes have flattered him by wishing: he used to be the butt of all the illustrious-obscure "who had a duty to perform" in the papers. The actual race only whisper where their predecessors would have roared. I begin to greatly appreciate the services of the Society which "furifies" these survivors of the *un*-fittest. What sort of notice would you expect Mr Furnivall to take of a scur[r]ilous article in the Saturday Review[2]—written, very probably, by one of the young men who lose no opportunity of spitting at me in its pages, while privately,—whenever there is an object to serve (—a monument to Spinoza, a Rabelais Club, a Tablet to Mr Spedding or the like—)[3] these very same vilifiers write fawningly to beg for my all-important patronage? No, no—"wince" whenever I get the "Batavian Grace" of approval in Mr Beresford Hope's[4] paper—which praises its proprietors rubbishly [*sic*] novels too assiduously to need a "Beresford Hope Society": when I set up a review and puff myself therein, I presume Mr Furnivall & his friends will think—and justly—that *their* "occupation is gone."[5] So, the flooding has extended even to Shalstone![6] I am sorry indeed. I could have written more at length about the Rosicrucians[7] but that time was wanting: as they pretended to derive their knowledge from Solomon—if not Moses or Adam—they had many intermediate transmitters of the doctrine. There is no more to be told about *Pen's* "Dryope" (not Ovid's, nor yet Virgil's) than he knows already: I hope for a very pretty & striking work.[8] Give my true sympathy and regard to Miss Smith[9] when you have occasion, and believe me ever aff^{y} yours

RB.

Manuscript: Carl H. Pforzheimer Library, RB 89

1. Very likely Keane (MPFG).

2. *The Saturday Review* makes slighting reference to Furnivall in its issue of November 1, 1884 (p. 561).

3. The invitation to join the Rabelais Association (dated June 23 [1879]) is printed in *Intimate Glimpses from Browning's Letter File,* assembled by A. Joseph Armstrong (Waco, Texas, 1934), p. 81.

4. Alexander James Beresford-Hope (1820–1887), politician, author, and conservative M.P., founded *The Saturday Review* in 1855. After he had called Disraeli an "Asian mystery," Disraeli told the House of Commons that "There are Batavian graces in all" Hope says, referring to Hope's Dutch ancestry and his awkward delivery (*DNB*).

5. *Othello,* III, iii, 357.

6. See Letter 25, n. 1.

7. Browning must have learned much about Rosicrucians when he was writing

Paracelsus (1835), for Paracelsus is sometimes regarded as the real founder of the movement (*Britannica*).

8. Perhaps Browning refers to Pen's 36″ bronze statuette, a replica of the 6′4″ *Dryope* (Sotheby, no, 1271, p. 149).

9. Laura Bullen Smith (see Letter 36, n. 11).

Letter 66

[*Palazzo Giustinian-Recanati*]
Venice, Nov. 5. '85.[1]

Dear Friend, your Dove and Olive-branch arrive very pleasantly opportune: I was just going to acknowledge with many thanks your letter from Geneva. You get back, I observe, to Shalstone this same day on which I write,—one of the worst and most rainy in my Venetian experience. I should be glad to know exactly how the weather was in London and at Shalstone at the time I am wondering here how two months can be so unlike as the November of two years ago, which was delightfully sunny without one interruption, and the present ill-conditioned season. I congratulate you on having made so long a journey[,] seen so many interesting places, and, above all, enjoyed the company of such a kind and accomplished friend as you have done.[2] You will now, I suppose, find the quiet of your Shalstone delightful and understand what Stendhal insists upon as one of the best results of travel—"l'étonnement du retour."[3] I am counting the days till your experience can be mine: not that I do not thoroughly love Venice and the friends I am surrounded with, but because I have work to finish at home. If possible, I may leave in a fortnight at latest: but I will forecast nothing, for fear of disappointment. We do not see many strangers, as during our visit two years ago: Mrs Bronson, having lost her husband this year, is in mourning and does not "receive" on the old scale, nor go out as before. My chief piece of so-called dissipation has been a rather sedulous attendance at the Goldoni Theatre, where a Venetian company play purely Venetian plays: the actors are capital, though I follow the voluble and by no means easy dialogue with a foreigner's difficulty — though I can read Venetian with tolerable ease: Pen gets on very well, both with Tuscan and this dialect. He has felt really the revival of old times in making acquaintance again with our servant (at Casa Guidi) [4] Ferdinando — his beloved for many years: who, in turn, assures me that he loves him "come un figliuolo." F. is in the service of an American family who duly value his honesty and culinary cleverness — which is considerable — as I judged by a dinner last evening. Well, dear friend, I hope soon to see you face to face, — and, I daresay, shall be able to tell you by word of mouth much more than suggests itself to the wearied pen of a pen-manager somewhat the worse for work. My Sister has a slight cold, but is well in the main: she sends her best love with mine: and I am, as ever,

affectionately yours RB.

Manuscript: Carl H. Pforzheimer Library, RB 90

1. In 1885 Browning and his sister spent their holiday in the Italian Alps and in Venice. They left London on August 18 and proceeded directly to Gressoney (D&K, p. 317). About October 1, they went to Venice, where they joined Pen and where they were the guests of Mrs. Bronson. They left Venice about November 23, arriving back in London about November 26 (Hood, p. 241).

2. There are references to Mrs. FitzGerald's having been to Germany and Switzerland in the fall of 1885 with Miss Bairnsfather (MPFG).

3. "A son retour à la vie, Octave fut saisi d'un long étonnement . . ." (Stendhal's *Armance,* 1827, chapter 23; p. 144 in the Pléiade edition).

4. The Brownings' home in Florence between 1848 and 1861.

Letter 67

19. Warwick Crescent, W.
Apr. 10. '86,

My dear Friend, S. tells me you wish to hear from me to-morrow: with all my heart? I have very little to say, for, though I am far better in health than I was of late, I still avoid any visiting which does not seem imperative on me, and there have been occasions this last week of what—under other circumstances—would prove enjoyable,—Liszt [1] two days ago, Joachim (at his Brother's house) [2] last evening,—and every evening some pleasure-promising party: but I will none of them—consequently there is nothing to tell about them. I don't know that I much care about seeing Liszt—whom I heard in his best days: but Joachim (in company with whom I dined on Wednesday) is the same now as before—so far as I remember. On Thursday I dined at a place where dinner was kept waiting for the French Minister,[3]—who was obliged to hear Gladstone's speech,—till 8¾: [4] and such arrangements do not suit me very well. The house was that of John Murray,[5] and, after all, there was compensation in seeing the III[d] Canto of Childe Harold in M. S. as it was written on odds and ends of all kinds of paper—I suppose he could not provide himself better while travelling. I noticed that the corrections were infinite and, so far as I could observe, all much for the better. We dined in the room which, in Byron's time, was the front-shop: the present drawing room being then the dining room—wherein Byron met Scott, for the first time: and the fire-grate is the actual one whereupon Byron's memoirs were burned.[6] Memories of all these events and persons and things come over one as one discusses one's glass of wine there.

I am having much trouble with my noble Marchese and his family about my purchase—they having *frankly* confessed that they want to get more money out of me than their agreement binds them to accept. I have determined to pay not one sixpence more, and to oblige these rascals to do as they engaged, and am assured they cannot possibly escape from their bond. But I mistrust law, and only resort to it from a natural indignation at avowed roguery.[7]

What weather! For five months not one wholly satisfactory day, that I can remember! We may have the Spring of a sudden,—and full Summer too soon after. I trust you are not the worse for this Siberian day!—and that you remember me as ever yours affectionately RB.

Manuscript: Carl H. Pforzheimer Library, RB 91

1. Franz Liszt (1811–1886) was in England from April 3 to 20, 1886. On April 8 he was honored by a Grosvenor Gallery reception, which Browning attended (see D&K, p. 324).

2. Lady Mary J. St. Helier speaks of Joachim's brother's house in Airlie Gardens (*Memories of Fifty Years,* p. 198).

3. Senator William-Henry Waddington (1826–1894), French ambassador to London (1883–1893) (*Larousse du XXe Siècle*).

4. On April 8, 1886, Gladstone spoke to the House of Commons on his Government for Ireland Bill. He "resumed his seat at 8 o'clock, having spoken for three hours and 25 minutes" (*Times,* April 9, pp. 5e–7c).

5. John Murray III (1808–1892), son of Byron's publisher, continued the publishing house at 50 Albemarle Street, where his father moved in 1812.

6. Byron died in Greece on April 19, 1824, and his memoirs were burned in May lest they compromise his reputation. The room of the burning is now the office of the present Sir John Murray, 50 Albemarle Street (Marchand, *Byron,* III, 1250).

7. In November of 1885, Browning was delighted to purchase from the Marchese Montecuccoli the Palazzo Manzoni, situated on the Grand Canal in Venice next to Browning's favorite hotel, the Albergo dell' Universo. It was the "most beautiful house in Venice" and worth double what Browning was paying for it (D&K, p. 321). Arrangements were completed, and Browning transmitted the purchase money to an Italian bank in February of 1886 (Hood, p. 252); but the Marchese had second thoughts, refused to receive the money, and continued to collect the rents (Hood, p. 250). After being assured that his adversary had no chance of winning a law suit, Browning went to law to force the Marchese to receive the purchase money, and Pen went to Venice to expedite matters (D&K, p. 335). When the owners permitted Pen to learn "on competent authority" that the palace foundations were shaky, Browning

at once withdrew from the suit (Orr, II, 526). However, since he was the retiring litigant, he was obliged to pay not only his own legal costs but the costs of the Marchese, both amounting to over £28 (D&K, p. 340). The palazzo still stands.

Although Browning did not get the palace, he did have the last word. His *Asolando* (1889) contains "Ponte dell' Angelo," a poem that retells the story of an unscrupulous Venetian lawyer who narrowly escaped being carried off by the devil because of his monstrous fees.

Letter 68

19. Warwick Crescent, W.
June 26. '86,

Dear Friend, I am far from being as "happy' [sic] as you suppose. My Sister still remains in bed—and although there is no fever, nor inflammation, the consequences of both continue. We called in Dr Broadbent [1] two days ago: his opinion entirely coincided with that of Frampton: [2] we must be patient—and recovery will be a long business. There is no danger—properly and immediately: but enough to be anxious about. The report is more favorable this morning than at any previous time: and I believe I shall go to Oxford on Tuesday—as I could be summoned thence by telegraph: there will be Fêtes enough and to spare. I go simply for the sake of Jowett, whose last occasion of officiating as Vice Chancellor makes it proper to be his guest if one can: [3] but I am weary of refusing invitations, almost as much as of accepting them. (I *think* (since writing the last word, on a sudden flash of memory occurring) I will run down to Osterley Park [4] for a breath of fresh air, returning to dinner,—since it is not an hour's journey by rail.) (Second thoughts,—probably I will only go to the Club) (?) [5]

I forgot to tell you that that silly paragraph about my "preference" for certain poems—was a misstatement of the simple fact that on an American lady writing to ask me which of my small pieces would represent me tolerably in a "Selection,"—which I could not prevent her from making,—I replied that those which I mentioned would do as well as any for that purpose.[6]

I must end, having more to write—but always

Affectionately yours,
Robert Browning.

Manuscript: Carl H. Pforzheimer Library, RB 92

1. Sir William Henry Broadbent (1835–1907), M.D., first baronet, well known London consultant, and Physician Extraordinary to Queen Victoria.

2. The Brownings' family physician.

3. Jowett's vice-chancellorship, from 1882 to 1886, ended in a "festive bouquet of fire-works" at the Oxford Commemoration (Hood, p. 250).

4. The house and grounds of Osterley Park, at Osterley, Middlesex, were given to the National Trust in 1949 by the ninth Earl of Jersey and are administered by the Victoria & Albert Museum. In 1886 Osterley was the property of Victor Albert Child-Villiers (1845–1915), seventh Earl of Jersey, and of Margaret, Countess of Jersey (1849–1945) (both in *DNB*).

5. The Athenaeum Club.

6. Perhaps the reference is to Jeannette Leonard Gilder's *Representative Poems of Living Poets American and English Selected by the Poets Themselves* (New York, 1886), which includes five of Browning's poems: "Abt Vogler," "Caliban upon Setebos," "A Forgiveness," "Saul," and "Clive." Browning gave Mrs. FitzGerald an autographed copy of this book for Christmas 1886 (MPFG).

Letter 69

19. Warwick Crescent, W.
Dec. 4, '86.

Dear Friend, you will not be much the gainer by my letter to-day, for, you must know, I am far from well,—have a something very like "spasmodic asthma,"—says the Doctor so that I need to guard myself troublesomely when I go out, and, if there be fog in the air, not go out at all. This is a new experience in my long life of easy-going health, and I shall not complain foolishly of taking my turn among the disabled ones. Clearly, the English — or perhaps London climate does not suit me: and in all likelihood I shall not spend the dark and dreary months here. I used to boast foolishly that my lungs would outlast my legs and arms, — and it is just these lungs that teaze me: I am, however, so ignorant about all these not unimportant matters, that I cannot tell you whether my complaint is a trifling incommodity or likely to prove an ever-increasing plague. You, as ever, were very good to send me that delicate bird which proved excellent yesterday and at this morning's breakfast.[1] Now, let me get on to something else than a report of coughing (not considerable) and wheezing (mainly troublesome at night). I am reading Dowden's Shelley,[2] with such an increasing irritation at the poor silly boy, — and not much respect for his biographer, — otherwise my friend and well-wisher, — that I hope to never again hear a word for or against Shelley. You will be sure to read the book earlier than I could get done with it and send it to you: otherwise you should have it at no distant period. I have been employing my enforced leisure this morning in beginning to somewhat arrange my books — such a chaotic mass, in real want of a good clearing fire! For how can I part with old tomes annotated by my Father, and yet how can nine out of ten of them do other than cumber the shelves like the dead weight they *are?* Oh that *helluo librorum* [3] my father, best of men, most indefatigable of book-digesters!

For one good thing, I have got rid of my new Poem [4] — it is gone to press, that is. So I can take my ease in all respects: there will be much to do with proof-correcting, but I manage that easily, with the thing in plain type before me. I am glad indeed that Tennyson's book [5] will appear at least a month before mine. Have you seen Hallam T's Jack and the Beanstalk? [6] It has been sent to me but I have not yet read it — as I will.

Ever affectionately yours

RB.

Here comes the day's first book-offering: I get, on an average, three books a day, and what table is sufficient for these things? Poetry, I see,—and let me say nothing!

Manuscript: Carl H. Pforzheimer Library, Shelleyana RB 4

1. "I should think this would be a Pheasant from a Shalstone Shoot. Such things were dispatched to R. B." (MPFG).

2. Edward Dowden, *The Life of Percy Bysshe Shelley* (London, 1886).

3. Perhaps suggested by Cicero's *De Finibus Bonorum atque Malorum* (III, ii, 7): ". . . quasi helluari libris, si hoc verbo in tam clara re utendum est" (as if to devour books, if this word may be used for such an exalted thing).

4. Browning's *Parleyings with Certain People of Importance in Their Day* was published on January 28, 1887.

5. Tennyson's *Locksley Hall Sixty Years After* was published in December of 1886.

6. *Jack and the Bean-stalk: English Hexameters* by Hallam Tennyson, Illustrated by Randolph Caldecott (London and New York: Macmillan and Co., 1886).

Letter 70

19. Warwick Crescent, W.
April 2. '87.

Dear Friend,

Your letter comes at "the beginning of the end" of poor 19. Warwick Cr[1]—a man is engaged at this moment on removing the tapestries,[2] which will be sent to Paris for repair. I shall cover the bare walls—which front me thus exposed for the first time these six and twenty years—with pictures of Pen, and so avoid unwelcome thoughts. Two days ago I completed (so far) the purchase of the new house, by signing the agreement, and Specification of improvements, and paying the deposit of £500: the rest will follow on the approval of the Title-deeds: and I daresay we may be enabled to take possession soon after the end of the month. Everybody competent to give an opinion thinks the bargain an excellent one: and Pen will have, in due course of time, a property pretty sure to increase in value. I heard from him yesterday,—poor fellow, was apprehensive for his monkey, Sophie,[3] who refused food and was evidently ill. His picture is not only accepted at the Salon[4] but carries a "numéro"—that is, direction for adequate hanging—a distinction accorded him for the first time. He will not be able to finish the picture intended for the "Grosvenor"—but sends the "Venetian Girl," you may remember, and the bronze bust of myself.[5] His hand is still swollen,[6] and incapable of continued work: a thing I cannot but be anxious about.

Here comes Easter, and, I hope, peace and quiet. I have tired myself thoroughly with quantities of pleasant things enough—had they presented themselves in moderation. Two dinners with Joachim—one with Mad[e] Schumann,[7] and, better, one afternoon of her very admirable performance at a private house: one concert of Miss Zimmermann's[8]—music in plenty: with one evening of bad music at a friend's—all within eight days. Last evening, an entertaining dinner at Trevelyan's: to-day, pictures, dinner at home, the Jewish-English Exhibition[9] last of all. To-morrow, luncheon at the Speaker's[10] to meet Jowett—so runs life away! After all, were you in Town—you would do as much—at least, have done as much in days not so long ago.[11] I am very glad indeed that you will be here, if but for a day: it will be delightful to see you: yes, there seems a return to winter—but perhaps to-day is a proof that Spring holds its own. I should like to be away for a day or two, but *that, you know,* is out of my power. L[d] Mount Temple invites me—and Pen also—to Broadlands, but I refuse—still determining to go to Shalstone whenever I *do* feel myself at liberty. You have not given me credit for this, but my conscience is a good one, as you would acknowledge did you know how often I have had the opportunity of paying country visits to even pleasant and friendly people—

not however the old and dear friend who thinks I am indifferent to her goodness! All love goes to her, however, from hers affectionately ever

Robert Browning.

Manuscript: Carl H. Pforzheimer Library, RB 93

1. Browning rented 19 Warwick Crescent from June 1862 to June 1887, when he moved to 29 DeVere Gardens, the house he purchased as mentioned in this letter. On the top of page 1 Mrs. FitzGerald wrote, "he has bought a house in South Kensington." Then, with reference to the encircled letterhead, "19, Warwick Crescent," she added, "my pleasantest hours spent here) E." At the top of page 2, she wrote, "He LITTLE thought then his son w[d] marry a rich American wife & buy a palace in Venice! Oh the vanity of human wishes!" (See appendix.) Browning's house in Warwick Crescent was demolished in 1960, and his house in DeVere Gardens is now Kiwi House, a private hotel.

2. The tapestries hung in the Brownings' apartment in Casa Guidi, then in the drawing room at Warwick Crescent (*Dearest Isa,* Letter 56, November 19, 1862), then in DeVere gardens, and were finally sold at auction (Sotheby, nos. 1385–1391, p. 159). The late James Deering purchased two of them (1385 and 1386) from P. W. French & Co. in 1916, and they now hang in his Miami home, Vizcaya (William H. Nicholas, "Vizcaya: An Italian Palazzo in Miami," *The National Geographic Magazine* [November 1950], pp. 595–604).

3. Pen painted a picture of two dogs and a monkey, entitled *Joe, Jim and Mademoiselle Sophia* (Sotheby, no. 47, p. 12).

4. At the Paris Salon of 1887, Pen showed his *After the Bath,* "a nude figure standing, one knee on a couch covered with a tiger skin" (Sotheby, no. 29, p. 10). Entry 368 of the catalogue (p. 31) reads, "Browning (Robert-Barrett), né à Florence, de parents anglais, élève de MM. J.-P. Laurens et A. Rodin. — Rue Campagne-Premiere, 15."

5. In 1887 Pen exhibited at the Grosvenor a bronze bust of his father and *Waiting for the Gondola,* an oil dated 1886 (*Grosvenor Notes,* 1887, pp. 44 and 63; Sotheby, no. 1268, p. 148 and no. 22, p. 8). The bust and the painting were also shown at the Paris Salon in 1888. (See Grace E. Wilson, *Robert Browning's Portraits . . .* [Waco, Texas, 1943], pp. 154–157.)

6. From rheumatism (D&K, p. 342).

7. Clara Josephine Schumann (1819–1896). She presented Mrs. FitzGerald with an autographed musical composition (MPFG), and Browning mentioned her in his "Founder of the Feast" (1884).

8. Agnes Marie Jacobina Zimmerman (1847–1925), German pianist and composer, resident in England (D&K, p. 323).

9. An exhibition illustrating Anglo-Jewish history and Jewish ecclesiastical art at the Royal Albert Hall. The catalogue (compiled by Joseph Jacobs and Lucien Wolf) mentions Browning as being a member of the General Committee (p. viii) and as lending two Hebrew Bibles to the exhibit (pp. 143 and 145). *The Jewish Chronicle* for April 8, 1887, described the brilliant opening, which was attended by three thousand guests, but did not include Browning in its list of distinguished Christian visitors.

10. Arthur Wellesley Peel (1829–1912), M. P. (1865–1895), speaker of the House of Commons (1884–1895), first Viscount Peel (1895).

11. Here Mrs. FitzGerald interlineated *"No—No. No!"*

Letter 71

Balliol College, Oxford
June 23, '88.[1]

Dear Friend, I had thought to leave this place for London earlier,—and, in that case, write from home where news may await me. Perhaps it will be better to say my extremely little say at once. We had a disastrous beginning of the week,—a rainy cold Wednesday, which spoilt the festivities, and a stormy next day, which prevented all walking. Yesterday was fine however—and the dinner to Ld. Lansdowne [2] went off exceedingly well. To-day is perversely fine—and but that I am engaged in the evening I should accept the kind Master's [3] invitation to stay longer: but I leave at 4. p.m. It has been pleasant to meet many old friends—besides the love I have for Oxford generally—perhaps all the more that I am an adopted child, and not an heir with his natural rights to sit at the dais, and be welcomed as a Fellow—so my chance was last night. Pen's portrait [4] is certainly good, as a likeness and a picture too. The artists generally decline to give the gown in its truthful aspect,—Millais refused to attempt it: Pen of course would refuse to try anything else: the fact is there,—and if my nose had been thrice as long as it is, would he be justified in making it more symmetrical than he found it? We had a little music in Hall—the fine Organ being the Master's gift: the room is excellently adapted for music.

All the same there is a soft sadness about this place,—such a perpetual remembrance is it of the fleeting state of mortal things. The Master said, last evening, in his speech—that already, since the last College dinner of the sort, he had to think of ten eminent members of the College whose places know them no longer. Even the three-years' stay of the undergraduates, the departure of the old and arrival of the new, in turn to become the old soon enough,—this is melancholy in some respects. "Well, we can smile and say—'my all was not laid here!'" Now, who wrote *that?* [5]—learned lady and my dear friend whose I remain ever

Affectionately
Robert Browning.

Manuscript: Richard L. Purdy, Yale University.

1. The text of this letter is from D&K (pp. 358–359). In addition to the reasons D&K give for saying it is addressed to Mrs. FitzGerald, one may add that it was dated on a Saturday, that it asks for the identification of a poetic quotation (as do other letters in this volume), and that the recipient is addressed as "learned lady" (as Mrs. FitzGerald is addressed in letter 27).

2. "The Marquis of Lansdowne was entertained at dinner last evening [i.e., June 22] by the Master and Fellows of Balliol College, of which he is a member, on the occasion of his appointment as Viceroy of India" (*Times,* June 25, 1888, p. 12a).

3. Jowett.

4. Pen's portrait of his father in academic dress was shown at the Grosvenor in 1885, presented to Balliol College, and hung in the Hall there in March 1886 (Wilson, p. 131). It now hangs in the new library.

5. Henry Kirke White, "On Disappointment."

Letter 72

Balliol College, Oxford.
June 30. '89.

My dear Friend, I have been here nearly a week, and shall stay till next Tuesday morning:[1] it did not occur to me that the "Academy" would be delayed in reaching you, and this is a word to explain why it happened so. I was much in want of a change, and have been greatly benefitted by a few quiet days with Jowett — we have been completely alone since the Commemoration. I stay for the "Gaudy"-Dinner[2] given to the Provost & Fellows of Eton[3] by this College of which the Provost was a member. Of old, on these occasions, there has been a crowd of entertainments, one after the other: this time, — no doubt on account of the Master's delicate health, — after the first two days, there was nobody, and I have had him to myself. I was at first glad to believe that his restoration to health was complete: but he is visibly unwell to-day. And to-day my Sister tells me you have been ill: I most truly grieve to hear it; and trust you are, or speedily will be, better. Indeed I have no good news — for my Daughter-in-Law's[4] condition is far from satisfactory. I feel myself unable to write the gossiping letters which I once was capable of — but you retain your old place in my affection and ever will: I might be more demonstrative with advantage — but I am truthful in what I manage to say. You must be benefitted, I will hope, by this fine weather — which I never remember the like of in this place. I was very tired and "washed-out," in German phrase, — but a few days have restored me. May you also recover as thoroughly is the earnest wish of yours ever

Most affectionately
Robert Browning.

Manuscript: Carl H. Pforzheimer Library, RB, 94

1. Browning went to Oxford on June 25 to attend the Commemoration and the Gaudy Dinner (D&K, p. 379).

2. The Gaudy (from *gaudeamus*) Dinner is held annually the week after the end of Trinity term in memory of the founders and benefactors of the college.

3. James John Hornby (1826–1909), headmaster of Eton from 1868 to 1884, and provost from 1884 to 1909.

4. Fannie (Coddington) Browning (1854–1935), Pen's American wife (*Dearest Isa,* p. 8). She was often in ill health but had recovered from this illness by July 17 (Hood, p. 314). On June 2 she had concluded a month's visit to Browning, Pen being there "about half the time" (letter of June 10, 1889, to Mrs. Bronson in the collection of the Count Rucellai).

Letter 73

29. De Vere Gardens. W.
Aug. 28. '89,

Dear Friend,

I must write a loving word of good bye to you,[1] and explain why you will not receive the Academy till late in next week: we leave to-morrow for "Asolo, Veneto,"—my address for the next few weeks, after which it will be at P° Rezzonico, Venice, till our return home. I shall forward the Journal from Venice, and you will only get it after much delay,—but the contents are not of a merely newspaper kind, and may bear waiting for, as the "Times" would *not.* Fortunately we travel under better auspices than last year: the rest after the close of the "Season" has been very serviceable to me, and I feel better than I have done for some years on the same occasion. We hope to be at Milan on Friday evening, at Vicenza the next; and last of all at Castelfranco and Asolo—two hours' drive distant: there good rooms have been secured for us at the Inn. I had a kind letter from you some little time back, with an interesting account of your visit to Castle Howard.[2] I am altogether "exceeded" as the French well say, by the letters which call every day for answer—and, of late, do not always get it: Friends' letters are different from the questions, and criticisms and so forth from all manner of Strangers, and I spend literally hours of precious time in attempting to make head against them: and what remains for the Friends indeed—who, after all, should understand and pity the sorrows of a poor old—Poet, and remember he is but worn-out flesh and blood. Be assured that I never forget your goodness nor my own duty of affection, although the assurances of it by letter get to be more and more sluggish.

My Sister is well—means to write, I think: in any case sends her true love—and my true love goes to you, Dear Mrs FitzGerald, as ever—so remember me always as

Affectionately yours
Robert Browning.

Manuscript: Carl H. Pforzheimer Library, RB 95

1. At the top of page 1 there is a note by Mrs. FitzGerald: "RB's last letter from London" (see appendix). In 1889 Browning and his sister spent their holiday at Asolo and in Venice. They left London on August 29 (Hood, p. 318), were in Milan on August 30 (Broughton, p. 386), and proceeded thence to Asolo. On November 1 they went from Asolo to Venice (G&M, p. 282), where they stayed with Pen in the Palazzo Rezzonico. There are references in Browning's letters to his intention to start for England on December 3 or 4 (Orr, II, 616), but he contracted his final illness and died in the Rezzonico on December 12.

2. The mansion of Castle Howard, near Malton in Yorkshire, designed by Vanbrugh, built 1701–1731, the seat of the Earls of Carlisle (*The Victoria History of the County of York* [London, 1923], II, 107).

Letter 74

[*Asolo*]
October 8, 1889.

*** Fortunately there is little changed here: my old Albergo [1] — ruinous with earthquake — is down and done with — but few novelties are observable — except the regrettable one that the silk industry has been transported elsewhere — to Cornuda and other places nearer the main railway. No more Pippas — at least of the silk-winding sort! [2]

But the pretty type is far from extinct.

Autumn is beginning to paint the foliage, but thin it as well; and the sea of fertility all round our height, which a month ago showed pomegranates and figs and chestnuts — walnuts and apples all rioting together in full glory — all this is daily disappearing. I say nothing of the olive and the vine. I find the Turret rather the worse for careful weeding — the hawks which used to build there have been 'shot for food' — and the echo is sadly curtailed of its replies; [3] still, things are the same in the main. Shall I ever see them again, when — as I suppose — we leave for Venice in a fortnight? ***

Text: Orr. II, 599–600. The letter is incomplete.

1. See Letter 15.
2. Browning's Pippa was employed in a silk mill at Asolo.
3. See Letter 15, n. 2.

Appendix

Bibliographical Descriptions
of Browning's Letters to Mrs. FitzGerald
now in the Pforzheimer Library

by
Marcelle Thiébaux

Bibliographical Appendix

In classifying this group of Robert Browning letters according to their physical, nonliterary features, I have turned to the scheme of bibliographical description devised by Dr. Kenneth Neill Cameron of The Carl H. Pforzheimer Library, in his edition of the Library's Shelley papers.[1] Like the manuscripts in those volumes, each manuscript here will be characterized in terms of its number of written pages; the condition of its sheets of paper, whether single or double, that is, folded, as well as their size; and the kind of paper, with its watermark if any. A description of imprinted letterheads or crests, when these occur, will accompany what is said about the paper.

The variety of writing papers used by Robert Browning in this collection of letters deserves comment. At least twenty different pieces of stationery are distinguishable: these fall into the general classification of laid or wove, and further differ according to watermark, ruling, crest, letterhead, and color. As for this last quality it will be here specified if a paper is cream, blue, or gray-blue; otherwise the reader may assume the paper to be white. Browning apparently used what he had at hand. When he was abroad he wrote on foreign papers, sometimes those provided by the hotel where he stayed. On two occasions when, presumably, he was a guest of his friend Mrs. Bronson, he wrote on stationery em-

[1] The reader may refer to Dr. Cameron's account of his work, explaining how he developed these descriptive formulae, in the essay, "Editorial Procedures," *Shelley and His Circle* (2 vols.; Harvard University Press, 1961), I, xxxvii-xlvi. I should like here to express my warm thanks to Dr. Cameron for his many valuable suggestions to me while I was engaged in the present work. My thanks are due, also, to Mr. Dard Hunter, Honorary Curator of the Dard Hunter Paper Museum, The Institute of Paper Chemistry, for his written response to my queries, in which he clarified for me several points on papermaking.

bossed with her initials, a letterhead which the guest took care to write over or cross out. One source of paper was Mrs. Skirrow, whom he thanks on May 8, 1884, for a gift of letter paper:

> Dearest Friend, the first use I make of your munificent gift is to shew you, by its help, on what beautiful paper my next year's letters will be written, however they may come short of the beauty in their black character.[2]

His note of May 13 a few days later shows that he has received "the envelopes."[3] Since Browning's birthday was May 7, the gifts from Mrs. Skirrow which he acknowledged other years at about this date may also have been writing paper. Earlier, writing to her from France on about September 1, 1881, Browning had added the postscript, "Look out for the proper envelopes when I get home again!"[4] In this group of letters to Mrs. FitzGerald, Browning writes intermittently on a blue wove paper engraved with a dark blue letterhead from June 5, 1880 (Letter 19, RB 47) to February 5, 1881 (Letter 32, RB 59), and on a blue wove paper with a light blue letterhead from July 23, 1881 (Letter 34, RB 61) to January 14, 1882 (Letter 41, RB 68). The dates reveal that he began to use these two batches of paper at some time after a birthday, and that the supply ceased six or seven months later; one can conjecture that it was these packets of letterhead paper that Mrs. Skirrow had sent him. In June and July of 1882 (Letter 42, RB 69—Letter 45, RB 71) Browning's letter paper was cream colored and bore a letterhead engraved in black. From this point on, stationery engraved with Browning's address continues to vary in color and letterhead color. In this collection the year 1883–1884 between birthdays yields three letterheads, but these are not uniform in color. Between May 1884, the year in which the writer thanked Mrs. Skirrow for paper, and May 1885, only two letters are contained in this group; one of them bears the letterhead. The correspondence with Mrs. FitzGerald in the collection now grows sporadic, but the engraved paper continues to appear along with other papers. Tactfully, Browning no doubt made certain to keep a supply of the engraved pa-

[2] D&K, p. 305. [3] *Ibid.*, p. 306. [4] *Ibid.*, p. 268.

per in reserve for his letters to Mrs. Skirrow. As for the other papers he used, a total list of writing papers will be found in the second part of this appendix (p. 220).

While the arrangement of these first three steps of manuscript description has been based upon a portion of the scheme established in the edition of the Shelley papers, I have elsewhere modified the scheme to suit the special needs of the present edition.[5] My system of classifying the Browning letters will incorporate the following manuscript irregularities: in Browning's hand, the placement of his additions or interlined words, his underscorings, corrections, deletions, postscripts, cross-written passages, and an instance of his misdating a letter. Where these occurrences are significant the editor has indicated them in the notes to the letters; thus the reader who does not wish to interrupt his perusal of a letter to learn of irregularities in the manuscripts need not do so, while the interested reader may look to an account of them. Mrs. FitzGerald's notes will also be recorded. She, it appears, went through her letters from Robert Browning some time after she received them, marking and annotating them for herself or for another reader. It may be inferred from her use of both pencil and pen that she did this on at least two different occasions. I have indicated the placing of her comments, stating, moreover, whether she wrote them in pen or pencil. Finally, such accidents as blotting or waterstaining, parts missing from letters, torn sections, or mended pages, are listed at the end of the description of each letter where they occur. A normal bibliographical scheme, one which includes all description mentioned above, is illustrated by the description of Letter 18, RB 45 (May 31, 1879):

> 4 pages.
> Double sheet, 8vo (8.9 x 7 inches).
> Laid paper. Watermark: J ALLEN & SONS/SUPER FINE/.

[5] Several steps of Dr. Cameron's scheme have been omitted. Inasmuch as all the manuscripts here are autograph letters signed by the writer, there is no purpose in beginning the description of each letter with this information. The later date of the Browning correspondence, hence the absence of seals, stamps, and postmarks from the letters themselves — the envelopes have not accompanied them — will preclude such remarks on postal matters as appeared in the Shelley volumes.

Addition, page 4, interlined: (She is far from well, I am sorry to say)/.

Annotation in pen, partly encircled, page 1, upper left margin, in the hand of Mrs. FitzGerald: The Roman/coil of hair/*from York*/.

I. THE MANUSCRIPTS

Letter 2 RB 31 (August 28, 1876)

4 pages.

Double sheet, 8vo (10.2 x 8.1 inches).

Laid paper.

Letter 3 RB 32 (December 30, 1876)

4 pages.

Double sheet, 8vo (8.8 x 7 inches).

Laid paper. Watermark: TOWGOOD'S/EXTRA SUPER/. Embossed crest [Lion rampant above shield above *virtute*].[1]

Cross-writing, page 1: 1 line along left margin, 11 short lines across upper margin; page 2: 1 line along left margin, 10 short lines across upper margin; page 3: 12 short lines including signature across upper margin.

Letter 5 RB 33 (March 10, 1877)

4 pages.

Double sheet, 8vo (9.1 x 7 inches).

Laid paper. Watermark: [crown above interlaced DLR]; countermark: IMPERIAL/TREASURY/DE LA RUE/.

Annotation in pencil, page 1, upper left margin, in the hand of Mrs. FitzGerald: E.FG/was there/to see him/take the/H *degree*/.

Letter 7 RB 34 (August 30, 1877)

4 pages.

Double sheet, 8vo (8.8 x 6.9 inches).

[1] Browning also used this crest (of the extinct Bruning family of Wiltshire) on his watch, signet ring, pickle forks, gravy ladles, and mustard pot (Sotheby, pp. 155–156).—E. C. M.

Laid paper.
Cross-writing, page 1: 1 line along left margin.
Annotation in pencil, page 1, upper margin, in the hand of Mrs. FitzGerald: Written/very shortly/before/Miss/Egerton/Smiths/ sad/death/; [following date:] La Saisiaz/.

Letter 8 RB 35 (June 9, 1878)
4 pages.
Double sheet, 8vo (8.9 x 7 inches).
Laid paper. Watermark: TOWGOOD'S/EXTRA SUPER/. Embossed crest: [Lion rampant above shield above *virtute*].
Annotation in pen, page 1, upper margin, left and right of embossed crest, in the hand of Mrs. FitzGerald: The Poets/son sold/his picture in/the Academy/for 300 £ which/was well//for a début/ & *encouraging/*.

Letter 9 RB 36 (August 3, 1878)
3 pages.
Double sheet, 8vo (9 x 7 inches).
Laid paper. Watermark: J ALLEN & SONS/SUPER FINE/.

Letter 10 RB 37 (August 9, 1878)
4 pages.
Double sheet, 8vo (9 x 7 inches).
Laid paper. Watermark: J ALLEN & SONS/SUPER FINE/.
Correction, page 2, interlined above a deletion: the earlier months./
Correction, page 3, written through another word: directing/.

Letter 11 RB 38 (August 24, 1878)
2 pages.
Single sheet, 8vo (8.2 x 5.2 inches).
Wove paper, ruled quadrille finish. Black printed letterhead, upper left margin: HOTEL BODENHAUS/SPLÜGEN/——/.

Letter 12 RB 39 (September 7, 1878)
4 pages.
Double sheet, 8vo (10.3 x 8.2 inches).
Wove paper, ruled quadrille finish. Black printed letterhead, upper left margin: HÔTEL BODENHAUS/SPLÜGEN/——/.

Annotation in pencil, page 4, interlined, in the hand of Mrs. FitzGerald: William Grove, the photographer/now./.

Underscoring in pencil, page 4: *as who is not, dear friend/.*

Letter 13 RB 40 (September 14, 1878)

2 pages.

Single sheet, 8vo (8.2 x 5.2 inches).

Wove paper, ruled quadrille finish.

Letter 14 RB 41 (September 21, 1878)

2 pages.

Single sheet, 8vo (8.2 x 5.2 inches).

Wove paper, ruled quadrille finish.

Postscript, page 1, upper margin: X) Oh, no! this place was suggested by nobody: we found it out for ourselves.

Underscoring in pencil, page 1: *wherever/*; triple underscoring: *Saturday/*.

Letter 15 RB 42 (September 28, 1878)

2 pages.

Single sheet, 8vo (8.3 x 5.3 inches).

Wove paper, press-marked linear ruling.

Annotation in pencil, page 1, upper margin, in the hand of Mrs. FitzGerald: He wrote again/from Asolo/; [following date:] Oct. 13. 1889/.

Letter 16 RB 43 (October 12, 1878)

4 pages.

Double sheet, 8vo (10.5 x 8.3 inches).

Wove paper, press-marked linear ruling.

Annotation in pen, page 1, upper left margin, in the hand of Mrs. FitzGerald: E. FG. then in/Paris for the Exhib^{n}/went there daily with/"Pen"/.

Letter 17 RB 44 (January 20, 1879)

4 pages.

Double sheet, 8vo (8.9 x 6.9 inches).

Laid paper. Watermark: TOWGOOD'S/EXTRA SUPER/. Embossed crest: [Lion rampant above shield above *virtute*].

Correction, page 4, written through "3": 4/.

Cross-writing, page 1: 1 line along left margin, 14 short lines, including signature across top margin.

Letter 18 RB 45 (May 31, 1879)

4 pages.

Double sheet, 8vo (8.9 x 7 inches).

Laid paper. Watermark: J ALLEN & SONS/SUPER FINE/.

Addition, page 4, interlined (She is far from well, I am sorry to say)/.

Annotation in pen, partly encircled, page 1, upper left margin, in the hand of Mrs. FitzGerald: The Roman/coil of hair/*from York*/.

RB 46 (See below, Letter 31, January 2, 1881)

Letter 19 RB 47 (June 5, 1880)

4 pages.

Double sheet, 8vo (8.8 x 6.9 inches).

Blue wove paper. Dark blue engraved letterhead, centered: 19, WARWICK CRESCENT,/W./.

Correction, page 4, written through "vo": book/.

Letter 20 RB 48 (June 19, 1880)

4 pages.

Double sheet, 8vo (8.8 x 7 inches).

Blue laid paper.

Letter 21 RB 49 (July 13, 1880).

4 pages.

Double sheet, 8vo (8.8 x 7 inches).

Blue wove paper. Dark blue engraved letterhead, centered: 19, WARWICK CRESCENT,/W./.

Letter 22 RB 50 (August 17, 1880)

2 pages.

Single sheet, 8vo (8.3 x 5.3 inches).

Wove paper, press-marked quadrille finish.

Letter 23 RB 51 (September 4, 1880)

5 pages.

Double sheet, 8vo (10.7 x 8.3 inches); single sheet, 8vo (8.3 x 5.3 inches).

Wove paper, press-marked quadrille finish.

Letter 24 RB 52 (September 13, 1880)

2 pages.

Single sheet, 8vo (8.3 x 5.3 inches).

Wove paper, press-marked quadrille finish.

Postscript, page 1, upper left margin: (Belgravia — Pig and all — / received this morning/.

Letter 25 RB 53 (September 19, 1880)

4 pages.

Double sheet, 8vo (10.6 x 8.3 inches).

Wove paper, press-marked quadrille finish.

Addition, page 3, interlined: my own letters/.

Letter 26 RB 54 (September 30, 1880)

4 pages.

Double sheet, 8vo (10.7 x 8.3 inches).

Wove paper, press-marked quadrille finish.

Addition in pencil, page 1, following "Sept. 3.," in the hand of Mrs. FitzGerald: 0/.

Letter 27 RB 55 (October 13, 1880)

4 pages.

Double sheet, 8vo (10.7 x 8.3 inches).

Wove paper, press-marked quadrille finish.

Correction, page 2, interlined above deleted "Nay": Oh/.

Cross-writing, page 4: single line along right margin, 3 words, including signature, upside down along top margin.

Letter 28 RB 56 (October 23, 1880)

4 pages.

Double sheet, 8vo (10.7 x 8.3 inches).

Wove paper, press-marked quadrille finish.

Letter 29 RB 57 (November 20, 1880)

4 pages.

Double sheet, 8vo (8.9 x 6.9 inches).

Blue wove paper. Dark blue engraved letterhead, centered: 19, WARWICK CRESCENT,/W./.

Letter 30 RB 58 (November 27, 1880)

4 pages.

Double sheet, 8[vo] (8.9 x 7 inches).

Blue wove paper. Dark blue engraved letterhead, centered: 19, WARWICK CRESCENT,/W./.

Letter 31 RB 46 (January 2, 1881)

4 pages.

Double sheet, 8[vo] (8.9 x 6.9 inches).

Blue wove paper. Dark blue engraved letterhead, centered: 19, WARWICK CRESCENT,/W./.

Correction, page 4, written through "bid": urging/.

Letter 32 RB 59 (February 5, 1881)

4 pages.

Double sheet, 8[vo] (8.9 x 6.9 inches).

Blue wove paper. Dark blue engraved letterhead, centered: 19, WARWICK CRESCENT,/W./.

Cross-writing, page 1: 1 line along left margin, 12 short lines including signature across upper margin.

Letter 33 RB 60 (April 20, 1881)

4 pages.

Double sheet, 8[vo] (8.9 x 7 inches).

Laid paper. Watermark: TOWGOOD'S/SUPERFINE/. Embossed crest: [Lion rampant above shield above *virtute*].

Postscript, page 4, upper margin: My sister is better,—thanks you and sends/her kind love. Pretty cards, too!/.

Correction, page 2, interlined above deleted "two," in the hand of Mrs. FitzGerald: 1:/.[1]

Letter 34 RB 61 (July 23, 1881)

4 pages.

[1] The correction is inaccurate. The word "two" should have been permitted to stand, and "March" should have been changed to "February." Browning dined with Disraeli at Lady Airlie's on that date. See D&K, p. 261.

Double sheet, 8vo (8.9 x 7 inches).

Blue wove paper. Light blue engraved letterhead, centered: 19, WARWICK CRESCENT,/W./.

Letter 35 RB 62 (July 30, 1881)

4 pages.

Double sheet, 8vo (8.8 x 7 inches).

Blue wove paper. Light blue engraved letterhead, centered: 19, WARWICK CRESCENT,/W./.

Letter 36 RB 63 (August 6, 1881)

4 pages.

Double sheet, 8vo (8.8 x 6.9 inches).

Blue wove paper. Light blue engraved letterhead, centered: 19, WARWICK CRESCENT,/W./.

Correction, page 4, over a waterstain obliterating "Lawr": Law/.

Annotation in pen, page 4, in the hand of Mrs. FitzGerald: Laurence/.

Letter 37 RB 64 (September 6, 1881)

3½ pages.

Double sheet, 8vo (10.5 x 8.3 inches).

Wove paper, ruled quadrille finish.

Letter begins on page 4, continues on pages 1 and 2, and concludes on page 3.

Letter 38 RB 65 (September 24, 1881)

4 pages.

Double sheet, 8vo (10.5 x 8.2 inches).

Laid paper.

Letter waterstained at edges.

Letter 39 RB 66 (November 5, 1881)

2 pages.

Single sheet, 8vo (6.9 x 4.4 inches).

Blue wove paper. Light blue engraved letterhead, centered: 19, WARWICK CRESCENT,/W./.

Letter 40 RB 67 (December 10, 1881)

4 pages.

Double sheet, 8vo (8.8 x 6.9 inches).

Gray-blue wove paper. Light blue engraved letterhead, centered: 19, WARWICK CRESCENT,/W./.

Postscript, page 4, continues cross-written on page 1: 1 line along left margin, 4 short lines across upper margin.

Letter 41 RB 68 (January 14, 1882)

4 pages.

Double sheet, 8vo (8.8 x 7 inches).

Blue wove paper. Light blue engraved letterhead, centered: 19, WARWICK CRESCENT,/W./.

Cross-writing, page 1: 1 line along left margin, 14 short lines across upper margin, 1 line including signature along right margin.

Addition in pen, page 4: ?/. [The question mark is written with an inverted caret under it.]

Letter 42 RB 69 (June 3, 1882)

4 pages.

Double sheet, 8vo (8.7 x 6.9 inches).

Cream laid paper. Black engraved letterhead, centered: 19, WAR–WICK CRESCENT,/W./.

Annotation in pen, page 2, interlined, in the hand of Mrs. FitzGerald: plants from Shalstone/.

Annotation in pen, page 2, interlined, in the hand of Mrs. FitzGerald: Geraldine/.

Letter 43 RB 70 (June 10, 1882)

4 pages.

Double sheet, 8vo (8.8 x 6.9 inches).

Cream laid paper. Black engraved letterhead, centered: 19, WAR–WICK CRESCENT,/W./.

Letter 45 RB 71 (July 15, 1882)

4 pages.

Double sheet, 8vo (8.7 x 6.9 inches).

Cream laid paper. Black engraved letterhead, centered: 19, WAR–WICK CRESCENT,/W./.

Letter incomplete, lacking conclusion and signature.

Letter 47 RB 72 (August 16, 1882)

4 pages.

Double sheet, 8vo (10.3 x 8 inches).

Wove paper, ruled quadrille finish.

Letter incomplete, lacking conclusion and signature.

Letter 48 RB 73 (August 23, 1882)

4 pages.

Double sheet, 8vo (10.3 x 8 inches).

Wove paper, ruled quadrille finish.

Additions, narrow strips and square patches of paper pasted along weak places, page 2: upper and lower margins; pages 2 and 3: center vertical fold, and center horizontal fold; page 3: upper, right, and lower margins. These mends occasionally obscure writing, especially, page 2, line 1: [I].

Letter 50 RB 74 (September 16, 1882)

4 pages.

Double sheet, 8vo (10.3 x 8.1 inches).

Wove paper, ruled quadrille finish.

Tear in surface of paper, page 4, removing a portion of the written side: Octo[ber]/.

Letter 51 RB 75 (March 17, 1883)

4 pages.

Double sheet, 8^{vo}(8.9 x 7 inches).

Laid paper. Watermark: TOWGOOD'S/SUPERFINE/.

Letter 52 RB 76 (March 24, 1883)

2 pages.

Single sheet, 8vo (7 x 4.4 inches).

Laid paper. Watermark: TOWGO[OD'S]/SUPER[FINE]/.

Letter 53 RB 77 (April 14, 1883)

4 pages.

Double sheet, 8vo (8.8 x 7 inches).

Laid paper. Watermark: TOWGOOD'S/SUPERFINE/.

Underscoring in pen, page 1: *no more*/and annotation in pen, page 1, lower margin, in the hand of Mrs. FitzGerald: X Yet I think he *does* say something more?/.

Letter 54 RB 78 (April 28, 1883)
1 page.
Single sheet, 8vo (7 x 4.4 inches).
Laid paper. Watermark: [ ]NSON/[ ]INE/.

Letter 55 RB 79 (May 5, 1883)
$3\frac{1}{2}$ pages.
Double sheet, 8vo (8.8 x 7 inches).
Laid paper. Watermark: TOWGOOD'S/SUPERFINE/.

Letter 56 RB 80 (June 23, 1883)
4 pages.
Double sheet, 8vo (8.9 x 6.9 inches).
Gray-blue wove paper. Black engraved letterhead, centered: 19, WARWICK CRESCENT,/W./.
Correction, page 1: "h" written through "H"/.
Correction, page 2: "tells" written through "has"/.

Letter 57 RB 81 (October 9, 1883)
4 pages.
Double sheet, 8vo (9 x 7.1 inches).
Laid paper. Watermark: J WHATMAN/. Embossed letterhead, diagonally crossing upper left margin: K. deK. Br./.
Letterhead obscured by writing.
Correction, page 1: "which" deleted, "it" interlined following "I see"/.
Cross-writing, page 1: 1 line along left margin.

Letter 58 RB 82 (October 22, 1883)
4 pages.
Double sheet, 8vo (8.5 x 6.4 inches).
Laid paper.
Addition, page 1, interlined: but one)/.

Letter 59 RB 83 (October 29, 1883)
4 pages.
Double sheet, 8vo (8.9 x 7.1 inches).
Laid paper. Watermark: 1882/.

Letter 60 RB 84 (November 8, 1883)

4 pages.
Double sheet, 8vo (8.9 x 7.1 inches).
Laid paper. Watermark: (Whatman cipher): [posthorn in shield, lower part visible]/W/. Embossed letterhead, diagonally crossing upper left margin: K. deK. Br./.
Letterhead deleted.

Letter 61 RB 85 (December 13, 1883)

4 pages.
Double sheet, 8vo (8.9 x 7 inches).
Gray-blue wove paper. Light blue engraved letterhead, centered: 22, PORTLAND PLACE. W./.

Letter 62 RB 86 (December 17, 1883)

4 pages.
Double sheet, 8vo (8.9 x 7 inches).
Embossed paper. Watermark: [crown above interlaced DLR]; countermark: IMPERIAL/TREASURY/DE LA RUE/.
Deletion, page 3: coupl/.

Letter 63 RB 87 (April 26, 1884)

4 pages.
Double sheet, 8vo (8.9 x 6.9 inches).
Gray-blue wove paper. Black engraved letterhead, centered: 19, WARWICK CRESCENT,/W./.
Blot, page 2: "Scot[s]man"/.

Letter 64 RB 88 (September 9, 1884)

4 pages.
Double sheet, 8vo (10.3 x 8.3 inches).
Wove paper, press-marked linear ruling.

Letter 65 RB 89 (November 4, 1884)

4 pages.
Double sheet, 8vo (8.9 x 6.9 inches).
Cream laid paper. Black engraved letterhead, centered: 19, WARWICK CRESCENT,/W./.

Letter 66 RB 90 (November 5, 1885)

4 pages.

Double sheet, 8vo (8.9 x 6.9 inches).

Gray-blue wove paper. Light blue engraved letterhead, centered: 19, WARWICK CRESCENT,/W./.

Letterhead deleted.

Letter 67 RB 91 (April 10, 1886)

4 pages.

Double sheet, 8vo (8.9 x 6.9 inches).

Gray-blue wove paper. Light blue engraved letterhead, centered: 19, WARWICK CRESCENT,/W./.

Letter 68 RB 92 (June 26, 1886)

2 pages.

Single sheet, 8vo (6.9 x 4.5 inches).

Gray-blue wove paper. Light blue engraved letterhead, centered: 19, WARWICK CRESCENT,/W./.

Letter 69 Shelleyana RB 4 (December 4, 1886)

4 pages.

Double sheet, 8vo (8.9 x 6.9 inches).

Cream laid paper. Watermark: [crown above PAPYRUS REGIA]. Light blue engraved letterhead, centered: 19, WARWICK CRESCENT,/W./.

Cross-writing, page 1: 13 short lines across top margin.

Addition, gray-blue wove paper rectangle (3.6 x 2.1 inches), with pin-holes corresponding to those at top of page 1, to which it had been fastened, with annotation in the hand of Mrs. FitzGerald: Would you/like this/letter as/an Autograph/written 3 years// before his/death in/Dec 1889—/he wrote to/me, till the/last week of/his life/.

Letter 70 RB 93 (April 2, 1887)

4 pages.

Double sheet, 8vo (8.7 x 6.9 inches).

Gray-blue wove paper. Light blue engraved letterhead, centered: 19, WARWICK CRESCENT,/W./.

Annotation in pen, partly encircled, page 1, upper margin, in the hand of Mrs. FitzGerald: he has bought a house/in South/Kensington. my pleasantest hours/spent here) E/. Annotation in pen, page 2, upper margin, in the hand of Mrs. FitzGerald: He LITTLE thought then/his son w[d] marry a/rich American wife &/ buy a palace in/Venice!/Oh the vanity/of human wishes!/Annotation in pen, page 3, between lines 17 and 18, in the hand of Mrs. FitzGerald: *No — No. No!/.*

Letter 72 RB 94 (June 30, 1889)

3 pages.

Double sheet, 8[vo] (8.8 x 6.9 inches).

Laid paper. Watermark: ORIGINAL/TURKEY MILL/KENT/.

Letter 73 RB 95 (August 28, 1889)

3¾ pages.

Double sheet, 8[vo] (8.8 x 7 inches).

Gray-blue wove paper. Embossed letterhead, upper right margin: 29 DE VERE GARDENS./W./.

Annotation in pencil, page 1, upper margin, in the hand of Mrs. FitzGerald: Last letter from London/One after/from Asolo/Oct. 1889./Eheu!/. Addition in pen, page 1, above "Last letter," in the hand of Mrs. FitzGerald: R. B's/. Underscoring in pen, page 1: *from London/.*

II. A CLASSIFICATION OF WRITING PAPERS

Laid and Embossed Papers:

(1) Laid paper. Watermark: TOWGOOD'S/SUPERFINE/.
RB 75, RB 76, RB 77, RB 79 (Letters 51, 52, 53, 55).

(2) Laid paper. Watermark: TOWGOOD'S/SUPERFINE/. Embossed crest: [Lion rampant above shield above *virtute*].
RB 60 (Letter 33).

(3) Laid paper. Watermark: TOWGOOD'S/EXTRA SUPER/. Embossed crest: [Lion rampant above shield above *virtute*].
RB 32, RB 35, RB 44 (Letters 3, 8, 17).

(4) Laid paper. Watermark: J ALLEN & SONS/SUPER FINE/.
RB 36, RB 37, RB 45 (Letters 9, 10, 18).

(5) Laid paper. Watermark: J WHATMAN/. Embossed letterhead, diagonally crossing upper left margin: K. deK. Br./.
RB 81 (Letter 57).

(6) Laid paper. Watermark: (Whatman cipher): [posthorn in shield]/W/. Embossed letterhead, diagonally crossing upper left margin: K. deK. Br./.
RB 84 (Letter 60).

(7) Laid paper. Watermark: ORIGINAL/TURKEY MILL/KENT/.
RB 94 (Letter 72).

(8) Laid paper. Watermark: [crown above interlaced DLR]; countermark: IMPERIAL/TREASURY/DE LA RUE/.
RB 33 (Letter 5).

(9) Embossed paper. Watermark: [crown above interlaced DLR]; countermark: IMPERIAL/TREASURY/DE LA RUE/.
RB 86 (Letter 62).

(10) Laid paper. Watermark: 1882/.
RB 83 (Letter 59).

(11) Laid paper. Watermark: [ ]NSON/[ ]INE/.
RB 78 (Letter 54).

(12) Cream laid paper. Black engraved letterhead, centered: 19, WARWICK CRESCENT,/W./.
RB 69, RB 70, RB 71, RB 89 (Letters 42, 43, 45, 65).

(13) Blue laid paper.
RB 48 (Letter 28).

(14) Miscellaneous laid papers.
RB 31, RB 34, RB 65, RB 82 (Letters 2, 7, 38, 58).

Wove Papers:

(15) Blue wove paper. Dark blue engraved letterhead, centered: 19, WARWICK CRESCENT,/W./.

RB 46, RB 47, RB 49, RB 57, RB 58, RB 59 (Letters 31, 19, 21, 29, 30, 32).

(16) Blue wove paper. Light blue engraved letterhead, centered: 19, WARWICK CRESCENT,/W./.
RB 61, RB 62, RB 63, RB 66, RB 68 (Letters 34, 35, 36, 39, 41).

(17) Gray-blue wove paper. Light blue engraved letterhead, centered: 19, WARWICK CRESCENT,/W./.
RB 67, RB 90, RB 91, RB 92, RB 93 (Letters 40, 66, 67, 68, 70).

(18) Gray-blue wove paper. Black engraved letterhead, centered: 19, WARWICK CRESCENT,/W./.
RB 80, RB 87 (Letters 56, 63).

(19) Gray-blue wove paper. Light blue engraved letterhead, centered: 22 PORTLAND PLACE. W./.
RB 85 (Letter 61).

(20) Gray-blue wove paper. Embossed letterhead, upper right margin: 29 DE VERE GARDENS./W./.
RB 95 (Letter 73).

Ruled Wove Papers:

(21) Wove paper, press-marked quadrille finish.
RB 50, RB 51, RB 52, RB 53, RB 54, RB 55, RB 56 (Letters 22, 23, 24, 25, 26, 27, 28).

(22) Wove paper, press-marked linear ruling.
RB 42, RB 43, RB 88 (Letters 15, 16, 64).

(23) Wove paper, ruled quadrille finish. Black printed letterhead, upper left margin: HÔTEL BODENHAUS/SPLÜGEN/.
RB 38, RB 39 (Letters 11, 12).

(24) Wove paper, ruled quadrille finish.
RB 40, RB 41, RB 64, RB 72, RB 73, RB 74 (Letters 13, 14, 37, 47, 48, 50).

Index

Index

Names are identified upon their first appearance in the text. References to the text include the notes.

Index

Index